6.08

THE CONDITIONS OF LEARNING

Third Edition

ROBERT M. GAGNÉ
Florida State University

HOLT, RINEHART AND WINSTON   New York   Chicago   San Francisco
Atlanta   Dallas   Montreal   Toronto
London   Sydney

Library of Congress Cataloging in Publication Data

Gagné, Robert Mills, 1916-
    The conditions of learning.

    Bibliography: p. 314
    Includes index.
    1. Learning, Psychology of.   I.   Title.
LB1051.G19 1977   370.15′2   76-45797
ISBN 0-03-089965-6

PREFACE

There have been many new research findings and theoretical developments since the publication of the second edition of this work. In addition, I have undertaken in the intervening years to examine what is known about learning conditions for five varieties of learning outcomes, some of which were only very briefly mentioned in previous editions. The emphasis in the present edition on interpretation of learning events in terms of the information-processing model will not come as a surprise to readers acquainted with my recent writings. I consider this form of learning theory to represent a major advance in the scientific study of human learning.

The considerable shift in orientation from its previous edition requires a very different organization for this one, and has occasioned its being largely rewritten to include much new material. This book, I feel, deserves a preface which is both frank and more than usually detailed.

In seeking to describe the conditions that affect human learning I have had in mind the question: What factors really can make a difference to instruction? The answer to this question is framed within two different themes that run throughout the book. The first of these themes is *varieties of learning outcomes*. A serious consideration of practical knowledge of learning, I believe, must go beyond the most general principles of the learning process, such as contiguity and reinforcement. One must recognize that learning results in retained dispositions which have different properties, different organizations, and which accordingly require that different conditions be established for their attainment. I call these learned dispositions by the general name of *capabilities*. Their five main varieties are called intellectual skills, cognitive strategies, verbal information, motor skills, and attitudes. Learning investigators and theorists often use these categories (not always by these names) in their accounts of learning—they are not entirely unfamiliar. Yet these same investigators often do not choose to make these distinctions explicit, as is done here. It should be noted that these five kinds of capabilities are simply different types of outcomes of learning. The five capabilities do not have simply ordered relationships with one another; and they are discussed in the order named mainly for convenience in presentation. As for how one kind of capability relates to another kind, that is a matter discussed within several chapters of the book.

The second main theme relating to the factors that make a difference to instruction may be identified as the *events of learning*. The description of these events begins with an account of the information-processing model of learning and memory, as posited by a number of contemporary investigators as a framework for learning research. This model, with its broad outlines of structures and processes, is shown to be both useful and illuminating as a basis for conceptualizing the conditions of learning. From the model, and from existing evidence regarding its functioning, one may form a description of conditions affecting the processes of learning and remembering. These conditions, some of which are internal to the learner and some external, make up the events of learning. Those events which are external, when deliberately planned and arranged, constitute *instruction*. Thus it is reasonable to define instruction as being made up of events external to the learner which are designed to promote learning.

The criterion of educational relevance for knowledge about learning results in a content which I recognize to be somewhat untraditional. Psychologists who study learning derive their problems for investigation from a variety of sources, not all of which relate to education. Sometimes, too, an original problem source which may have been educational in nature has over a period of years been virtually lost sight of, while the problem itself has become subtly altered in its definition. As a consequence, one cannot simply or automatically assume that names for topics in learning research (such as "verbal learning," "concept identification," "reasoning," and so on) are closely relevant to an understanding of planned instruction. By saying this, I do not mean to deprecate such research, which often has the most worthy purpose of finding explanations for general characteristics of the learning process. Selection of research findings for this book on the basis of their relation to instruction, however, is not the same as answering the question: What have investigators of learning been studying?

The initial chapter of this edition, like that of the previous one, is a bridge providing knowledge about the history of learning research, with which many students may have a hearsay acquaintance, and is intended to assure a minimal background. The two main themes—varieties of learning outcomes and events of learning—are then outlined in Chapters 2 and 3. Chapter 4 summarizes evidence about learning conditions for what are called "basic" forms of learning—classical conditioning, operant conditioning, and chaining. The point of view is adopted that basic principles of associative learning have been investigated by studies of these forms, and that the resulting principles are applicable to the "associations" usually assumed as components of more highly organized kinds of learning outcomes.

Succeeding chapters discuss the nature and conditions of learning for the five types of human capability introduced in Chapter 2, from intellectual skills to attitudes. These learning outcomes are described as learned capabilities exhibiting themselves as human performances, and as being supported in their learning by particular sorts of internal and external events. The latter are related to the processes of learning which comprise the information-processing model presented in Chapter 3. Thus the unity aimed for in these chapters is one which deals with each type of learned capability in terms of the events that support its learning.

Two final chapters, 11 and 12, have an applied orientation, directed particularly at the interests of students in understanding how knowledge of learning can be employed in the planning, design, and development of programs of instruction.

The book is addressed to a fairly broad audience and, it must be supposed, one which is heterogeneous in prior knowledge. I hope, first, that it will be used by those who are preparing for, or already pursuing, the teaching profession. Students in this category will need to acquire many new concepts and principles about learning and about their applications to education. This group of readers, I trust, will be rewarded by gaining a set of internalized models of human learning and instruction into which they will be able to incorporate the most important features of their varied experience with the practical affairs of teaching and learning.

A second group of students for whom the book is intended is of somewhat mixed composition, although possessing common goals. These are students of education who see their future careers as being concerned with educational management in its broadest sense. They may have teaching specialties in particular content areas, such as language, mathematics, science, or social studies. They may have chosen to orient their careers toward the establishment of educational quality in elementary, secondary, post-secondary, or adult education, or in vocational or industrial training. A knowledge of human learning is of value in all of these pursuits. Such knowledge is relevant to the practices of education that are known by such names as curriculum planning and development, instructional systems design, assessment of learning outcomes, and program evaluation. Educational leadership which includes a concern for the quality of instruction and the competence of student graduates must take into account the conditions of human learning and the means available for establishing them. Students of education in these varied fields will, I believe, profit from an understanding of learning conditions as described in this volume.

A substantial segment of the book's intended audience is expected to be composed of students of educational psychology at both undergraduate and graduate levels. For these students, a word of orientation perhaps needs to be said. The psychology of learning described in this book represents that body of theoretical and empirical knowledge about learning which, in my view, is most highly relevant to education. The selection of this knowledge has been made against the criterion of relevance to what I perceive to be taking place in classrooms or other places where deliberately planned instruction occurs. There is, in addition, some information which provides a historical-intellectual background, occurring chiefly in Chapters 1 and 4. This may be reviewed very briefly, or skipped, by students of educational psychology if it is already familiar to them. Otherwise, the contents of the book present an organization of knowledge about human learning that I consider worthy of appreciation by the student of educational psychology, and most promising as a basis for future research.

Naturally, it would please me as an author to learn, as this book is put to use, that students of a variety of backgrounds and interests in education have found it possible to acquire an organized schema of human learning as it occurs in situations of instruction. While I would expect each such student to contribute his or her own interpretations, and amendments, I would nevertheless anticipate that such a schema will be valuable as a referential model against which the complex events of teaching and learning can be compared and evaluated.

Tallahassee, Florida   **ROBERT M. GAGNÉ**
December 1976

CONTENTS

1

INTRODUCTION

Human beings acquire most of their human qualities through learning. Although shared with other animals, the capacity for learning makes possible the remarkable differences in patterns of behavior of humans, as well as their enormous adaptability to change.

Few things are so intriguing as the development of human behavior. Adult human beings are marvelously adaptable, competently functioning persons within a complex society. How they progress to this point from a beginning as highly dependent and relatively uncapable infants is a question of great intellectual interest and importance. One part of the answer to this question, to be sure, lies in an understanding of the processes of growth and devel-

1

opment, characteristic properties shared by all living things. The other part, relating to a different set of circumstances in the life of the individual, is learning. The human skills, appreciations, and reasonings in all their great variety, as well as human hopes, aspirations, attitudes, and values, are generally recognized to depend for their development largely on the events called learning.

One may, if one wishes, cease to wonder about learning at this point, having confirmed to one's own satisfaction that human development in all its manifestations must depend on the twin factors of growth and learning and their interactions with each other. One can say about a child, "He'll learn," just as one says, "She'll grow into it (or out of it)," and such a statement is difficult to deny. But to equate learning and growth as natural events is to overlook the most important difference between them. The factors that influence growth are to a very large extent genetically determined, whereas the factors that influence learning are chiefly determined by events in the individual's living environment. Once the individual's genetic stock has been chosen at the moment of conception, growth cannot be altered very much, except by rather extreme measures. But members of the human society, which itself is responsible for the care of a developing person, have a tremendous degree of control over events that affect learning. Experience, we are told, is the great teacher. This means that the events the developing individual lives through—at home, in the geographical environment, in school, and in various social environments—will determine what is learned and therefore to a large extent what kind of person he or she becomes.

This enormous dependence of learning on environmental circumstances implies a great responsibility for all members of human society. The situations in which developing children are placed, whether deliberately or otherwise, are going to have great effects on them. In fact, there is not a very clear understanding at present of what the limits of these effects may be. Are the situations in which the growing person is nowadays customarily placed the sort that will encourage the development of disciplined thinkers, of great artists and scientists? Or will they discourage such development and inhibit the full exploitation of human thought and intellect?

The realization that learning is largely dependent on events in the environment with which the individual interacts enables us to view learning as an occurrence that can be examined more closely and understood more profoundly. Learning is not simply an event that happens naturally; it is also an event that happens under certain observable conditions. Furthermore, these conditions can be altered and controlled; and this leads to the possibility of examining the occurrence of learning by means of the methods of science. The conditions under which learning takes place can be observed and described in objective language. Relations can be detected between these conditions and the changes in human behavior that occur in learning, and thus we can make inferences about what has been learned. Also, scientific models and theories can be .constructed to account for the changes observed, just as for other types of natural events.

Learning and Its Conditions

This book is about the *conditions of learning*. We shall consider the sets of circumstances that obtain when learning occurs, that is, when certain observable changes in human behavior take place that justify the inference of learning. A number of different kinds of changes brought about by learning will be described, and related to the situations in which they occur. We shall not present a theory of learning, but will draw some general concepts from various theories. Our major concern is to find a reasonable answer to the question, What is learning? This answer is to be phrased in terms of an objective description of the conditions under which learning takes place. These conditions will be identified, first of all, by reference to the situations of ordinary life, including those of the school, in which learning occurs. Their identification will also be aided in certain instances by reference to experimental studies of learning.

Learning is a change in human disposition or capability, which persists over a period of time, and which is not simply ascribable to processes of growth. The kind of change called learning exhibits itself as a change in behavior, and the inference of learning is made by comparing what behavior was possible before the individual was placed in a "learning situation" and what behavior can be exhibited after such treatment. The change may be, and often is, an increased capability for some type of performance. It may also be an altered disposition of the sort called "attitude" or "interest" or "value." The change must have more than momentary permanence; it must be capable of being retained over some period of time. Finally, it must be distinguishable from the kind of change that is attributable to growth, such as a change in height or the development of muscles through exercise.

The Elements of the Learning Event

Students in the sixth grade may learn to write sentences which use the participial form of verbs to modify the subjects of sentences, as in the example, "Seeing no obstacles, he went ahead with the plan." By such learning, they may acquire an alternate way of expressing thoughts which otherwise would require a separate clause, such as "Since he saw no obstacle, he went ahead with the plan." When they have learned to the extent that they can use this alternative, learners should have no difficulty in turning sentences with clauses into sentences which use participial phrases, and vice versa. In addition, they will readily be able to detect the incorrectness in a sentence such as "Trying to catch up, the tight skirt slowed Ruth's progress." In other words, learning has made it possible for students to use a new form of a sentence correctly, whatever its content may be.

How has this learning been brought about? What are the elements of the situation that can be abstracted as having to do with learning?

1. First there is a *learner*, who is a human being (It would be possible for the learner to be an animal, but that is another story, or more exactly, several others.) The learner possesses sense organs, through which he receives stimulation; a brain, by means of which the signals originating in his senses are transformed in a number of complex ways; and a set of muscles, by means of which he exhibits the various performances that show what he has learned. The stimulation that is constantly being received is organized into various patterns of neural activity, some of which are stored in his memory in such a way that they can be recovered. Such memories may then be translated into action that may be observed as the movement of muscles in executing responses of various sorts.
2. The events that stimulate the learner's senses are spoken of collectively as the *stimulus situation*. When a single event is being distinguished, it is often called a *stimulus*.
3. Another important "input" to learning consists of content recovered from the learner's *memory*. Such content, of course, has an already organized form which has resulted from previous learning activities.
4. The action that results from these inputs and their subsequent transformations is called a *response*. Responses may be described more or less specifically; for example, one can speak of the movement of a particular muscle or of the action of the whole

body in walking. For this reason and others, responses are often described in terms of their effects rather than in terms of their appearances. When so classified, they are called *performances*. For example, a response might be "moving the finger rhythmically over a small area of the scalp." But it may often be more useful to refer to the performance of "scratching the head."

A learning occurrence, then, takes place when the *stimulus situation* together with the *contents of memory* affect the learner in such a way that his *performance* changes from a time *before* being in that situation to a time *after* being in it. The *change in performance* is what leads to the conclusion that learning has occurred.

At this general level of description, the students' learning to use a participial phrase correctly may be said to have come about in the following way. Before the learning, the students' performances in writing sentences showed no tendency to use participial phrases. Then a stimulus situation was introduced, which may have included a teacher who used verbal communications to get the students to attend to certain stimulus features of sentences and to make certain responses to them. A number of different sentences, some containing participles and some not, were also used as part of the stimulus situation. Students were required to recover certain concepts from memory, such as "subject," "modifier," "phrase," and "participle." A sequence of stimulus events was made to occur, at the end of which the students succeeded in using participial phrases and in distinguishing a sentence containing such a phrase from one using a clause. The teacher then verified to herself, and also to the students, that learning had taken place by asking the students to repeat their performances with some additional examples. The performance was again exhibited successfully, and the inference was made that learning had taken place. What had been produced by this activity was a new *capability*, to be stored in the learner's memory.

This example is markedly oversimplified, of course. But the framework for the events of learning exhibits a constant set of elements. External to the learner is the stimulus situation, which may initiate and influence learning. Internally, the learning is affected by organized contents recovered from the learner's memory. Various transformations of these inputs result from internal processing, and finally exhibit themselves in the learner's performance. As our discussion of the conditions of learning proceeds, many occasions will call for reference to these elements of the set of learning events.

This brief introduction to the events of learning shows that there are two main ideas which need to be understood, and these the following chapters will try to illuminate. First is the question of the nature of new *capabilities* established by learning and stored in memory. There are, of course, as many different learned capabilities as there are human performances. Also, there are different levels of complexity of organization of these capabilities. If we are to make sense of them, we must have a way of dealing with *general types of capabilities* having common characteristics, rather than with each individually learned performance. Chapter 2 will introduce the major types of learned capabilities. The second main idea pertains to the processes involved in learning, which are described initially in Chapter 3 as the *events of learning*. As the previous example has indicated, a single instance of learning is made up of a number of events, some of which are internal to the learner, while others are external. Before dealing with these matters, however, it will be useful first to review briefly some historical trends in learning psychology that have influenced thought about the processes and outcomes of learning.

SOME TRENDS IN LEARNING PSYCHOLOGY

The view of learning to be presented in this book arises out of a relatively long history of thought and investigation. Since it is likely that readers will have differing degrees of acquaintance with this history, we include here a brief review. Our purpose is to indicate the continuinty of earlier conceptions, but more especially their contrasts, with contemporary learning theory.

How people learn, and the conditions under which they learn, are questions that have been investigated by several generations of learning psychologists. Learning has been a favorite problem particularly for American writers and researchers, partly no doubt because of a philosophical tradition that places great emphasis on experience as a determiner of human knowledge. It is of some value, therefore, to spend a little time in describing these historically important ideas about the nature of learning, since they will point the way to the influences that have shaped current learning theory, and that will undoubtedly affect future developments as well.

Research on learning has generated several typical models, or *prototypes*, which are frequently referred to by writers on the subject. Prototypes of learning have been based upon the conditioned response, trial-and-error learning, insight, the reinforcement model, and others. These prototypes are often used to communicate basic similarities or contrasts among situations in which learning occurs. Knowledge of the prototypes of learning (and the situations in which they are typically observed) is an aid to understanding the varieties of learned capabilities that are discussed in subsequent chapters.

The Associationist Tradition

One of the oldest lines of thinking reflected in modern learning psychology derives from the British associationist psychologists, who formulated theories about how ideas are linked. These theorists were primarily concerned with how complex ideas, such as flower or number, are constructed in the human mind from elementary sense impressions. In other words, they were interested in how such "complex ideas" are learned in the first place. On this latter point, they were generally agreed that acquiring a new idea necessitated (1) *contiguity* of the sense impressions or simple ideas that were to be combined to form the new idea, and (2) *repetition* of these contiguous events. Some of these psychologists also discussed "mental concentration" (which is now usually called attention) as an important condition for learning new ideas by association (Mill, 1869).

American psychologists like William James and John Dewey added some distinctly new interpretations to this associationist tradition. The ideas of Darwin concerning the functions of living organisms in adaptation exerted a considerable influence on these American scholars. Accordingly, they sought to discover the *functions* of behavioral events like learning and thinking, rather than simply the composition of these events. A most important characteristic of learning was considered to be its function in the life of the organism. This view led them to place the *nervous system,* rather than "the mind," in a position of central importance in understanding how sense impressions are connected with behavior. And perhaps most significant, they assigned a critical role to *action* as a factor in learning. Action did not simply follow ideas, as British associationists had proposed, but became an essential feature of the process of behavioral organization called learning.

As other developments in learning psychology occurred, "association" came to mean something other than relations among ideas. The strong tendency to avoid mentalistic conceptions of learning led to the formulation of "associations" as inferred links between the stimulus and the response (Robinson, 1932). They were also called, at one time or another, "connections," and "bonds." This conception of associations has persisted to the present day, when many investigators consider the association the simplest form of learned capability, constituting a fundamental "building block" for other more complex types of learned capabilities.

Trial-and-Error Learning

A most important trend in the scientific study of learning was established in the use of animals for experiments on learning. Edward L. Thorndike (1898) was a pioneer in these efforts to understand the learning of animals by performing experiments, rather than by collecting anecdotes about animal behavior. From his controlled observations of cats, dogs, and chickens escaping from problem boxes, he concluded that many previous accounts of animal thought were erroneous in that they attributed too much power to animal intelligence. His investigations suggested that all that was necessary to explain animal learning were specific bonds between "sense impressions" and "impulses to action." These associations he considered to be stamped in by the consequences resulting from the completed act (such as escape from the problem box). Thorndike believed that these associations also made up a large part, although not all, of what human beings learned and remembered.

A hungry animal, such as a cat, is placed in a box with slatted sides and a door that can be opened by pressing a wooden lever to release a latch, allowing the animal to reach food placed within his view outside the box. At first, the cat is observed to engage in a variety of acts, including scratching at the sides and door of the box. Sooner or later, these activities lead by chance to the depression of the latch that opens the door. The animal then immediately leaves the box and eats the bit of food. When placed in the box again, the animal's behavior is obviously changed. He spends less time scratching at the sides of the box, and more time making movements in the region of the latch. On this second trial, the animal takes much less time to release the latch and get to the food. Subsequent trials reduce the time still more, until the cat is releasing the latch only a few seconds after being placed in the box.

The view of learning represented by this prototype situation may be described briefly as follows. When confronted with a novel situation, the motivated animal engages in various "tries" to attain satisfaction. Sooner or later, largely by chance, he makes a set of responses that lead to motive satisfaction. The particular responses that are immediately followed by motive satisfaction (eating the food, in this case) become "stronger" in relation to others. Thus, when the animal is placed in the box a second time the latch-pressing responses occur sooner, whereas the other responses (such as scratching the floor of the box) tend to be shorter in duration or entirely absent. On subsequent trials in the box, these "errors'" progressively weaken and disappear. The correct responses, in contrast, are progressively strengthened by being followed immediately by motive satisfaction. This generalization was called the "law of effect" by Thorndike. The learning situation does not differ in basic characteristics from that of the rat pressing a lever, employed later by Skinner (1938). "Reinforcement" is the term Skinner uses to identify the events that Thorndike called the law of effect.

Is the animal trial-and-error prototype representative of human learning? The answer is clearly in the negative. It is, in fact, rather difficult to relate this prototype to the learning that might occur in a human being. If a person is put in a problem box, we know that he is likely to adopt a strategy of searching for a way out. He recognizes latches, knobs, or other devices as having certain functions. He "thinks out" the consequences of his actions before he takes them, and chooses the most likely alternative. Once he finds his way out, he will remember it under most circumstances, and there will be no gradual error reduction on subsequent trials. How can such human behavior be in any sense comparable to "trial and error"? The strategies, the recalling, the recognizing, thinking, the choosing, are all there in the person's behavior; they can readily be observed if the proper experimental conditions are provided.

By searching hard, one can probably find some degree of comparability between the trial-and-error prototype and young children's acquisition of a motor skill, such as balancing blocks, making a simple knot, or learning language sounds. Insofar as the prototype helps us to understand such learning, it is useful. But this usefulness is, of course, limited for the field of learning in general.

A number of more modern learning theorists have made the individual association, as seen in animal behavior, the basis of their ideas on learning. Among these are Edwin R. Guthrie (1935), Clark L. Hull (1943), and B. F. Skinner (1938), each of whom has proposed somewhat different interpretations of the basic idea that the *association*, as observed in animal learning of simple acts, is the typical form of learning. Other investigators of animal learning have opposed this tradition, however. Chief among these was Edward C. Tolman (1932), whose experiments convinced him that Thorndike and those who followed him were wrong in asserting that nothing but an "association" existed between a situation and the response that followed it. Tolman's theory maintains that association is an internal connection between a representation (within the animal's nervous system) of the stimulus situation and a representation of the alternatives of action to be taken. He thus attempted to restore to animal behavior the "ideas" (although this was not his term) that had been considered unnecessary by Thorndike.

One modern theorist, Neal Miller (1967), has provided evidence to indicate that strong and lasting single associations can be learned as rapidly by rats in a single trial as they often are by human beings. Thus there is good reason to believe that the speed of forming such associations does not differ in man and the lower mammals. Differences in capacities of learning between men and animals must presumably be sought in the greater complexity of human intellectual processing, and perhaps in the size of the memory store, rather than in the basic mechanism for learning.

The Conditioned Response

I. P. Pavlov (1927) found that when a signal such as a buzzer was sounded at the time food was shown to a hungry dog, and this set of events was repeated several times, the dog came to salivate at the sound of the buzzer alone. Whereas the salivation at the sight of food could be considered a natural (or unconditioned) response, salivation to a buzzer had to be acquired as a conditioned response. This learning occurred when the new signal (the buzzer) was presented together with the food in a number of trials.

John B. Watson (1919) championed the view of learning suggested by Pavlov's studies of conditioning in dogs. In Watson's writings, learning is viewed as a matter of establishing individual associations (conditioned responses) firmly based in the nervous system. More complex human acts are considered to be chains of conditioned responses.

Some investigators of Pavlovian conditioning believe it to be a very special kind of learning, representative of the establishment of *involuntary* "anticipatory" responses such as the startled eyeblinking that may follow a threatening gesture (Kimble, 1961). It is likely that human beings acquire many conditioned responses of this sort in the course of their lives. One may find oneself, for example, waking with a start at the slight click the alarm clock makes before it actually rings. Hearing an automobile horn from an unexpected direction may evoke a tensing of muscles in the hands on the wheel and in the foot on the brake. In the schoolroom, the teacher's pointing to an object to be described may become a conditioned signal for students to be alert for other stimuli from that direction. It is even possible that learned anticipatory responses may be largely what we mean when we speak of "paying attention" to something. Conditioned emotional reactions of an involuntary sort may be involved in reactions to snakes, spiders, or in other events accompanied by unexpected signals. Perhaps they also play a part in the determination of attitudes.

Despite the widespread occurrence of conditioned responses in our lives, the prototype remains unrepresentative of most learning situations. The learning of voluntary acts cannot adequately be represented by the pairing of conditioned and unconditioned stimuli. If a child wants to learn to ride a bicycle, she will get little help from some deliberate arrangement of conditions in accordance with the prototype of the conditioned response, because voluntary control of her actions is not acquired in this way. The same is true, needless to say, for most other kinds of things she must learn, beginning with reading, writing, and arithmetic. There can be little doubt that Watson's idea that most forms of human learning can be accounted for as chains of conditioned responses is wildly incorrect, primarily because it is an overly simple conception of what is learned.

The Learning of Verbal Associates

Hermann Ebbinghaus (1913) carried out an ingenious set of experimental studies of learning and memorization. He used himself as an experimental subject, and series of nonsense syllables of the sort NOF-VIB-JEX, as materials. These constructed syllables were employed in the attempt to gain control over the unwanted variable of previous practice, since it was apparent to Ebbinghaus that an association like BOY-MAN was already more or less well learned. In committing to memory these series of nonsense syllables, he was able to study the effects of the variables of length of series, order of presentation, and many others. Later investigators saw in the nonsense syllable a versatile tool for the study of *verbal association*.

An important and productive line of investigation of the learning of nonsense syllables and other verbal units was carried on by Robinson (1932) and McGeoch (1942) and down into the present day by Melton (1940, 1964), Postman (1961), Underwood (1964a), and many others. Generally speaking, investigators in this tradition have championed empirical research rather than the development of comprehensive theory.

For some years, investigators of verbal associate learning apparently believed that their findings could account for the learning of *single* associations. But even Ebbinghaus's results showed that the commission of one syllable to memory was strongly influenced by the presence of other syllables. During the many years of research following Ebbinghaus, the factors that have been found to affect the learning of nonsense lists have constantly increased, and the difficulty of experimental control has similarly become greater. The learning of any single association in a sequence has been shown to be markedly affected by the *interference* of other associations both within the list and outside it. A great many characteristics previously thought to describe the learning of single associates are now attributed to the effects of interference.

The verbal associate prototype must also be considered to represent a very limited range of actual learning situations. The differences in learning and retaining logically connected prose and poetry, as opposed to nonsense lists, have been apparent for many years (see Ausubel, 1968); and it is doubtful whether the interference that occurs within these two types of material follows the same laws. There may be a limited number of instances in which human beings engage in the learning of material whose members are arbitrarily related, as in learning the alphabet, or π to ten places. But the vast majority of verbal learning that occurs must be affected strongly by its meaningfulness, as experiments on verbal associates have demonstrated.

Insight

Opposed to these associationist trends in studies of learning has been the Gestalt tradition, reflected in the writings of Max Wertheimer (1945), Wolfgang Köhler (1929), and Kurt Koffka (1929). As conceived by these writers, learning typically takes the form of an *insight*, which is a suddenly occurring reorganization of the field of experience, as when one "has a new idea" or "discovers a solution to a problem."

Köhler used a variety of problem situations to study insightful learning in chimpanzees (1927). For example, a banana was suspended from the top of the animal's cage, out of reach. Several wooden boxes were available within the cage, but the animal could not reach the banana by standing on any one of them. A great variety of restlessness and trial and error was exhibited. On occasion, however, an animal was observed to act suddenly, as though he were carrying out a plan, by placing one box on top of another, then immediately climbing on this structure to reach the banana. As another example, one chimpanzee was observed, again after much trial and error, to put together two jointed sticks, which he then used as a single long stick to reach a banana placed outside his cage. Köhler called such learning *insight*, and emphasized its discontinuity with the previous trial-and-error behavior. The total successful act was put together and exhibited suddenly, without error, and as if by plan. Köhler's interpretation was that insight involved a "seeing" of relations, a putting together of events that were internally represented.

This form of learning in human beings has also been described by other Gestalt writers like Wertheimer (1945) and Katona (1940). For example, Wertheimer describes children's solutions, insightful and otherwise, to a geometric problem. Children who knew the formula for the area of a rectangle as $h \times b$ were asked to derive a means of finding the area of a parallelogram. Some proceeded in a rote fashion to multiply the length of the base times the length of the side, which, of course, is incorrect. Others were able to obtain the correct solution by cutting a right triangle from one side of the parallelogram, and attaching it to the other side, thus reconstructing a known figure, the rectangle. Still others were able to see the problem as one of dividing the entire parallelogram into little squares (a very sophisticated solution). Although a child may have tried several wrong approaches, a "good" solution was arrived at, according to Wertheimer, when the child could see the essential structure of the problem situation.

The most frequent criticism of the insight explanation of these learning events is, however, a very serious one. This is that animals and children solve these problems by *transfer from previous learning*. The chimpanzee is able to pile boxes one upon another because he has previously learned to do this, although not necessarily in the test situation. The child is able to identify the triangles as similar because she has previously done this with other right triangles. It cannot be said that such an explanation is not true, because in these Gestalt examples the factor of prior learning was not controlled. Despite the neatness of a theory that accounts for insight on the basis of the structure of the observed situation, the phenomena of insight in one instance after another have been shown to be affected by previous learning.

One of the most impressive modern evidences of the effects

of prior learning on insightful behavior occurs in Harlow's studies (1949) of *learning set*. Harlow trained monkeys to solve problems in which the correct choice among three objects was the "odd" one, the object dissimilar to the others. By trial-and-error learning, in which they were consistently rewarded for doing so, monkeys learned to choose the odd one of three objects. In the next problem, three new objects were presented, including an odd one, and the monkeys again learned to choose the odd one, somewhat faster this time. A third problem, again with a new set of objects, was solved faster than the second. After solving a few more of these oddity problems, the animal was able to solve oddity poblems (involving objects he had not previously encountered) at once, without any hesitation. He had acquired, Harlow said, a learning set that enabled him to solve oddity problems correctly without trial and error.

This evidence implies that previous learning, acquired through a number of encounters with similar problems, can establish an internal capability that makes the animal quite different from naive monkeys of the same age and strain. He becomes an "oddity-problem solver" monkey, who displays insight when given an oddity problem to solve. Obviously, this capability for insight did not arise because of "structuring of the situation." Rather it came from accumulated experience based on many individual trials of previous learning.

What can be said about the representativeness of insight as a prototype of learning? On the one hand, it does appear to represent some common learning occurrences which are rather easy to identify. When children are led to "see" relations, such as those between addition and multiplication or between weight and the "pull" of gravity, they often display insight. On the other hand, it is difficult to find insight in the learning of a great variety of other things. A child cannot learn the names of plants or stars in an insightful manner. He cannot learn to read by insight, nor to speak a foreign language. A student of biology does not learn the structures and functions of animals by insight. In short, insight cannot be a prototype for a vast amount of learning that human beings ordinarily undertake. Perhaps it occurs when we learn by "solving problems," but we also learn many, many things that are not problems. They may simply be facts or propositions or principles.

Reinforcement Theory

The term *reinforcement* has played a prominent role in determining the prototype situations studied by learning investigators.

It is important to note, first, that reinforcement has several different meanings, and it is doubtful at the present time that these can be conceived as similar to each other. Thorndike's classic statement of the law of effect has already been mentioned. Learning was thought to be influenced positively when the animal attained through its activity a "satisfying state of affairs." One direction of theory that represented a somewhat more precise statement of reinforcement has been proposed by Hull (1943) and also by Spence (1956) and N.E. Miller (1959). In this theory, reinforcement is typically considered to occur when a motive is directly satisfied—for example, when the fundamental drive of hunger undergoes a reduction in intensity. The effect of such reinforcement may be to strengthen a learned association or its recall or both. This general conception of motivation is often called *drive reduction theory*. Obviously, in the prototype learning situation to which it leads, the newly acquired response of the learner is followed as immediately as possible by the satisfaction of a drive. In the case of an animal, the intensity of the drive may be reduced by changing some internal state, as food reduces hunger. With human beings, however, various other stimuli may acquire reinforcement properties simply because they have been associated with drive reduction; these other stimuli become what are called "secondary reinforcers."

Skinner's conception (1968) of reinforcement, which constitutes a central part of his theoretical view of learning, is really quite different from that of Hull and Neal Miller. It does not necessarily depend on the notion of reward. To Skinner, "reinforcement" is the name for a particular arrangement of stimulus and response conditions that bring about the learning of a new association. Specifically, a response that one wants the individual to learn must be made *contingent* on the occurrence of certain *stimulus conditions*, which in turn bring about another response. This theory may appropriately be called the *contingency of reinforcement* theory. Typically, in the learning situation the response desired from the individual is deliberately made to precede the occurrence of some other response which has a high probability of being made. Thus the cat's obtaining food (as in Thorndike's puzzle box) is made contingent upon his pressing the lever. The child's activity of coloring pictures is made contingent upon his reading the names of the colors printed within the picture outlines. Various arrangements of contingencies (some of which will be referred to later) are possible. They have the common characteristic that the activity to be learned must be followed by the occurrence of some chosen event. This event shortly comes to exert control over the activity, and one can then say that learning has occurred.

Modern ideas of reinforcement are thus by no means unitary in their meaning. Yet it seems likely that the concept of reinforcement will continue to play a prominent part in learning theory. The common feature of the idea of reinforcement is its emphasis on the *aftereffects* of the response that is to be learned. To Thorndike, the satisfying aftereffects strengthened the association. To Hull and his associates, learning was influenced by aftereffects that brought about drive reduction (or motive satisfaction). To Skinner, the activity to be learned must be made to take take place in such a way that aftereffects are made contingent on its occurrence.

Learning and Memory as Information Processing

Contemporary theories of learning and memory reflect a rather distinct break with the tradition of learning prototypes so far discussed. The latter models give small emphasis to the *internal* processing supposed to occur when something is learned and retained. As is apparent, they are largely based upon the idea that *associations* are formed and stored as a result of learning. A marked contrast is shown by a number of newer learning theories, some of which are described by Tulving and Donaldson (1972). These theories propose an elaborate set of internal processes to account for the events of learning and retention. The contrast between old and new conceptions is so great, particularly in terms of the number and variety of internal structures and processes proposed, that one pair of authors has suggested the phrase "the new mental forestry" (Greeno and Bjork, 1973).

Contemporary theories of human learning and memory propose that the stimulation encountered by the learner is transformed, or *processed* in a number of ways by internal structures during the period in which the changes identified as learning take place. The initial stimulation is transformed by the receptors into a *registration* of the events seen, heard, or otherwise sensed. A second transformation takes place when this information is temporarily stored in what is called the *working,* or *short-term memory.* Still another kind of processing occurs when the information is put into *long-term memory.* Again, a different transformation takes place when the information is *retrieved* from short-term memory, and when it generates the responses that lead to the observed performance of the learner. These theoretical notions will be described in greater detail in Chapter 3, where we shall consider their implications for identifying optimal learning conditions.

The conceptions of information-processing models of learning and memory derive from a number of sources. In part, they have arisen from the attempts of learning psychologists to formulate "mathematical" learning theory, that is, to represent the variables of the learning process in mathematical equations. In large part also, they derive from the formulations of computer science, particularly its attempt to explore the limits of "intellectual" processing possible to the computer. A third source of thought reflected in information-processing theories is that of linguistic science, which attempts to understand how human beings learn and use language. Modern theories of learning appear to have revived a concern with how "ideas" are learned and stored, as opposed to how stimuli are associated with responses. Initial stages of internal processing, for example, are often conceived as operating on *propositions*, in which form "information" is to be stored in memory.

The information-processing model of learning has important implications for an understanding of instruction. The stimulating conditions that are brought to bear on the learners are not viewed simply as stimuli to which they "react." Instead, these external stimuli may be conceived as initiating, maintaining, or otherwise *supporting* several different kinds of ongoing internal processes involved in learning, remembering, and performing. A second and related implication is the conception that several *phases of processing* occur during a single act of learning. The external stimulation involved in instruction may be designed to support a single phase of such processing, or a combination of phases.

The Significance of Learning Prototypes

Throughout the scientific investigation of learning, there has been frequent recourse to certain typical experimental situations to serve as *prototypes* for learning. These prototypes have been derived from a number of sets of investigations, including animal learning, the conditioned responses, verbal associates, and the phenomenon of insight. A distinct change in these trends has occurred with the emergence of an information-processing model, which derives in part from computer and linguistic sciences. The choice of prototype has had considerable influence on the course of learning research. When contrasting predictons are made by theories, these prototypes are often appealed to as concrete ways of settling the issues. And it is from these prototypes that experiments are designed to test theoretical predictions. In other words, these prototypes continue to be the models that investigators of learning think about when they set out to study learning experimentally.

As examples, the prototypes themselves represent a variety

of kinds of learning. It has not been possible to "reduce" one variety to another, although many attempts have been made. In addition, there are many instances of learning that these prototypes apparently do *not* represent. There seem, in fact, to be varieties of learning that are not considered by these standard examples; their representativeness of actual learning phenomena is not at all comprehensive.

These learning prototypes all have a similar history in this respect: each of them started out as a representative of a particular variety of learning situation. Thorndike wanted to study animal association. Pavlov was studying reflexes. Ebbinghaus studied the memorization of verbal lists. Köhler was studying the solving of problems by animals. By some peculiar semantic process, these examples became prototypes of learning, and thus were considered to represent the domain of learning as a whole, or at least in large part. Somehow, they came to be placed in opposition to each other: either all learning was insight or all learning was conditioned response. Such controversies have continued for years, and have been relatively unproductive in advancing our understanding of learning as an event.

THE VIEW OF LEARNING PRESENTED IN THIS BOOK

How can one determine what learning is? The plan followed in this volume is twofold. First of all, it is to identify the general *types of human capabilities* that are learned. These are the behavioral changes that a truly comprehensive learning theory must explain (and which no theory as yet does encompass). Once these varieties of learning outcome have been identified, an account can be given of the *conditions* that govern the occurrence of learning and remembering. This leads to a description of the factors that determine learning, derived insofar as possible from available evidence in controlled experimentation. By this means it is possible to differentiate the sets of conditions that support the learning of different human capabilities.

Types of Learned Capabilities

From a naturalistic viewpoint, we shall describe the major kinds of learning outcomes, that is, five types of human capabilities that are learned. The traditional prototypes described in the previous section are considered to represent only parts of the situations in which learning of these capabilities occur, and therefore to depict mainly the elemental forms of learning. The information-processing model has a great deal more flexibility, and apparently greater relevance, in accounting for the learning of major types of capabilities. The kinds of questions to be raised and answered by subsequent chapters are suggested by the following set:

1. How does an individual learn the skill of threading a needle, of parking an automobile?
2. What conditions are necessary for the student to learn to "understand" Newton's laws of motion?
3. How can one account for the learning of factual information, such as the events of history, or descriptions of the natural world?
4. How does a learner acquire increased competence in finding new solutions to the many practical problems of life?
5. How can conditions be arranged to bring about the learning of positive social values such as honesty and respect for others' feelings?

All these human activities are learned. To suppose that one set of conditions governs their occurrence is to ignore the facts of common observation. A serious and comprehensive attempt to describe learning must take all these varieties into account. Naturally, it must make differentiations among them, and classifications of them, if these are possible. But to begin with the premise that "all learning is the same" would be quite unjustifiable.

The Conditions of Learning

The occurrence of learning is inferred from a difference in a human being's performance before and after being placed in a "learning situation." One may, for example, think of designing some conditions of learning to teach children how to form the plurals of nouns. The children could then be placed in the learning situation, and following this, their performance in making plural nouns could be observed. But it would be embarrassing to discover that their performance in making plurals was no better than that of children of equivalent age and ability who had *not* been placed in the same learning situation. The presence of the performance does not make it possible to conclude that learning has occurred. It is necessary to show that there has been a *change in performance*. The capability for exhibiting the performance *before* learning must be taken into account as well as the capability that exists after learning.

One set of factors contributing to learning is the capabilities that already exist in the individual before any particular new learning begins. The child who is learning to tie her shoelaces does not begin this learning "from scratch"; she already knows how to hold the laces, how to loop one over the other, how to tighten the loop, and so on. The theme is the same for other kinds of performances. The student who learns to multiply whole numbers has already acquired many capabilities, including adding and counting and recognizing numerals and writing them with a pencil. The student who is learning how to write clear descriptive paragraphs already knows how to write sentences and to choose words.

Previously learned capabilities make up the *internal conditions* necessary for learning. These internal conditions are brought into play by a set of "transforming" processes (as conceived by learning theory) which are to be described in Chapter 3.

A second major category of learning conditions is *external* to the learner. Let us suppose an individual possesses all the prerequisite capabilities needed for learning the English equivalents of ten foreign words. Another individual possesses all the prior capabilities for learning how to multiply two negative numbers. There is no particular reason to suppose that the external conditions needed for learning in one case are the same as the external conditions needed for learning in the other. In the first case, common observation would lead us to expect that the pairs of words would need to be repeated a number of times in order for learning to occur. But in the second case it is not apparent that repetition would have a similar effect. The differences between these two sets of external conditions, among others, will be discussed more completely in the chapters to follow. At this point, the important thing to note is that the conditions are not the same. Two different *types of capabilities* are being learned. They require not only different prior capabilities, but also different external conditions for learning.

The point of view to be expanded on in this book is probably apparent from previous paragraphs. Restated, it is this: there are several varieties of performance types that imply different categories of learned capabilities. These varieties of performance may also be differentiated in terms of the conditions for their learning. In searching for and identifying these conditions, one must look, first, at the capabilities internal to the learner and, second, at the stimulus situation outside the learner. The learning of each type of new capability starts from a different "point" of prior learning, and is likely also to demand a different external situation. The useful prototypes of learning are delineated by these descriptions of learning conditions.

ORGANIZATION OF THE BOOK

The first theme, varieties of what is learned, is introduced in Chapter 2. There, five major categories of learning outcomes are defined and exemplified. These five classes of outcome form a descriptive basis for many of the later chapters. Next, in Chapter 3, there is a shift to a second theme, the events which take place during learning. These events, as conceived by the information-processing model of learning and memory, must be related to *each* of the kinds of learned capabilities described in Chapter 2. By considering these events in relation to each kind of learning outcome, we describe in subsequent chapters the *conditions* for their learning.

The relationship of events of learning to learning conditions and to varieties of learning outcome is shown schematically in Figure 1.1. This figure intends to show that the two themes, categories of learning outcomes (as initially described in Chapter 2) and the events of learning (Chapter 3), together provide a framework for our account of learning conditions. Both Chapters 2 and 3 therefore have "foundational" functions. They examine human learning from two different viewpoints, which are to be related in the remainder of the volume.

One more topic must also be introduced before we proceed to the main substance of the book. Our discussion of the conditions of learning begins with what we call *basic forms* of learning. A great deal of research on learning has been devoted to investigating the establishment of *associations* and *response chains*. It should be

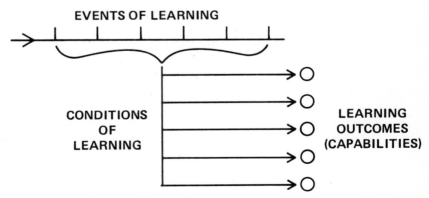

EVENTS OF LEARNING

CONDITIONS OF LEARNING

LEARNING OUTCOMES (CAPABILITIES)

FIGURE 1.1 The relations between events of learning, outcomes of learning, and conditions of learning, as these topics are to be treated in subsequent chapters.

noted that these kinds of learning do not, in our view, result in classifiable learning outcomes corresponding to the categories of Chapter 2 (and Chapters 5–10). Associations and response chains may best be considered, we believe, as *components* of learned human capabilities. In fact, they are usually treated as components in most contemporary learning theories. Since a great deal of research has been done on these components, much is known about the conditions of their learning. Furthermore, the characteristics of associations and response chains—how they behave once they are learned —are thought to be of fundamental importance to an understanding of the organized capabilities they compose. For these reasons, it is desirable to devote some attention to a description of the conditions of learning for these behavioral components, and to some of their major properties, in Chapter 4.

Having set these foundations, we proceed to provide descriptions of the conditions of learning for each type of human capability. Chapters 5 and 6 consider these conditions as they apply to several subvarieties of *intellectual skills*. (This and other categories of capabilities are defined in Chapter 2). Chapter 7 deals with *cognitive strategies* and their relation to problem-solving activities. Chapter 8 describes learning conditions for *verbal information;* Chapter 9 for *motor skills*, and Chapter 10 for *attitudes*.

In Chapter 11, we turn our attention to *analyzing learning requirements*. Given any specific human performance to be established by learning, how can such a task be analyzed to reveal its nature as a human capability, and the conditions necessary for its learning? Finally, in Chapter 12, we develop a general view of the application of knowledge about conditions of learning to the design of instruction. Although educational implications are discussed in each chapter, the intention in Chapter 12 is to explore the main outlines of systematic instructional planning.

EDUCATIONAL IMPLICATIONS

The identification of varieties of learning in terms of the conditions that produce them obviously has some definite implications for education and educational practices. Some of these may be immediately evident as the reader becomes acquainted in subsequent chapters with the conditions of learning for each variety. Others, however, need to be separately specified, since they are so fundamentally related to educational procedures.

The discussion of educational problems in later chapters

uses the fewest possible assumptions about the mechanics (or "logistics") of education. None of these logistic elements is assumed as a "given." Quite to the contrary, the point of view presented is that these features of the educational process should be determined by the requirement of getting students to learn efficiently. In discussing implications, therefore, it is assumed that neither a school building nor a set of books nor desks nor chalkboards nor even a teacher is necessarily needed. If these components of the educational system are shown to be necessary because of the requirements of learning, well and good. The only thing that must be assumed is the existence of a student who is capable of learning. This is the starting point.

How learning operates in everyday school situations is a most valuable kind of understanding. Such knowledge can make possible the successful accomplishment of activities of the following sorts:

1. *Planning for learning.* One important implication of the identification of learning conditions is that these conditions must be carefully planned *before* the learning situation is entered into by the student. In particular, there needs to be planning in terms of the student's capabilities both before and after any learning enterprise. Where does the student begin, and where is he going? What are the specific prerequisites for learning, and what will the learner be able to learn next? The planning that precedes effective instructional design includes carefully specifying these prerequisites.

2. *Managing learning.* How can the student be motivated to begin and to continue learning? How should the direction of interest and effort be guided? What can be done to assess the outcomes of learning? These questions pertain to the management of learning and the learning situation. They are general questions, in the sense that their answers are not specifically dependent on the content to be learned, or on the conditions of learning which prevail for that content. The management activities implied by these questions are necessary for any system whose purpose is to accomplish learning in an effective manner. Clearly, they are among the most important functions to be carried out by a teacher.

3. *Instructing.* The function of instructing derives in a specific sense from a description of the required conditions of learning. Instructing means arranging the conditions of learning that are external to the learner. These conditions need to be constructed in a stage-by-stage fashion, taking due account of each stage of

the just previously acquired capabilities of the learner, the requirements for retention of these capabilities, and the specific stimulus situation needed for the next stage of learning.

In the most general sense, instruction is intended to promote learning. This means that the external situation needs to be arranged to activate, to support, and to maintain the internal processing that constitutes each learning event. At one point, instruction may support the process of attending, an early phase of learning. At another point, the external stimulation provided by instruction may activate an internal strategy for "encoding" a mass of facts. And at still another point, instruction may primarily function to provide cues that make a newly learned skill memorable, or readily applicable to a novel problem encountered by the student. Whether instruction is given by a teacher, or is in some fashion provided by the student, it has several important functions in influencing the ongoing processes of learning.

GENERAL REFERENCES

LEARNING AND LEARNING THEORIES

Deese, J., and Hulse, S. H. *The psychology of learning,* 3rd ed. New York: McGraw-Hill, 1967.

Gagné, R. M. *Essentials of learning for instruction.* New York: Holt, Rinehart and Winston, 1974.

Hilgard, E. R., and Bower, G. H. *Theories of learning,* 4th ed. Englewood Cliffs, N.J.: Prentice-Hall, 1975.

Kimble, G. A. *Foundations of conditioning and learning.* New York: Appleton, 1967.

Melton, A. W. (Ed.) *Categories of human learning.* New York: Academic Press, 1964.

Travers, R. M. W. *Essentials of learning,* 3rd ed. New York: Macmillan, 1972.

WHAT IS LEARNED
-VARIETIES

During their lifetimes, people learn many things. In early childhood, they learn to interact with their environment in basic patterns of sensorimotor coordination—to move their bodies and limbs in space, to manipulate objects, to respond appropriately to their caretakers and protectors. Quite early, children learn to speak and to use language, an enormously powerful set of skills that will have the most profound effect on all their subsequent learning, and that will set them apart from all other animals for the remainder of life.

As beginning schoolchildren, human individuals face two major learning tasks. One is to continue their "socialization" by learning to interact with other children and adults in ways that will achieve moment-to-moment goals without conflict, and that will support the needs of others with kindness and consideration. A second task is to learn to respond appropriately to symbols which represent the environment in miniaturized fashion—pictures, diagrams, printed words, and numerals. This last is the intellectual task of reading, writing, and manipulating numbers. While the children continue to elaborate and supplement what they have learned of oral language, this distinctly new form of symbol use adds another dimension to their capabilities as human beings.

Once these basic language and symbol-using skills are acquired, schoolchildren are capable of learning many things. They learn about the earth, its peoples, and its geographic and physical properties. They learn about human society and its institutions. They learn how to deal with the environment not only by direct interaction with things and people, but by solving problems constructed in imagination. As they continue to acquire competence in symbol-using activities, children learn skills which prepare them for adult life: comprehending passages of printed language, composing communications in both oral and written form, solving practical quantitative problems with numbers.

As education continues, human individuals learn more and more specialized knowledge and more highly complex skills. They may learn things that will be useful in pursuing an occupation—such as typing or drawing or the procedures of real estate transfer. They may learn knowledge and skills that pertain to the role of a citizen—such as the structure of local government, the rules of jury trial, and the laws of voter registration. And the chances are that they will learn things that give them pleasure—such as listening to music, reading fiction, and participating in sports.

FIVE VARIETIES OF CAPABILITY

How is it possible to think about learning in all the varieties in which it occurs during the lifetime of the individual? How can we find common ground among the many instances of learning, considering the vast array of differences that are so apparent in what is learned?

As a first step, we must focus on *what is learned*, rather than upon the conditions that obtain when learning occurs. Learning conditions are not the same for different varieties of what is learned. Therefore, it is first necessary to distinguish as clearly as possible the *types* of outcomes that learning has—the *varieties of learned capabilities.* These capabilities, as we have seen in Chapter 1, must be observed as human performances. What must be looked for, then, are types of human performances that have common characteristics, even though their specific details vary. From these performances, inferences can be made about the learned capabilities which make them possible.

Consider, then, what major categories of human performance may be established by learning. The following list will be expanded upon in the remainder of this chapter.

1. An individual may learn to interact with the environment by *using symbols.* As a child, she uses oral language to deal with her environment symbolically, as when she says "Open!" as a request to her parent to open a door, or as a response to such a parental request. Reading and writing and using numbers are basic kinds of symbol use learned in early grades. As the learning of school subjects continues, symbols are used in more complex ways: distinguishing, combining, tabulating, classifying, analyzing, and quantifying objects, events, and even other symbols. Mentally translating 24 ounces into pounds is a simple example; making a singular verb agree with a singular subject in a written sentence is another. This kind of learned capability is given the name *intellectual skill.*

2. A person may learn to *state* or *tell* some information. He may tell someone a fact, or set of events, by using oral speech; or he may accomplish the telling by writing, typewriting, or even drawing a picture. Now, obviously, he must *have* some intellectual skills in order to do this stating. In other words, he must ordinarily know how to construct at least simple sentences. But the purpose of the learner's act is to *tell information*, not to display the intellectual skill of sentence construction. The stating done by two different people may vary in its skill, yet the information (the ideas) conveyed may be indistinguishable. What is stated may be a single idea, or a set of ideas which are ordered in some way (as in recounting a set of events). Being able to *state* ideas is a learned capability called *verbalizable information*, or simply *verbal information.*

3. The individual has learned *skills which manage her own learning, remembering, and thinking.* She has learned certain ways of attending to different parts of a text, for example. When asked to learn a set of apparently unrelated object-names, she approaches the task by searching for relationships among the names, or relationships among the names, or relationships with other more

familiar names. Perhaps the learner has acquired a particular skill which enables her to recapture the details of a scene she has witnessed, or to remember the main points of a lecture she has heard. She has also learned certain techniques of thinking, ways of analyzing problems, approaches to the solving of problems. These skills, which control the learner's own internal processes, are given the general name of *cognitive strategies*.

4. The human learner has learned to *execute movements* in a number of organized motor acts, as in threading a needle or throwing a ball. Often these individually coherent acts form a part of more comprehensive activities such as playing tennis or driving an automobile. The unitary acts are referred to as *motor skills*.

5. The learner has acquired mental states which *influence his choices of personal actions*. He may tend to choose actions that increase the likelihood of his choosing golf, for example, as a preferred recreation. Or he may choose to study physics rather than English literature during the time available for study. Such "tendencies," which are observed as *choices* on the part of the learner, rather than as specific performances, are called *attitudes*.

Here, then, are the five major categories of capabilities that human beings learn. These categories are intended to be comprehensive. Any learned capability, regardless of how it is otherwise described (as mathematics, history, economics, or whatever), has the characteristics of one or another of these varieties. We shall see in later chapters what conditions support the learning of each of these types of capability. First, though, we shall give some additional examples of each type.

INTELLECTUAL SKILLS

A person who takes a saw and cuts a piece from the end of a board is, of course, interacting with the environment in a *direct* manner. The possibilities are, though, that this action was preceded by planning which involved measuring a length like 22 3/16 inches, finding the difference between that distance and 24 1/8 inches, and perhaps using a tool with a straight edge to draw a line at a right angle to the board's edge. Many of the activities involved in such planning require the individual to interact with the environment *indirectly*, by using symbols. The learner represents linear extents by the symbols "22 3/16" and "24 1/8," and proceeds to operate on these symbols, rather than directly on the lumber itself. Some symbolic operations done "in the learner's head"; others may need to be worked out on a small writing surface. But these operations are very different from the actions that would need to be done directly to the wood, were such symbolic activity not possible. The capabilities that make symbol use possible are what we mean by *intellectual skills*.

The human individual learns many kinds of intellectual skills, simple and complex. The content of school mathematics, for example, is virtually all intellectual skills. However, intellectual skills pertain also to symbols other than numerals and number operations. In a larger sense, the symbols used to represent the environment to the learner constitute *language*. A relatively simple intellectual skill in the use of language symbols is the grammatical rule of the objective form of a pronoun following a preposition ("from her"). A more complex skill is involved in using a metaphor ("seeking the bubble reputation"). Since language is used to record and communicate the relationships (concepts, rules) that exist in any subject, the learning of such relationships can be expected to involve the learning of intellectual skills. It may be seen, therefore, that such skills are in many ways the most important types of capability learned by human beings, and the essence of what is meant by "being educated."

Conditions of Learning

How do individuals learn to use symbols in an intellectual skill? It is apparent that some conditions for this learning must exist within

Applying a rule: A performance involving an *intellectual skill*.

the learners (*internal* conditions), while others are *external* to the learners, and may be arranged for in instruction. These conditions will be described in subsequent chapters. Here, we shall give a few examples to illustrate what is meant by the "conditions of learning."

Suppose that some youngsters are expected to learn how to find the difference between a linear extent measured as 22 3/16 and another measured at 24 1/8; and assume that they don't already know how to do this. They can learn this particular skill (applicable to all mixed numbers containing eighths and sixteenths) quite readily, provided certain internal conditions are present. Particularly significant among these conditions is the availability of certain *component* or *subordinate skills*, which may be identified as "forming equivalent fractions by multiplying numerator and denominator by the same (small) number" ($1/8 \times 2 = 2/16$), "forming equivalent fractions by dividing numerator and denominator by the same (small) number" ($6/16 \div 2 = 3/8$), and "finding a difference by subtracting fractions having common denominators" ($4/8 - 1/8 = 3/8$). Of course, if these subordinate intellectual skills have not been previously learned and stored in memory, they will not be available to the learners, and must therefore be learned. But if they are present as internal conditions, learning of the new skill can proceed with little difficulty or delay.

The external conditions for acquiring the new skill may begin with a reminder that the subordinate skills will need to be recalled. Often this is done by means of verbal communications, such at "Remember how to subtract fractions like 3/16 from 4/16." A second kind of verbal communication may be used to inform the learners of the *objective* of their learning, that is, of what the specific purpose of the performance will be after they have learned it. This may be represented by some such statement as "The distances 22 3/16 and 24 1/8 are different; what you want to do is to find the amount of this difference." A picture and an example might also be used to convey this objective.

The next event which makes up the external conditions of learning for this skill is a communication that suggests "putting things together," that is, combining subordinate skills to make the new one. Actually, the learners may already see how to do this, or may be able to "discover" it themselves—in which cases no additional stimulation is needed. Often, though, some statement or "hint" may be valuable, such as "If you change 1/8 to 2/16, can you then find the difference?" Then, if the learners state the difference they seek as "1/16," only one more step is needed. This is the provision of a new example (such as the distances 1 7/8 and 1 1/4 on which the learners can demonstrate the application of their newly learned skill.

Thus, the *internal conditions* for learning an intellectual skill consist of (1) the previously learned skills which are components of the new skill and (2) the processes which will be used to recall them and put them together in a new form. Several distinct events make up the *external conditions*, and some of the most important have been mentioned in the example described. Notice that these external events have the purposes of (1) stimulating recall of the subordinate skills; (2) informing the learner of the performance objective; (3) "guiding" the new learning by a statement, question, or hint; and (4) providing an occasion for the performance of the just-learned skill in connection with a new example. These events are perhaps the most obvious features of the external conditions of learning; they serve to illustrate a set which will be described more fully in later chapters.

The Nature of Intellectual Skill

The most typical form of an intellectual skill, exemplified by the instance just described, is called a *rule*. When human learners have acquired a rule, they are able to exhibit behavior that is *rule-governed*. Such behavior does not mean that the learners are able to formulate or state the rule. Quite the contrary is often the case; young children evidence rule-governed behavior in their use of oral language, and in many other ways. The external observer of behavior (the learning investigator, for example) is able to draw the conclusion that a rule has been learned.

Performance is rule-governed when its regularity can be described only by a rule statement, rather than by the relation of a particular stimulus to a particular response. A rule statement relates *classes* of stimuli to *classes* of responses. In the fraction example mentioned previously, the learners acquired a capability which does not relate to the *particular* stimulus situation (22 3/16, 24 1/8), but to a *class* of situations having certain characteristics (mixed numbers including eighths and sixteenths). Accordingly, the performance of which the learners become capable does not consist of a *particular* response (1/16), but of an entire class of responses (any differences of the mixed numbers presented, expressed as eighths or sixteenths). Thus the performance made possible by learning is perfectly regular, and it can be described by a rule statement ("finding the differences in mixed numbers containing eighths and sixteenths as fractional parts") which relates an entire class of stimuli (any mixed number of the sort described) to a class of performances (any difference obtained). This is what is meant by rule-governed behavior. The individuals, then, can be said to have *learned a rule*.

It should be emphasized that when learners have acquired a rule (as shown by its use), they may be quite incapable of describing what has been learned, in other words, of *stating* the rule. In fact, learners are likely to think that stating the rule is a rather silly thing to do. It may also be a very difficult thing to do, because rule statements can quickly become enormously complicated in a linguistic sense. The most straightforward way of determining whether learners have learned a rule is to simply ask them to perform on an instance of the rule not previously encountered during learning. If the rule is one of finding differences in mixed numbers of the sort described, then a new instance such as 3 1/16 and 3 5/8 may be given. If the rule is one of using pronouns in the objective case following prepositions, an example might be "The captain was silent, and I waited to receive a signal from ―――.''

Subcategories of Intellectual Skills

We have seen that when component skills are already available in the learner's memory, rule learning is typically a matter of *combining* simpler component skills into a new pattern. Are these component skills also rules, which are analyzable into even simpler skills? In general, the answer to this question is affirmative. A complex rule may usually be shown to be composed of simpler rules, each of which in turn may be further analyzed into previously learned components. However, as this process continues, the nature of the components changes somewhat, and they need therefore to be separately identified and described.

CONCEPTS.   A fairly simple rule is represented by the statement "Air produces rust on iron." It can be seen that a rule is a *relation* between two or more *things*. In this case, there are three *thing-concepts:* air, rust, and iron. The primary *relational concept* is the verb "produces," with a secondary relation represented by the preposition "on." Thus, an initial step in the further analysis of a *rule* produces the new category of intellectual skill called a *concept*. The concept is a component of a rule, and is thus subordinate to it. Learning the simplest rule is a matter of combining some previously learned concepts in a particular way. If the learner has previously learned the concepts *air, rust, iron, produces,* and *on,* learning the new rule "Air produces rust on iron" may be readily accomplished.

(Note particularly, however, that learning the new rule does not mean learning to *state* the rule, which is not the same capability. Rather than stating it, the learner who has acquired this rule will be able to show that rust will appear on a piece of iron that is exposed to air).

DISCRIMINATIONS. Intellectual skills can be analyzed still further. Concepts can be seen to require even simpler skills, which are called discriminations. The things concepts represent have characteristics which may be described (in the ultimate sense) in physical terms. For example, a dime posseses certain object properties: it is round, of a certain thickness and diameter, a particular weight, silver in color, and metallic in its "feel." (As we shall see in a later chapter, these object properties are themselves concepts of a basic sort called *concrete concepts*). In order to learn to identify a dime, that is, to learn "dime" as a concept, these object properties must be distinguished from each other and from those of other objects. The learner must be able to *tell the difference* between objects varying in these particular qualities: between a color that is silver and one that is not silver, between shape that is small and round and one that is not, and so on. Telling the difference between variations in some particular object-property is called a *discrimination.*

Obviously, colors, shapes, sizes, texture, and most other discriminations important for further learning are learned very early in our lives. Kindergarten children are likely to have learned to "tell the difference" between the color red and some other color, as shown by an exercise in which they match the reds in an array of various colors with a red "sample." But not all the necessary discriminations have been learned; the children may need to learn to "tell the difference" between tones of nearby pitch, or letter-sounds that are similar (such as the short vowels "e" and "i"). Quite a few children must learn discriminations of printed letter patterns (for example, L and ⌐) as prerequisite capabilities for learning the letter concepts *d* and *b*. The necessity for learning additional discriminations sometimes becomes apparent in later school grades and in adult learning. For example, the pronunciation of certain sounds in a foreign language may need to be preceded by discrimination learning, so that the students first learn to "hear" the differences between the new sounds and sounds more familiar to their native languages. Consider also how many fine discriminations must be learned by a tea taster or a wine taster!

HIGHER-ORDER RULES. Just as rules may be analyzed to reveal the necessity for simpler skills (concepts, discriminations), the reverse process also occurs. Rules may be combined by learning into more complex rules, which may be called *higher-order rules*. Such rules have greater generality, that is, they apply to a greater variety of situations than do any of the component rules which make them up. Higher-order rules may be learned under conditions similar to those for other rules. It is often true, however, that higher-order rules result from the learner's *thinking* in a *problem-solving* situation. In attempting to solve a particular problem, the learner may "put together" two or more rules from very different content domains in order to form a higher-order rule which solves the problem.

Prerequisites in the Learning of Intellectual Skills

The very important learned capability called *intellectual skill* has a number of forms, some simple and some more complex. Distinguishing these forms of intellectual skill is important for two reasons. First, a significant characteristic of intellectual skills is that the learning of any one depends upon the prior learning of some other, simpler ones. Second, as we shall see in later chapters, certain notable differences exist in the conditions of learning required for each type of intellectual skill.

A summary of the interdependence of intellectual skills, and their dependence upon basic forms of learning, may be given as follows:

Higher-order Rules
require as prerequisites

|

Rules
which require as prerequisites

|

Concepts
which require as prerequisites

|

Discriminations
which require as prerequisites

|

```
┌─────────────────────────────────┐
│    Basic Forms of Learning:     │
│    Associations and Chains      │
└─────────────────────────────────┘
```

Subsequent chapters will devote attention to conditions for learning the following forms of intellectual skill: discriminations, concepts, rules, and higher-order rules. The significance of the internal conditions brought about by prior learning of prerequisite skills will again be emphasized in these descriptions. Preliminary to a discussion of these intellectual skills, we will begin in Chapter 4 with an account of basic forms of learning. While the latter (for example, conditioned responses and response chains) are seldom of consequence in deliberately planned instruction, their role as fundamental components needs to be recognized and their properties noted.

COGNITIVE STRATEGIES

A second and most important kind of capability learned by human beings is called a *cognitive strategy*. These are the skills by means of which learners regulate their own internal process of attending, learning, remembering, and thinking. These internally organized skills have been given different names by various authors. Bruner (1971) refers to them by the name "cognitive strategies," which he relates primarily to processes used in finding and solving novel problems. These strategies appear to be related to the "mathemagenic activities" described by Rothkopf (1971), and to the "self-management behaviors" referred to by Skinner (1968). They are called "executive control processes" by a number of learning theorists who favor information-processing conceptions (Greeno and Bjork, 1973).

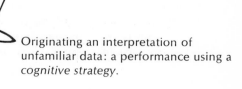

Originating an interpretation of unfamiliar data: a performance using a *cognitive strategy*.

Besides the increasing repertoire of competencies for dealing with their environment (intellectual skills), human learners acquire increasingly skillful strategies which they use to activate and regulate the learning, retention, and use of their own skills. Rather than being oriented to specific kinds of external content, such as language or numbers, cognitive strategies are largely independent of content, and generally apply to all kinds. If learners have improved their strategies of attending (one kind of cognitive strategy), this strategy will apply to the learning of any subject, regardless of content. Similar generality of application would be true of strategies of encoding, strategies of memory search, strategies of retrieval, and strategies of thinking.

A "mnemonic system" for remembering the sequence of ideas in a speech is an example of a cognitive strategy for retrieval. Such a system is of limited usefulness, and is not advocated here as something to be learned. Nevertheless, mnemonic systems of this sort have been used by prominent orators for a great many years. One strategy is to "locate" each point to be made in an imagined part of a highly familiar room. For example, the speaker might begin with the high cost of oil, imagining that this idea is located at the left of the doorway to the room. Then, proceeding clockwise, he might locate his next point (say, the scarcity of food supplies) as the closet door along the lefthand wall. If his next point concerns the incidence of starvation, this might be located in the left corner of the room. He would continue this process until he had completed the location of the main points of his speech. The imagined locations become cues for the retrieval of the speaker's points in the proper order. In using this method of cueing for speech remembering, the speaker has deliberately chosen a cognitive strategy, in this case a strategy for retrieval.

This particular cognitive strategy for remembering a sequence of ideas apears to have limited usefulness. The cognitive strategies that apply to remembering in a more general sense are undoubtedly more complex and subtle in their operation. It is likely, though, that everyone has learned *some* strategies for remembering, as well as some for attending, learning, and thinking. The strategies that some people possess appear to be better than those of other people, because the *quality* of their learning and thinking is better or faster or more profound. How to bring about improvement in cognitive strategies, so that every learner is "working up to potential" is one of the challenging problems of education.

Surely, not enough is yet known about how to arrange the conditions of learning so that effective cognitive strategies will be learned. For one thing, the strategies themselves have not been identified and described—most of them are obviously more complex than our example of the mnemonic system. It seems probable, too, that a learner's cognitive strategies improve in increments over long periods of time, rather than being totally learned in a few days, weeks, or months.

INTERNAL CONDITIONS.   Since cognitive strategies are internally organized skills, they must have some internal "stuff" to work on. Thus, it is reasonable to suppose that if an encoding strategy for the learning of facts is being learned, and if the strategy involves putting the facts in familiar categories, the learner must have a repertoire of convenient categories, previously learned and recallable for use. Similarly, if what is being learned is a strategy of thinking which can be used to solve problems of light refraction, the learner needs to have available some previously learned rules relevant to light refraction. Thus, although cognitive strategies are themselves free of specific content they cannot be learned or applied without some specific content. These mental operations, in other words, must have something to work on—they cannot be exercised in a vacuum.

The capabilities that need to be recalled from previous learning, in support of the learning and refinement of cognitive strategies, are usually intellectual skills. This necessity is illustrated in the previous examples: in one instance concepts (such as categories) must be recalled by the learner, in the other rules of light refraction. In addition, information is sometimes the kind of capability that must be recalled. For example, the exercise of cognitive strategies in composing an original essay on the distribution of electric power obviously requires the recall of a great deal of information about the subject. The effectiveness of the learner's cognitive strategies may be indicated by the *originality* of the essay, but the facts must be available in any case.

EXTERNAL CONDITIONS.   The identification of specific external conditions affecting the learning of cognitive strategies is perhaps least well known. In view of the absence of exact knowledge of what these strategies are, and how they operate internally, it is perhaps not too surprising that our knowledge of these external factors is limited. Arranging external conditions to establish and improve cognitive strategies is, after all, an attempt to exercise external control in an indirect fashion over the learning of capabilities that are internally managed.

Practical means of arranging optimal external events for

learning cognitive strategies usually come down to encouraging the learners to "practice" using cognitive strategies in a variety of novel situations. For example, various kinds of learning materials may be presented, so that the learners are faced with decisions about strategies for attending, strategies for encoding, or strategies for retrieving. A succession of extremely varied, novel problem-solving situations may confront the learners, requiring them to select and use different strategies in solution. The educational implications of these approaches call for the inclusion in courses of instruction of frequent occasions on which the students are "challenged" to discover new ways of managing their own learning and thinking (cf. Bruner, 1961, 1971).

VERBAL INFORMATION

A third major category of learned capability is *verbal information*. We expect individuals to learn verbal information during the course of their lives, and to retain a great deal of such information so that it is immediately accessible.

We know that individuals have learned some verbal information when they are able to "tell about it," or to state it. What they state, of course, is basically in the form of one or more sentences (or propositions) having a subject and a predicate. Information is thought of as *verbal*, or more precisely, *verbalizable*, because we know it in sentence form. Learner's statements often have the purpose of "telling" some other person or persons. However, it is often the case that learners may be "telling" themselves.

Information is an important capability for a number of reasons (cf. Gagné and Briggs, 1974, pp. 53–60). First, the individual may need to know certain facts—such as the days of the week, the months of the year; the names and locations of cities, states, and countries—simply because they are "common knoweldge" which every adult is expected to have. Second, verbal information functions as an aid and accompaniment to learning. The study of the principles of economics, for example, requires that the same is true for virtually every subject of the school curriculum. And third, information is important as specialized knowledge, which must be possessed by experts in any field. A trained chemist, besides knowing how to use the rules of chemistry, also knows a great deal of information about the subject.

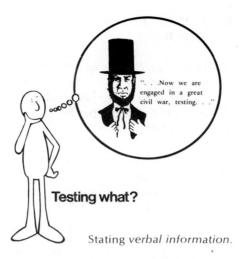

Testing what?

Stating *verbal information.*

Conditions of Learning: Verbal Information

The learning of verbal information requires its own set of internal and external conditions. Consider the following passage as containing information to be learned:

> The action of a volcano consists of the expulsion of heated materials to the surface of the earth from the interior. A volcano is a conical hill composed mainly of materials which have been thrown up from underground, and have built up around a central vent of eruption. The volcano has a truncated summit, and a cup-shaped cavity called a crater. In large volcanoes, rents appear on the sides of the cone, from which steam, hot vapors, and streams of molten lava are poured out.

This passage may be perceived as being composed of several propositions, which may be listed as follows:

Proposition 1: Function of volcanic action (expulsion of heated materials, etc.)

Proposition 2: Characteristics of a volcano (conical hill)

Proposition 3: Function of volcanic hill materials (thrown up from underground, etc.)

Proposition 4: Characteristics of conical hill (truncated summit, cup-shaped crater)

Proposition 5: Relation of cone to rents (rents form on sides of cone)

Proposition 6:   Function of rents (hot vapors and lava pour out
                  from them)

Let us assume that we are not immediately concerned with how the previous passage is presented—whether in print or by some aural source. How are these propositions learned? What conditions must be present in order for the learner to "tell" someone what the passage contains?

INTERNAL CONDITIONS.   Certain internal conditions for learning this material are immediately apparent. The learner must have available, from previous learning, linguistic rules (intellectual skills) which make possible the comprehension of sentences as structures composed of agent, action, location, object, and so on. If the passage itself has a complex syntactic structure, the learner must be able to interpret it as a proposition with conjunctions, dependent clauses, modifiers, and other elements. Apparently, the learner must also "know the meaning" of at least some of the words, although the extent of this requirement cannot be clearly specified. For example, the sentence "*Tilgem reduces gorbil*" is readily learnable as information even though the thing-concepts "tilgem" and "gorbil" are not known from previous learning.

Still another internal condition influencing the learning of information has been emphasized by a number of learning theorists, particularly by Ausubel (1968). This is the availability to the learner of "cognitive structures" of meaningfully organized information. Such structures of organized knowledge are considered to have been previously learned. They are related in some meaningful sense to the new information to be learned. For example, the passage about volcanoes would, according to Ausubel, be related to a more inclusive cognitive structure, previously learned, probably pertaining to hills, mountains, and other geographical features of the earth, including those having the name "volcano." The new information is conceived as being acquired when it is *subsumed* in this larger meaningful structure.

EXTERNAL CONDITIONS.   Two sets of conditions are of particular importance to the learning of information. The first is stimulation which makes the "cognitive structure" readily accessible to the learner—which reminds one of the larger meaningful context into which the new information will fit. Studies by Ausubel and his associates (Ausubel, 1960; Ausubel and Fitzgerald, 1962) have shown the effectiveness of what is called an *advance organizer* in accomplishing this purpose, and thus improving learning and retention of information. The advance organizer is a communication given to the learner prior to the encounter with the to-be-learned set of information. Its purpose is to remind the learner of the meaningful context already available in memory, and relevant to the new learning.

A second condition which may be externally arranged is that of *informing the learner of the objective* of the learning. In any passage of meaningful propositions, certain features of the information may represent the desired goal of learning, while others may be incidental. For instance the objective may be to learn definitions of new technical terms or to learn the dates of the events described or to learn new names for familiar things. The particular objective chosen, of course, will be reflected in the "test" given to assess the learning of the information. Informing the learner of the objective may be done in a number of ways, including a directly informing statement. A way which has been much investigated is to include within a passage of text the type of questions the learner will be expected to answer once the learning is completed (Frase, 1970; Rothkopf, 1970, 1971).

What about repetition as an external condition? Will not the information be better learned and retained if it is "gone over" several times? Practically speaking, repeated hearing or reading of an informational passage does improve its learning. The weight of evidence, however, attributes this result to variations in the internal processing of the information from one occasion to another. Certain "facts" within a total paragraph, may be processed when it is read the first time, certain others when it is read a second time, and so on. But the reading of the *same* fact more than once does not make it "stronger" in memory. Thus if a learner is asked to learn ten disconnected facts, repetition of the list increases the number of facts learned. It does so, according to most modern theories, because additional facts are "taken in" with additional repetitions.

Varieties of Information Learning

Just as intellectual skills come in varieties that are more or less complex, one might expect similar degrees of complexity among sets of information. It is true that certain distinctions can be made along this dimension of information, although the categories are primarily for convenience of description.

The simplest kind of information is a *label*, or *name*. This elemental form of information probably should be conceived as a *verbal chain* (see Chapter 4), in which an instance of the object is associated with its name. The verbal response itself may be of any variety: *Mark 2, telephone, James Grover,* or *laser beam.* It is important to note that learning the *name* of an object is not the same as learning the *concept* that the object represents.

The most typical form of unitary information is the *fact*, which is expressed as a simple proposition such as "Jet engines generate noise," or "The boy captured the model airplane." Single facts appear to depend for their learning on the internal presence of the "larger meaningful structure." Their learning may also be strongly influenced by the simultaneous presentation of other related facts. Information may also be learned sets of interrelated facts, or *bodies of knowledge.* The organization of these sets of facts, the ways in which the individual components are related to each other, may have a considerable effect on learning and retention.

MOTOR SKILLS

We turn now to a different and familiar kind of capability, usually easy to distinguish in human performance, a motor skill. (Note that there is no particular reason for considering this type of learning outcome, or any other type, in a particular order; each type is different). Many examples of motor skills come to mind. In the young child, there are the motor skills involved in such activities as dressing and eating. At the start of school, if not before, the child learns to make particular kinds of designs, including letters, with pencil and paper. Throughout the years of school, the individual learns the various motor skills involved in games and sports: throwing a ball, hitting a ball, jumping over hurdles, climbing. In courses in science, industrial arts, home economics, the student is likely to learn a number of tool-manipulation procedures which include motor skills. While not often given a central place in the curriculum, motor skills of many kinds are often involved in school learning.

We say that an individual has acquired a motor skill, not simply when she can perform certain prescribed movements, but when these movements are organized to constitute a total action that is smooth, regular, and precisely timed. The smoothness and timing of performances reflecting motor skills indicates that these

Planing the edge of a board:
a *motor skill.*

performances have a high degree of internal organization. As a consequence, it is typical for a motor skill to improve in precision and smoothness with continued practice over long periods of time (Fitts and Posner, 1967).

INTERNAL CONDITIONS.   Motor skills are usually composed of a sequence of movements. Thus, the action of driving a golf ball consists of the sequence of (1) positioning the body and the club, (2) raising the club over the shoulder, (3) aiming the club at the ball, and (4) making a full swing with involvement of arms and body. Printing the letter *E* requires a sequence of movements in which each of the four lines composing the letter is first (1) positioned and then (2) drawn to a particular length. The *procedural sequence* of a motor skill must be learned. Often, it is learned along with the motor skill itself. This procedure, which has been called the "executive sub-routine" (Fitts and Posner, 1967), has the character of a *rule* by which the learner knows "what comes after what." A procedural rule of this sort must be available to the learner as he continues to improve his motor performance by practice.

The separate parts of a motor act can often be learned and practiced separately as *part-skills.* These too may be prerequisites which have been established by previous learning. Swimmers, for example, sometimes practice separately the part-skills involving leg movements and those involving arms and head. A child who is learning to draw a square may "put together" the previously learned part-skills of line drawing and corner drawing.

EXTERNAL CONDITIONS. The most important set of external conditions for motor skill learning is provided by periods of *practice*. The sequence of motor acts gets repeated again and again in a situation which provides *feedback*, or *knowledge of results*. Sometimes, the feedback is an inherent part of the act being performed, as is the case when a musical instrument is being played. In other instances, additional feedback may be provided by a coach or instructor. In any case, an important part of the stimulus situation for motor skill learning is provided by internal feedback from the muscles. Apparently, it is this system of kinesthetic sensing over successive periods of practice which brings about the gradual improvement in smoothness and timing of motor skills.

ATTITUDES

The final kind of learned capability to be introduced in this chapter is attitude. We define *attitude as an internal state that influences (moderates) the choices of personal action* made by the individual. Attitudes are generally considered to have *affective* (emotional) components, *cognitive* aspects, and *behavioral* consequences (Triandis, 1971). Some investigators consider attitudes to have their origin in discrepancies of beliefs and ideas; others presume that attitudes arise from emotional states. Here, we empasize the effects of attitudes upon behavior, that is, upon the choices of action made by the individual. The internal states which influence these actions may well possess both intellectual and emotional aspects. However, it is their outcomes in human performance which provide the point of reference for our description of attitudes as learned dispositions.

The kinds of actions taken by human beings are obviously influenced greatly by attitudes. Whether one listens to classical music or rock, whether one obeys the posted speed limit while driving, whether one encourages one's spouse to express independent ideas, whether one votes for candidates who demonstrate concern for the public good—all are influenced by attitudes. These internal moderating states are acquired throughout life from situations encountered in the home, in the streets, in the church, and in the school.

Of course, the course of action chosen by an individual in any particular situation will be largely determined by the specifics of that situation. An individual who has a strong attitude of obedience to laws may nevertheless exceed the highway speed limit when he is in a hurry and no patrol cars in sight. A child who has a strong

Making a choice of
personal action: the
influence of an *attitude*.

attitude of honesty may steal a penny when she thinks no one will notice (Hartshorne and May, 1928). But the moderating tendency which persists over a period of time, and which tends to make the individual's behavior consistent in a variety of specific situations, is what is meant by an attitude. Obviously, observing and measuring the strengths of such tendencies is not an easy matter, since the effects of specific situational variables must be ruled out.

Attitudes are learned in a variety of ways. They can result from single incidents, as when an attitude toward snakes is acquired by an instance of fright, experienced in childhood at the sudden movement of a snake. They can result from the individual's experiences of success and pleasure, as when someone acquires a positive attitude toward doing crossword puzzles by being able to complete some of them. And frequently, they are learned by imitation of other people's behavior, as when a child learns how to behave toward foreigners by observing the actions of his parents. Regardless of these variations, there are some common factors in the learning and modification of attitudes.

INTERNAL CONDITIONS.   Attitudes must have some behavioral means of expression; this implies that certain capabilities appropriate to that behavior must be available to the learner. If the personal action to be influenced involves intellectual skill, these skills obviously must have previously been learned. For example, if an attitude of liking to solve mathematical puzzles is to be acquired, the learner must have some previously learned skills of numerical computation. If someone is to develop a strong attitude toward avoiding harmful drugs, some information about the drugs (such as their appearance and names) is a prerequisite. The learner who is to learn to like playing the piano must already have the motor skills to make such a choice of action possible.

When attitudes are acquired by imitation, or "human modeling," it is necessary that the learner have respect or admiration for the person whose behavior is being imitated. This condition often exists between child and parent, or between child and teacher. As is well known, the imitation of peers is likely to replace the imitation of parents during the preadolescent and adolescent periods, when the earlier unquestioning admiration for parents is replaced by a kind of rejection. In adults, attitudes are often established by modeling of people who are respected or admired for various qualities: physical attractiveness, virtuosity in sports, moral probity. But admiration for the model must exist, if the attitude exhibited in his on her behavior is to be acquired by the learner.

EXTERNAL CONDITIONS.   Since a variety of situations may lead to the modification of attitudes, their common features are not easy to identify. Apparently, there must either be (1) an emotionally toned experience on the part of the learner in following a course of action or (2) the observation of a "good" or "bad" effect of the behavior of a human model. The latter condition leads to the presumption that the success (or, alternatively, the failure) of the model is vicariously exprienced, that is, the learner is "vicariously reinforced" (Bandura, 1971).

A word should be said here about the inadequacy of certain external conditions in bringing about changes in attitudes. It has frequently been found that verbal statements intended to persuade are quite ineffective in changing listerners' attitudes (Hovland, Lumsdaine, and Sheffield, 1949). Whether based upon appeals to moral principles, to emotional states, or to rational arguments, these statements appear to be equally ineffective. Thus, it seems that a frequently important condition for attitude change is the presence of a human being who can serve as a "model," whether in actuality or in the learner's imagination. When the persuasion is attempted by a respected human model, a change in the learner's attitude is likely; persuasive statements without such a model are notoriously ineffective.

As is true for other learned states, the feedback of accomplishment, reward, or success is also an important condition for the learning of attitudes. The learner who succeeds at ice skating will very likely acquire a positive attitude toward that activity. The learner who has modeled an attitude of kindness toward animals will be more likely to maintain this attitude if his own acts of kindness to animals are rewarded in some fashion.

A SUMMARY OF TYPES OF LEARNING OUTCOMES

The five major categories of learning outcomes have now been described and exemplified. As a summary, we include Table 2.1, which lists these learned capabilities and gives a single example of each. The first category, intellectual skill, contains a number of subordinate categories, listed in order of their increasing complexity. The five major categories, however, are arbitrarily ordered in the table. They are simply *different* capabilities.

Subsequent chapters of this book describe conditions of learning for the categories of human capabilities shown in Table 2.1. Chapters 5 and 6 are devoted to *intellectual skills,* from discriminations to rules. Chapter 7 considers the higher-order rules involved in human problem solving, and goes on to discuss the

TABLE 2.1   Five Major Categories of Learned Capabilities, Including Subordinate Types, and Examples of Each

Capability (Learning Outcome)	Examples of Performance Made Possible
Intellectual Skill	Demonstrating symbol use, as in the following:
Discrimination	Distinguishing printed *m*'s and *n*'s
Concrete Concept	Identifying the spatial relation "underneath"; identifying a "side" of an object
Defined Concept	Classifying a "family," using a definition
Rule	Demonstrating the agreement in number of subject and verb in sentences
Higher-Order Rule	Generating a rule for predicting the size of an image, given the distance of a light source and the curavature of a lens
Cognitive Strategy	Using an efficient method for recalling names; originating a solution for the problem of conserving gasoline
Verbal Information	Stating the provisions of the first Amendment to the U.S. Constitution
Motor Skill	Printing the letter *R*
	Skating a figure eight
Attitude	Choosing to listen to classical music

category of *cognitive strategies* as it applies to problem-solving performance. The learning of *verbal information*—the stating or "telling" of names, facts, and ideas—is taken up in Chapter 8. Next we consider the learning of the class of capabilities called *motor skills*, in Chapter 9. The category of *attitudes*, in Chapter 10, completes the roster of major classes of learning outcomes.

EDUCATIONAL IMPLICATIONS

Human beings learn many different things during their lifetimes. One way to make sense of the enormous variety of outcomes learning produces is to consider them as *performance categories*. Although these categories cut across the subject matter (content) of what is learned, they possess certain distinguishing features. Each category implies that a different kind of capability has been learned.

When viewed in this manner, there are five major categories of learned capabilities: intellectual skills, verbal information, cognitive strategies, motor skills, and attitudes. Not only do these differ in the human performances they make possible; they also differ in the conditions most favorable for their learning. These learning conditions are partly *internal*, arising from the memory of the learner as a consequence of previous learning. In addition some learning conditions are *external* to the learner, and may be deliberately arranged as aspects of *instruction*. In the following paragraphs, we summarize some of the main points made in this chapter which apply to the planning of instruction. These points will be elaborated in subsequent chapters.

For the learning of intellectual skills, the most important internal condition is the recall of prerequisite skills which are components of the new skill to be learned. External conditions, often in the form of verbal directions, guide the "combining" of these simpler skills. Intellectual skills have several varieties, increasingly in complexity from *discriminations*, to *concepts*, *rules*, and *higher-order* rules.

The learning of *verbal information* depends upon the recall of internally stored complexes of ideas which constitute "meaningfully organized" structures. In addition, certain basic linguistic skills must be present so that information can be stored in propositional form. Externally, the conditions of learning operate to relate the to-be-learned information to these previously learned structures, which serve as cues for retrieval and as organizing schemes.

Cognitive strategies are internally oganized skills which the learner uses to manage his own processes of attending, learning, remembering, and thinking. They require as internal conditions the recall of intellectual skills and information relevant to the specific learning tasks being undertaken. Externally, what is apparently required is frequent opportunity to practice these strategies; over the course of practice, their use is refined and improved.

The learning of *motor skills* is attended by the recall (or prior learning) of an executive subroutine which provides the sequence and pattern for the performance, and often by the recall of part-skills which are combined into the total motor act. External conditions are mainly provided by repetition of the performance, that is, by practice.

Attitudes are internal states that modify choices of personal action toward objects, persons, or events. They are learned in a variety of ways. One of the most dependable is by "human modeling," which requires a pre-existing, or previously learned, respect for a real or imagined person. When this method of attitude change is employed, the external conditions consist of display of the desired behavior by the model, and the observation of a successful outcome (or reward). The experience of success following a behavior choice usually has a direct positive effect upon the learner's attitude.

GENERAL REFERENCES

VARIETIES OF LEARNED CAPABILITIES
Gagné, R. M. Domains of learning. *Interchange,* 1972, *3,* 1–8.
Gagné, R. M., and Briggs, L. J. *Principles of instructional design.* New York: Holt, Rinehart and Winston, 1974.

INTELLECTUAL SKILLS
Bourne, L. E., Ekstrand, B. R., and Dominowski, R. L. *The psychology of thinking.* Englewood Cliffs, N.J.: Prentice-Hall, 1971.
Klausmeier, H. J., Ghatala, E. S., and Frayer, D. A. *Conceptual learning and development: A cognitive view.* New York: Academic Press, 1974.

INFORMATION
Ausubel, D. P. *Educational psychology: A cognitive view.* New York: Holt, Rinehart and Winston, 1968.
Anderson, J. R., and Bower, G. H. Recognition and retrieval processes in free recall. *Psychological Review,* 1972, *79,* 97–123.

COGNITIVE STRATEGIES
Rothkopf, E. Z., and Johnson, P. E. *Verbal learning research and the technology of written instruction.* New York: Teachers College, 1971.

Bruner, J. S. The act of discovery. *Harvard Educational Review,* 1961, *31,* 21–32.

Bruner, J. S., Goodnow, J. J., and Austin, G. A. *A study of thinking.* New York: Wiley, 1956.

MOTOR SKILLS

Singer, R. N. (Ed.) *Readings in motor learning.* Philadelphia: Lea & Febiger, 1972.

Singer, R. N. *Motor learning and human performance,* 2nd ed. New York: Macmillan, 1975.

ATTITUDES

Bandura, A. *Principles of behavior modification.* New York: Holt, Rinehart and Winston, 1968.

Fishbein, M. (Ed.) *Readings in attitude theory and measurement.* New York: Wiley, 1967.

Triandis, H. C. *Attitude and attitude change.* New York: Wiley, 1971.

3

THE EVENTS OF LEARNING

In the previous chapter, we described the five major kinds of *outcome* learning can have. In this chapter we take a different view of learning, this time as a *process*, or more precisely a *set of processes*. A single act of learning has (at least for purposes of analysis) a beginning and an end. Each instance of learning takes a certain time, although that may in some cases be only a few seconds. During the course of an act of learning, a number of different processes are at work. One can analyze these processes into phases, each of which performs a different kind of processing. The occurrence of phases of processing is what is meant here by the *events of learning*.

The processes of learning form the basic structure of information-processing theories of learning. These theories have adopted a model which posits internal *structures* of the human learner, and the kinds of *processing* accomplished by each of these structures. The processes and structures described by learning theories are inferred from empirical studies of learning. Presumably, these processes and structures reflect the action of the human central nervous system, and are compatible with what is known about the neurophysiology of the nervous system. The structures and their activities remain as postulated entities, however, since they have not yet been related to particular locations or operations of the brain.

From the model of learning and memory employed in modern theories, one can identify the phases of processing which take place from the beginning to the termination of an act of learning. These events of learning provide us with valuable indicators of what conditions of learning are needed for the completion of each phase. The purpose of this chapter is to describe the events of learning postulated by the information-processing model, and the conception they provide of human learning and memory.

THE INFORMATION-PROCESSING MODEL

The model of learning and memory which forms a basis of information-processing theories (for example, J. R. Anderson and Bower, 1973; Atkinson and Shiffrin, 1968; Rumelhart, Lindsay, and Norman, 1972) postulates a number of internal structures in the human brain, and some corresponding processes that they carry out (Greeno and Bjork, 1973). A version of this model is shown in Figure 3.1.

The Flow of Information

From the environment, the learner receives stimulation which activates his receptors and is transformed to neural information. Initially, this information enters a structure (or structures) called the *sensory register*, where it persists for a very brief interval. The investigations of Sperling (1960) and Crowder and Morton (1969) have shown that information from the various senses is "registered" in more or less complete form for a few hundredths of a second. The components of this sensory representation which persist for a longer period must be the object of the process of *attention* (often equated

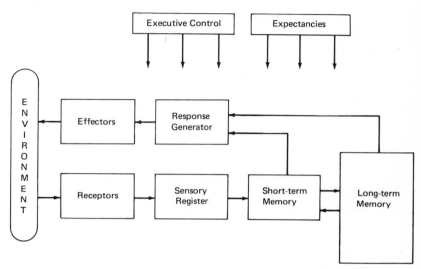

FIGURE 3.1   Model employed by information-processing theories of learning and memory. (From R. M. Gagné, *Essentials of learning
for instruction.* Copyright © 1974 by The Dryden Press, a division of Holt, Rinehart and Winston. Reproduced by permission of Holt, Rinehart and Winston.)

with *selective perception).* The remaining components simply die
away and no longer affect the nervous system.

THE PROCESS OF ATTENDING: SELECTIVE PERCEPTION.   The
entire "picture" recorded in the sensory register does not persist
into subsequent phases of learning processing. Instead, patterns of
this stimulation are perceived. Instead of random arrays of stimuli,
such invariances as edges, textures, slants, and three-dimensional
objects are synthesized (J. J. Gibson, 1950). Essentially, this process
is known as *selective perception,* and depends upon the learner's
ability to *attend* to certain features of the contents of the sensory
register, while ignoring others (Lindsay and Norman, 1972, pp. 355–
370). Attending therefore accomplishes a transformation which
forms a new kind of input to the short-term memory.

SHORT-TERM MEMORY STORAGE.   The transformed information
next enters the short-term memory, where it can persist for a limited
period, generally thought to be up to twenty seconds. Some evi-

dence exists for two forms of storage in the short-term memory: (1) an acoustic form, in which the information is internally "heard" by the learner, and (2) an articulatory form, in which the learner "hears himself saying" the information. In retrieving a telephone number for the time needed to dial it, for example, one has the impression of hearing onself repeat the number (cf. Lindsay and Norman, 1972, pp. 337–355). It is also quite possible, however, that the learner uses other kinds of storage, such as visual imagery, in remembering pictures of scenes he has witnessed (Paivio, 1971).

The capacity of the short-term memory is limited. A number of studies have suggested its capacity may be similar to that of the "immediate memory span," that is, a number of individual items equal to seven plus or minus two (see Klatzky, 1975). The items themselves may be letters, numbers, or single-syllable words. Once this capacity has been exceeded, old items must be "pushed out" when new items are added to the store. However, an interesting additional property of the short-term memory is its ability to carry out silent, mental repetition of the information, a process called *rehearsal*. Obviously, rehearsal extends the capacity of the short-term memory to store items for longer time intervals. The rehearsal process may also aid the encoding of information as input to the next structure, the long-term memory. But the *number* of items stored in the short-term memory is not increased by rehearsal.

ENCODING.   From the standpoint of learning, the most critical transformation of the information occurs when it leaves the short-term memory and enters the long-term memory. This process is called *encoding* (cf. Melton and Martin, 1972). The information which is available as certain perceptual features in short-term memory is now transformed into a *conceptual*, or meaningful, mode. Apparently it is stored not as sounds or shapes, but as concepts whose meaning is known and can be correctly referenced in the learner's environment. The information that is stored is *organized* in various ways, rather than being merely collected. A number of modern theories, for example, postulate that one basic form in which learned material is encoded is as meaningful *propositions* (J. R. Anderson and Bower, 1973; Kintsch, 1972; Rumelhart, Lindsay, and Norman, 1972). Some propose even more complex forms of encoding, involving hierarchical relations of concepts (Quillian, 1968) or topical organization of the sort occuring in paragraphs (Crothers, 1972). At the same time, it is generally recognized that visual and other kinds of imagery may form a basis for the encoding that characterizes the input to long-term memory (Bower, 1969; Paivio, 1971).

Apparently, then, many forms are taken by the process of encoding. What is learned may be encoded in meaningful verbal units like sentences or perhaps even more comprehensive units. Encoding processes may take the form of tables, spatially arranged matrices, diagrams, or detailed images, or "pictures," of the information being learned. The main characteristic of encoded material (for entry into long-term memory), is that it is *semantic*, or meaningfully organized.

STORAGE. In encoded form, the information is stored in long-term memory. Some evidence suggests that storage is permanent and does not suffer loss through time (cf. Adams, 1967). However, it is evident that what is stored may become inaccessible, for a number of reasons. *Interference* between newer and older memories may block the accessibility of stored information. Mainly, though, the phenomenon of forgetting may be due to the ineffectiveness of search and retrieval processes (to be described next). Other than these few points, little is known about what specifically happens to learned material during the time it is stored in long-term memory.

RETRIEVAL. In order to be verified as learned, entities must be retrieved from long-term memory. It is generally supposed that the process called retrieval requires that certain *cues* be provided, either by the external situation or by the learner (from other memory sources). The cues are employed to match or "link" what is learned, in a process of *search*. The entities so located are considered to be "recognized," and may then be retrieved.

Often, what is retrieved is returned to the short-term memory, which has the character of a "working memory," or perhaps a "conscious memory" (Atkinson and Shiffrin, 1968). Here the learned material becomes readily *accessible* to the learner. So that it may be combined with other inputs to form new entities (that is, new encodings). Or it may be transformed to activate the *response generator*, which provides an oranization for various human performances. Sometimes, as in the case of "automatized" skills, learned entities are directly transformed as inputs to the response generator.

Recall of what has been learned may be exhibited within a short time after the internal events of learning have taken place. Within limits, such a performance is spoken of as being "immediate." Many times, however, the performance is not called for until a future time—hours, days, or weeks later. In such circumstances, the internal processing that occurs may be somewhat different. Presumably, search and retrieval processes of the long-term memory are involved in both cases, but additional kinds of processing may be necessary in "delayed" recall.

The processes of recall apparently sometimes require a *reconstruction* of the events remembered, rather than simply a reinstatement of them. For example, people can usually answer correctly a question about the number of windows in the house or apartment in which they live. How do they do this? Apparently, they first retrieve a visual image of each room, and then, while holding it in mind, count the windows. When asked to recount a set of events observed months ago or a story read in the distant past, the learner may "flll in the gaps" by a *construction* which "makes sense," and at the same time be quite convinced that his remembering is accurate (cf. Bartlett, 1932).

When the recall of what has been learned involves application to a new situation or to a novel problem, *transfer of learning* is the phenomenon of interest. Although this matter has not been extensively studied as an information-processing problem, it appears that special processes, or particular combinations of processes, must be involved. An individual who is required to bring her knowledge or skill to a novel problem must often conduct a *search* process that is more complex and extensive than that used for familiar situations. It is likely also that the *cues* which she employs to retrieve what is learned (and to be "transferred") are of a different sort than those used for immediate, or even delayed, recall. Novel problem situaations requiring transfer of learning may involve internal processing of the sort called "interpreting," as well as that of active "construction" (cf. Lindsay and Norman, 1972, pp. 381–385).

RESPONSE GENERATION.   The next transformation along the route of information flow is accomplished by the *response generator*. This structure determines, first, the basic form of human responding—that is, whether the performance will involve speech, the large muscles of the trunk, the small muscles of the hand, or whatever. Second, it determines the pattern of the performance—the sequence and timing of the movement involved in the action to be accomplished. In general, the processes associated with the response generator insure that an organized performance will occur.

PERFORMANCE.   The penultimate stage of information processing consists in the activation of the effectors; this results in patterns of activity that can be externally observed. If what has been learned is a capability of stating the sense of a set of propositions, then "telling" is the performance that shows learning has occurred. If a motor skill such as writing with a pen has been acquired, then this performance may be exhibited, and its occurrence verifies (to an external observer) that the capability has been learned.

FEEDBACK.   Learning is a process which appears to require the closing of a "loop" which begins with stimulation from the external environment. The final link of this loop is an event which also has its origin outside the learner, in his environment. *Feedback* is provided by the learner's observation of the effects of his performance. This is the event that provides the learner with the confirmation (or verification) that his learning has accomplished its purpose. If someone has set out to learn to ride a bicycle, feedback is provided by her observation that she can ride it. If the purpose of learning has been to acquire the intellectual skill of finding the area of triangles, feedback is provided by the successful computation of the area of one or more triangles. Although feedback usually requires a check which is external to the learner, its major effects are obviously internal ones, which serve to fix the learning, to make it permanently available. This is the phenomenon called *reinforcement*, about which we shall have more to say later.

A SUMMARY OF INFORMATION-PROCESSING FLOW.   Our account of the internal processing that constitutes the events called learning and memory is not complete, and some very important processes have yet to be described. Nevertheless, it appears desirable to review the main features of the flow of information from the external environment through the learner's nervous system, out to his environment, with another link to internal processes through feedback.

Figure 3.2 displays the structures of the information-processing model (Figure 3.1) in a vertical linear fashion. Its right-hand column indicates the processing associated with each structure; we have described these processes in the previous paragraphs.

Stimulation from the learner's environment activates receptors to produce *patterns of neural impulses*. These patterns persist in the sensory register for a brief interval (some hundredths of a second), from which they may be processed by *selective perception* into perceived objects and object-qualities, or features. This "information" may then be stored in short-term memory as auditory,

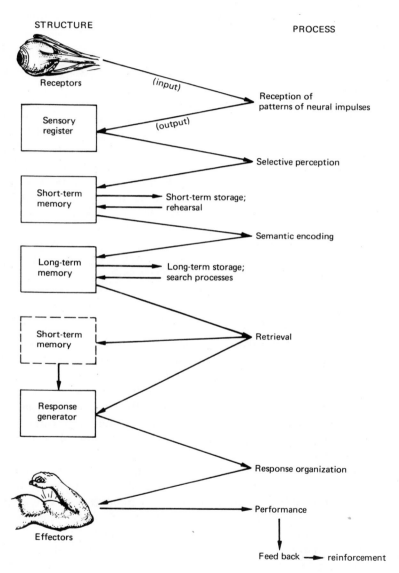

STRUCTURE

PROCESS

Receptors

(input)

Reception of
patterns of neural impulses

Sensory
register

(output)

Selective perception

Short-term
memory

Short-term storage;
rehearsal

Semantic encoding

Long-term
memory

Long-term storage;
search processes

Short-term
memory

Retrieval

Response
generator

Response organization

Effectors

Performance

Feed back ➔ reinforcement

FIGURE 3.2   Processes of learning and memory as inputs to and outputs
from postulated structures of the information-processing
model.

articulatory, or visual images, which are subject to *rehearsal*. As input to the long-term memory, the information is *semantically (or meaningfully) encoded*, and then stored in this form. Processes of *search* may be instituted, followed by the process of *retrieval*. At this point, the information may be returned to the short-term memory, which is conceived as a "working" or "conscious" memory. From this structure, or directly from long-term memory, the response generator is brought into play to generate a suitable *response organization*. The signal flow from this structure activates effectors which exhibit the human *performance*. Feedback is provided via the learner's observations of this performance, and the phenomenon of *reinforcement* establishes the learned entities as capabilities available for future recall, exercise, and use. Since these events are displayed linearly in the figure, the feedback loop is not indicated as part of the diagram, but must be imagined by the reader.

Control Processes

Our description of information flow and the processes involved in it provides a conception of the internal events of learning. In computer language, these processes might be called "routines." Obviously, though, as these processes occur in human learning, they have a richness and complexity that goes beyond their basic functioning. The ways in which an individual learner may approach, engage in, and execute an act of learning all display the characteristics of variability, flexibility, and ingenuity. How are these qualities of learning, remembering, and generalizing to be conceived and brought into the total picture?

The answer lies in the processes listed at the top of Figure 3.1, *executive control processess* and *expectancies*. Both these processes have been largely acquired by the individual in previous learning. For that reason, they constitute another separate portion of long-term memory. Their function is to determine (or choose) the particular kinds of information processing in which the learner engages to accomplish particular kinds of learning tasks. In other words, they determine the learner's approach to one or more ways of processing information—how he goes about attending and storing and encoding and retrieving information.

It may be noted that the arrows leading from the boxes labeled *executive control processes* and *expectancies* are not connected with other structures in the model. Actually, this incompleteness is intended to illustrate, on the one hand, that these control processes are capable of affecting any and all of the phases of information flow; and on the other, that their interconnections have not yet been fully worked out.

EXECUTIVE CONTROL PROCESSES. The *cognitive strategies* described in the previous chapter are executive control processes. They are called by various names by different writers. For example, they appear to be equivalent to the *mathemagenic activities* described by Rothkopf (1970) and the *self-management behaviors* referred to by Skinner (1968). Bruner (1971) makes frequent reference to cognitive strategies, and considers their learning a most important educational goal. As control processes, they occur prominently as part of the model of information-processing theories of learning and memory (Greeno and Bjork, 1973).

Control processes influence attention and selective perception by determining what features of the contents of the sensory register will be entered into the short-term memory. They may determine what is rehearsed in short-term memory, and thus what is retained for longer storage. They may influence the choice of an encoding scheme—whether the learner finds meaning in small chunks or large—and thus determine how the information is stored in long-term memory. They may affect the learner's scheme of search and retrieval, and thus determine how much or how well one remembers. Probably also, they have an effect on the choice of a format for responding, and so influence the kind of response organization chosen for the learner's performance. And by no means of least importance, they determine the learner's strategies for generalizing and problem solving, and so influence the quality of the individual's thought.

A simple example from the psychological laboratory may illustrate the essential nature of an executive control process and its functioning in learning. Rohwer and Lynch (1966) gave children the task of learning twenty pairs of words such as LION-HORSE, STICK-COW. The subjects studied the total list and later were asked to respond with the second word when given the first. The encoding strategy deliberately employed with half the children was to use the words in a sentence such as "The STICK hurts the COW." For the other half of the children, randomly chosen, a different encoding strategy was used; the words were presented in a phrase such as "the STICK and the COW." A considerably greater number of words were remembered after two review trials by the group using the first strategy than by the group using the second. Of course, these children did not choose the strategies in this instance. But these approaches are examples of strategies which can be readily learned and employed as executive control processes for this particular kind of learning task.

EXPECTANCIES. Expectancies are another subclass of executive control processes. They represent the *specific* motivation of learners to reach the goal of learning which has been set for them, or which they have set for themselves. What learners intend to accomplish can influence what they attend to, how they encode the learned information, and how they organize their responses. An expectancy is a continuing set, oriented toward the goal accomplishment, which enables learners to select the outputs of each processing stage. Thus, if learners have the expectancy of learning how to find resistances of electric circuits, they may selectively reject the perception of the shape of the resistors or the location of the circuit in a piece of equipment. They will encode certain characteristics of the circuit relevant to its resistance, and ignore others. They will choose a response organization which reports or identifies a numerical value of ohms, and not some other physical property. In other words, all of their internal processes will be responsive to the goal that these learners "have in mind," which is an expectancy.

Although the concept of expectancy is not commonly included as an integral part of information-processing theories of learning, it has figured prominently in the work of one modern theorist, namely, Estes (1972). His proposal has been adopted for the account given here. Estes considers that the feedback effects of reinforcement influence learning and memory not because they are "rewarding," but because they convey information to the learner. Information that informs the learner if he has reached his goal, or how close he has come to it, has a reinforcing effect. In other words, feedback is useful because it *confirms the learner's expectancy*, and this is what is meant by the term *reinforcement*. While this view of reinforcement denies none of the empirical facts about reinforcement (cf. Skinner, 1969), it provides a novel interpretation of this important concept.

THE ROLE OF EXECUTIVE CONTROL. The two interrelated sets of processes called "executive control" and "expectancy" play crucial roles in any information-processing account of human learning and memory. It is apparent to the theorists who use the model shown in Figure 3.1 (or a similar one) that learning and remembering cannot be fully accounted for in terms of a simple diagram of information flow. There must also be processes by which the learner *selects* the nature of processing at each of the stages shown. How the attention of the learner is directed, how the information is encoded, how it is retrieved, and how it is expressed in organized responses are all matters that require a choice of strategies. This choice is the function of the executive control processes, including the expectancies which have been established before learning is undertaken. These processes have the effect of making the learner a truly intelligent being—one who can "learn to learn," and therefore one who can engage in a large measure of self-instruction.

It is of interest to note that control processes must themselves be learned, as we indicated in the last chapter when cognitive strategies were being described as one type of learning outcome. Of course, some very elemental control processes are probably determined largely by innate genetic factors (for example, the organization of visual perception or the basic structure of language). Nevertheless, learning most probably plays a major part in the formation of useful strategies of learning, remembering, and thinking, particularly as they apply to the subjects acquired in school. As for expectancies, these too are influenced by learning in the sense that they must be related to various persisting motives possessed by the learner. In addition, though, expectancies are capable of being changed in their specific content in the manner of a set (or "mental set"). Thus, an expectancy to "find the multiplication product of two-place numbers" on one occasion may give way to an expectancy to "convert decimals into fractions" on another occasion. The two expectancies do not conflict with each other, since they are temporary. Both may be equally effective in selecting specific processes to serve the learning goals they represent.

EFFECTS OF EXTERNAL EVENTS ON LEARNING PROCESSES

Up to this point, our account of the events of learning has been concerned almost entirely with the *internal* structures of learning and memory and with the processes they mediate. To be sure, we have assumed that some external stimulation is present to begin the information flow, and that feedback from the external environment reinforces the learning. But our account of learning events is still incomplete; while these internal processes are occurring other things can happen *externally*, and these have only been hinted at. Of utmost importance is the fact that these additional external events can have substantial effects on learning—on how it takes place, and on how effectively it accomplishes its purpose.

External events that transpire, or are made to transpire, during the course of a single act of learning can have the effect of *promoting* learning and memory. Alternatively, of course, external events may do the opposite; they may hinder learning. But we are mainly concerned here with the positive aspects of these events, with the effects that lead to the furtherance of learning and remembering.

Apprehending Phases of Learning

In the very brief period before something is stored (and therefore "learned"), the learner's processes are concerned with "taking in," or *apprehending*, the stimuli relevant to learning. These preparatory phases consist, first, of an alertness to stimuli which goes under the general name of *attention*. Second, there is the very important screening and organizing of the raw stimulation, or what we have described as *selective perception*; this leads to a storage of relevant stimulus features in the short-term memory. From this point, the transformed information is ready to be again transformed (encoded) to enter the long-term memory.

EXTERNAL EVENTS IN ATTENDING.   It is easy to grasp the idea that learners who must respond to some stimulation in order to learn must first *receive* this stimulation. This means that their senses must be oriented toward the source of the stimulation, and that they must be ready to take it in. Attending may be thought of as the initial event of learning, made possible by an internal state that can often be detected by observing what learners are looking at or listening to. This internal state is believed to be in part a function of a central neural system called the *reticular activating system* (Lindsley, 1958), and the state itself is one of "arousal" or "alertness."

The kinds of external stimulation that produce alertness are fairly well known. Increases in the intensity of stimulation, such as those made by bright lights or loud sounds are usually dependable stimuli for the command of attention. More generally, any sudden change in stimulation, up or down, is likely to constitute an effective stimulus to alert the learner. The sudden dimming of lights in a theater alerts the audience; a sudden turning off of the sound of a radio similarly commands the attention of a listener.

EXTERNAL EVENTS IN SELECTIVE PERCEPTION.   The processing of information that has been registered in the *sensory register* proceeds with *perception*, which is selective in its operation. One who is looking at another person may selectively perceive her face or hands or clothing or, under other circumstances, her totality as a person. Similarly, one may perceive a window as a part of a wall or, alternatively, as twelve individual panes of glass. Selective perception is guided by a control process that includes a temporary (mental) *set* (see Hebb, 1966, pp. 82–101), which may be activated by verbal instructions or other forms of stimulation. Thus, a common external event affecting perception is the verbal communication that activates such a mental set.

Other kinds of stimuli are frequently used to influence selective perception. For example, the learner who is reading a text may encounter pictures which illustrate key concepts, and italic type or underlining which indicates important terms. If pictorial material is being presented, diagrams may emphasize important features. Or arrows and heavy outlining may be employed to differentiate the features to be learned. In general, the purpose of these additional stimuli is to facilitate selective perception by increasing the differences between relevant and irrelevant features of the objects or events being observed.

The process of perceiving implies that the individual is differentiating the stimulus from other stimuli, or parts of the stimulus from other parts. The limits to what someone is able to do in this respect depends largely on previous learning of stimulus discriminations. This prior learning, determining the limits of what can be perceived, is often called *perceptual learning* (see E. J. Gibson, 1969).

Acquisition

In order to enter and be stored in the long-term memory, the material of learning must be *encoded*. That is, it has to be transformed into a form that is *semantic*, or *meaningful*. The directional meaning of *starboard*, containing no inherent clues to the landlubber, may be encoded as "The *star boarder* is always right." A long sequence of numbers such as 1 4 9 1 6 2 5 3 6 4 9 6 4 8 1 may be encoded as "squares of successive whole numbers."

The process of encoding, and the subsequent entry of the encoded information into long-term memory, may be considered the central and critical event in an act of learning. The phases of processing that precede this one are preparatory; the phases that follow it are confirmatory, in the sense that they "prove" that learning has occurred. Encoding, however, is the critical process by which incoming information is transformed into learned and memorable capabilities.

This pivotal process of encoding may obviously be affected by events in the learner's environment or events planned as a part of instruction. A particular scheme for encoding may be directly communicated to the learner. For example, a teacher may organize a set of facts about the farm products of the various states in a table which divides the states into regions, and the products into several convenient categories. The table then becomes an encoding scheme, and quite an effective one. As a second possibility, learners may be encouraged to provide their own individual encoding schemes. Some may use visual images, others rhymes, others a network of superordinate concepts. In this case, the external stimulus is functioning to activate a *set* of the learners, which thereafter brings to bear one of the learner's cognitive strategies for encoding.

Storage, Search, and Retrieval

Having been acquired, the new capability must be *stored* in order to qualify as something that has truly been learned. The change that has been brought about by the process of encoding now is retained, over a period that might be a few minutes or a lifetime.

One intriguing possibility, supported by some clinical evidence, is that retention in long-term memory persists for a lifetime, and in this sense is permanent. Penfield (1951) has reported instances in which patients whose brains are electrically stimulated under medical treatment have reproduced in startling detail childhood memories—episodes involving recall of situations, sounds, conversations, and other aspects of past events. Such events have been forgotten in a practical sense, but traces of them may persist in the brain. If memory traces are in some sense permanent, the reasons for forgetting must be sought in other events such as interference from other stored memories, or obstacles to retrieval.

The storage of learned items in long-term memory can presumably be influenced by external events, particularly by the learning of other items. Research has been conducted on the retention of verbal information (of the sort which forms meaningful propositions), to determine whether *interference* (Postman, 1961; Underwood, 1964) occurs, and whether it follows the same course as it does with unconnected words or word-pairs. Previously learned propositions might conceivably influence the storage of propositions to be newly learned (*proactive interference*); or the learning of new propositions might interfere with the storage of some that are already learned (*retroactive interference*). Evidence for interference of both types has been obtained with meaningful information (Crouse, 1971; Slamecka, 1959, 1960). However, it appears that such interference occurs when the specific propositions learned directly negate each other (R. C. Anderson and Myrow, 1971). Under conditions in which entire passages of text contain different, or conflicting, information, evidence of interference is not found. For example, Ausubel, Robbins, and Blake (1957) found that the retention of ideas learned from a passage on Buddhism was not diminished, but slightly enhanced, when followed by the reading of a passage on Christianity.

SEARCH AND RETRIEVAL. The processes of *search* and *retrieval* seem to be definitely subject to the influence of events external to the learner. Having learned a set of verbal items (in this case, unconnected words) the learner's retrieval of these items is markedly improved when *cues* in the form of categories are provided (Tulving and Pearlstone, 1966). For example, the recall of words in the category "vegetable" may be cued by that category name. Cues of this general sort may also be provided by the learner himself, when such a strategy is suggested to him (Dong and Kintsch, 1968).

The provision of cues to search and retrieval is obviously an external event of great importance to remembering. Such cues can be incorporated into the situation designed for initial learning and encoding (Thomson and Tulving, 1970). Presumably, they can also be effective at the time of recall, if they are able to suggest to the learner a search strategy which is relevant to the encoding already accomplished. Cues for retrieval can take a variety of forms. Besides the "categorization" function already referred to, cueing can be accomplished by matrix or tabular organizations or by pictures (see Paivio, 1971).

Performance and its Organization

The transformations brought about by the structure called the response organizer (Figure 3.1) are surely affected by events external to the learner. Somehow, these external events must indicate to the learner the general form of this performance is usually established by the initial learning situation and is typically a verbal communication. (Of course, in the case of young children, other means may be used). The kinds of performances indicated to the learner are those described in the previous chapter. That is, the external communication establishes a set for the learner (1) to *tell* something, (2) to *demonstrate* how to do something, (3) to *execute* a skilled movement sequence, (4) to *choose* a course of personal action, or (5) to *originate* a solution to a novel problem.

Establishing the correct set for the learner's performance is normally done in instruction by "informing the learner of the objective" of the learning. It is easy to understand that gross errors of performance are avoided by the learner who possesses a correct impression of the performance aimed for. If the student has learned about Ohm's law, telling about it is one kind of performance; demonstrating its application to an electric circuit with particular values of voltage and resistance is quite a different kind of performance. Originating a way of teaching Ohm's law understandably to sixth-graders would be still another kind of performance.

Processes of Executive Control

We have now considered the ways in which external events may influence the flow of information in the model of Figure 3.2. What about the executive control processes of this model? Can they also be influenced by external events? What can be done outside the learner to affect the operation of these control processes (which we equate to the *cognitive strategies* of Chapter 2)?

Executive control operations can be selected and activated by external events. One example of such effects is to be seen in the activation and selection of particular kinds of *attentional sets* by instructions or by questions (Frase, 1970; Rothkopf, 1970). When questions interspersed in textual passages refer to particular categories of content (such as technical terms or dates), these categories are selectively perceived by the learner. Apparently as a consequence of these external events, classes of content involved in the interspersed questions are learned and remembered to a greater extent than other kinds of content. Thus, particular strategies for selective perception are activated and selected as a result of these events.

Activation and selection of a similar sort may be seen in the effects of instructions or hints on encoding strategies. When learners are encouraged to encode items to be learned in terms of vivid imagery, learning and retention are improved over items learned without such instructions (Bower, 1970; Rohwer, 1974; Wittrock, 1974). Again, the activation of particular types of sets for retrieval of information, such as the use of concrete or "picturable" cues, sets into motion strategies of retrieval that are superior to other strategies in their effects on recall (Paivio, 1971). Over periods of practice in problem solving, instructions to children demonstrating the use of such strategies as "waiting until all the evidence is in" and "systematically reviewing the facts" have been shown to activate strategies leading to improved solving of "detective story" problems in fifth-grade children (Olton and Crutchfield, 1969). Thus, external instructions, suggestions, and other similar events appear unmistakably to affect the selection and use of various control processes, and to exert influence on many different internal learning processes.

Expectancies, too, are often influenced by external events such as verbal instructions. Typically, verbal communications that "inform the learner of the objective" of learning establish specific expectancies. This sort of communication, externally delivered, may influence any or all of the internal processes of learning by enabling the learner to "keep on the track" and to avoid gross errors. A specific expectancy established in this manner enables the learner to know when his learning is complete—he is able to perform in the desired manner and to receive reinforcement thereby.

A SUMMARY OF EXTERNAL EVENTS
WHICH INFLUENCE INTERNAL PROCESSES

Table 3.1 summarizes the relationships described in the previous section, indicating the kinds of external events which can affect ongoing internal processes.

TABLE 3.1   Internal processes of learning, and the effects which can be exerted upon them by external events

Internal Process	External Events and Their Effects
Attention (Reception)	Stimulus change produces arousal (attention)
Selective perception	Enhancement and differentiation of object features facilitates selective perception
Semantic encoding	Verbal instructions, pictures, diagrams, suggest encoding schemes
Retrieval	Suggestion or display of cues such as diagrams, tabular arrays, rhymes, aids retrieval
Response organization	Verbal instructions about the objective of learning inform the learner about the class of performance expected
Control processes	Instructions establish sets which activate and select appropriate strategies
Expectancies	Informing the learner of the objective establishes a specific expectancy for performance

In early stages of the learning act, abrupt stimulus changes can arouse the learner's attention. Once the information is received in the sensory register, emphasis on features of objects (by underlining, colored printing, or other forms of enhancement) contributes to the process of selective perception. Beginning with the process of semantic encoding (for entry into long-term memory), a variety of forms of "learning guidance" may be employed. Often, instructions are delivered orally or by printed text. Pictures, diagrams, tables, lists, or combinations of these vehicles may be employed as external stimuli. Their purpose is to provide, or to suggest, schemes for encoding and cues for search and retrieval. Verbal instructions are also frequently used to define for the learner the pattern of responding, that is, the type of performance expected (in particular, one of the five kinds of learning outcomes described in the previous chapter).

Executive control processes, including expectancies, are also influenced by external events. Verbal instructions establish (mental) sets which put in operation various cognitive strategies available to the learner. These strategies (or control processes) may in turn influence any and all phases of information processing involved in an act of learning. Expectancies are also established, typically, by verbal communications which tell the learner what the objectives of learning are.

EDUCATIONAL IMPLICATIONS

The information-processing model of learning and memory is of great significance for the planning and design of instruction in educational programs. The model tells us that an act of learning, however brief or extended it may be in time, is composed of several phases. Learning begins with the intake of stimulation from the receptors, and ends with the feedback that follows the learner's performance. Between these events are several stages of internal *processing*. Instruction, then, is not simply a matter of presenting an initial stimulus—instead, it is composed of several different kinds of external stimulation which influence several different processes of learning.

As a whole, the stimulation provided to the learner during instruction has the function of *supporting* the various kinds of internal processing which are taking place in the learner. The external events called instruction may support internal processes by *activating* a mental set which affects attention and selective perception. Or an external event may *enhance* the internal process of encoding, by providing an organization that is adopted by the learner. Another possibility for instruction is to *maintain* the operation of an executive control process, such as an expectancy of performance outcome, so that internal processing preserves a particular direction. As the learning act is completed, the external event called *feedback* is a particularly important function of instruction. Taken together, these various external events make up what is called "instruction." In appropriate ways, they support the operation of internal learning processes.

Assuming that some motivation exists, the internal processing that constitutes learning is ongoing. When the outcomes of learning are deliberately planned, the events of instruction can likewise be planned to achieve these outcomes. Naturally, the learner can influence the internal processes by means of his own executive control processes (cognitive strategies). In fact, as experience is gained, the learner can be expected to gain an increasing degree of control over his own processes, and this control will probably become more and more effective. Thus, the learner becomes capable of engaging in self-instruction to an increasing extent as learning continues. The kinds and amount of support required in externally provided instruction may be expected to vary with the learner's own sophistication in self-instruction.

The five varieties of learning outcome described in the previous chapter are supported by some instructional events which affect their learning in the same ways, and by some events which affect them differently, depending on what is being learned. An example of the former sort is feedback, which is an essential condition for all learning. An example of the latter sort is instruction that supports encoding, the nature of which differs for each kind of learning outcome. The conditions of learning to be described in subsequent chapters are concerned with the external events that support the different types of learned capabilities, as well as with the internal events (processes) these external events influence. These conditions provide a basis for the design of effective instruction.

GENERAL REFERENCES

THE INFORMATION-PROCESSING MODEL OF LEARNING AND MEMORY
Atkinson, R. C., and Shiffrin, R. M. Human memory: A proposed system and its control processes. In K. W. Spence and J. T. Spence (Eds.), *The psychology of learning and motivation,* Vol. 2. New York: Academic Press, 1968.

Gagné, R. M. *Essentials of learning for instruction.* New York: Holt, Rinehart and Winston, 1974.

Greeno, J. G. and Bjork, R. A. Mathematical learning theory and the new "mental forestry." *Annual Review of Psychology,* 1973, *24,* 81–116.

Klatzky, R. L. *Human memory: Structures and processes.* San Francisco: Freeman, 1975.

Lindsay, P. H., and Norman, D. A. *Human information processing: An introduction to psychology.* New York: Academic Press, 1972.

PROCESSES OF LEARNING

Adams, J. A. *Human memory.* New York: McGraw-Hill, 1967.

Gibson, E. J. *Principles of perceptual learning and development.* New York: Appleton, 1969.

Melton, A. W., and Martin, E. (Eds.) *Coding processes in human memory.* Washington, D.C.: V. H. Winston, 1972.

Paivio, A. *Imagery and verbal processes.* New York: Holt, Rinehart and Winston, 1971.

Trabasso, T., and Bower, G. H. *Attention in learning.* New York: Wiley, 1968.

EXTERNAL EVENTS AND THEIR EFFECTS ON LEARNING

Gagné, R. M. and Briggs, L. J. *Principles of instructional design.* New York: Holt, Rinehart and Winston, 1974. Chaps. 7, 8.

4

BASIC FORMS OF LEARNING

The important varieties of learning outcomes have been described in Chapter 2. We shall find these five categories and their subcategories of major interest throughout this book. Considerably more information needs to be given about them, and about the external and internal conditions needed to bring them about, which have been briefly suggested in Chapter 3.

Up to now, however, we have not made further reference to the kinds of learning studied by generations of learning psychologists mentioned in Chapter 1. What about the learning of the connections described by Thorndike, the verbal associations of Ebbinghaus, the conditioned responses studied by Pavlov, or the operant responses of Skinner? We return to these "simple" prototypes of learning in this chapter. We do so in order to present as comprehensive a picture as possible of learning processes and conditions; and in order to reflect the continuities that exist between these models of learning and those to be described in the remaining chapters.

In following this course, we need to provide a reasonable point of view towards these "basic" conceptions of learning. Are the association, the conditioned response, the learned connection, so outdated by modern discoveries that they must be rejected and abandoned completely? Were investigators of learning pursuing blind alleys in their study of these prototypes of learning?

THE STATUS OF BASIC LEARNING FORMS

What investigators of basic forms of learning intended to investigate was the *characteristics of learning by association.* Thus, the study of the conditioned response was undertaken to find and verify the conditions which governed the "association" of a new stimulus (such as the sound of a buzzer) with a response such as salivating. Those who studied animal trial-and-error learning were seeking to explore the conditions leading to an "association" between a stimulus situation (such as a maze or a problem box) and the animal's response of running or pushing. And those who investigated the learning of word-pairs were seeking to describe the conditions of "association" of the first word as a stimulus with the learner's response of saying (or writing) the second word.

The study of learning employing these prototypes, whether conducted with animals or human beings, was dominated by the requirement of employing learning situations in which an identifiable stimulus was in fact associated with a relatively invariant response. It was usually assumed, or sometimes deliberately postulated, that the learner was internally "associating," or "connecting," a stimulus (S) with a response (R). Thus the psychology of learning came to depend on what is called "S-R theory," in which interest centered upon accounting for the dash between the S and the R, which represented the learned association.

It is now generally recognized by those who conduct scientific investigations of learning that even the most deliberately simplified learning situation cannot be adequately accounted for as an association between an S and an R. Over a period of thirty years, for example, the brilliant theoretical account of paired-associate learning formulated by E. J. Gibson (1940) in S-R terms has given way to the recognition that such learning is an exceedingly complex act that requires the postulation of a number of different internal processes (Battig, 1968), each of which may be affected by a distinct set of external conditions (see, for example, S. E. Newman, 1964; Saltz, 1963).

The Role of Association in Learning

It is virtually a certainty that more than association is involved in learning, even when learning is apparently of a very simple type. Nevertheless, the idea persists, with considerable justification, that association is *one* of the processes that occurs in learning. Furthermore, association seems to occur with such frequency that it deserves to be called a *basic* process.

The British associationist psychologists were impressed with the fact that when two "ideas" are commonly experienced together, the presentation of one tends to arouse a thought of the other. Thus, an individual seeing a picture of a dog is likely also to think of a cat, since the two have commonly been experienced as household pets. People do possess these associations, which are to a considerable extent predictable on the basis of known common experiences (Deese, 1966). For this reason alone, it may be expected that associations are involved as processes in learning.

Information-processing theories of learning and memory often begin with the assumption that what is learned (that is, what is "stored in long-term memory") are propositions (see several examples in Tulving and Donaldson, 1972). When attempting to account for the storage of propositions and their retrieval, however, such theories find it necessary to assume that association is a basic process in learning. Propositions and their components may require the existence of "peg-words," "category names," and "associative networks" of words, to account for the ways in which new items of information are learned and old ones recalled.

If association remains, even in modern theories, as a basic learning process, how shall its characteristics be studied? We have seen that various attempts to investigate association are now thought to be inadequate, because the simplified learning situations employed were not really simple. How to study a process like association is a puzzling problem to which no ready answer has yet been suggested. The study of basic forms of learning has provided a number of suggestions about how association "works," and what conditions govern the learning of associations. It is worthwhile to take some note of characteristics of association that have been revealed by these studies. At the same time, the reader must be aware of the possibility that what appear to be studies of "S-R learning" may turn out to have much more complex explanations than that implied by words such as "association" or "connection."

Varieties of the Basic Forms of Learning

There are three prototypes of learning which have been examined with the intention of revealing the characteristics of "associative learning." First, there is the conditioned response studied initially by Pavlov (1927), and by many learning psychologists throughout the world. This type is here called *signal learning*, to emphasize that the learner is associating an already available response with a new stimulus, or "signal." Second, there is the learning called *operant conditioning* by Skinner (1938), which is also frequently called *instrumental conditioning* (Kimble, 1961). This kind of learning is to be found in Thorndike's work (1898) with animals in problem boxes, as well as in many other animal learning studies involving mazes, compartments, levers, and other devices in which a response of the learner is "instrumental" to a subsequent reinforcing event. Here, this type of learning is called *stimulus-response learning*.

A third way of studying associative learning has been with human beings learning to make verbal responses to stimuli which are words, or pairs of words. Again, the intention has been to investigate the characteristics of association as a learned "connection" betwen one word and another, following the tradition of Ebbinghaus (1913). We call this *verbal association learning*.

To these three basic types of learning situations, we add another which is closely related to, and sometimes difficult to distinguish from, the basic three. This is *chaining*, in which the individual associations are connected in sequence; rather than S-R the learner is exhibiting S-R~S-R~S-R, and so on. Chains of S-R's are readily learned by animals, for example, as successive turns in a maze. In human beings, similar sequences may be learned as "mental mazes." Chaining is also exhibited in *verbal sequences*, such as lists of words or nonsense syllables.

SIGNAL LEARNING

There is a wide acquaintance with signal learning, whether in common domestic animals or in other human beings. Most people have observed one or more instances of signal learning in household pets; for example, the cat or dog may run to the kitchen when he hears his food dish placed on the floor. A cat runs from the driveway when he hears a car approaching. George Bernard Shaw (1959) thought that these things were completely obvious and could not see why Pavlov had to "discover" them. Of course, in a real sense, Pavlov did not discover them; but true scientist that he was, he attempted to measure them under carefully controlled conditions. In so doing, he gave us an account of the conditions and characteristics of signal learning that is as valuable today as ever.

The Phenomenon of Signal Learning

The learning of Pavlov's dog to salivate in response to a signaling buzzer is known to most educated adults. However, the example of a signal learning situation used here is one that has been extensively studied in human beings, namely, the eyeblink. There are many precise data on the learning of this connection, and the results are particularly instructive concerning the question of what is learned.

When a small puff of air is delivered to the cornea of a person's eye, the eye blinks rapidly. This is the connection Pavlov called the *unconditioned reflex*, meaning that the action is there to begin with and is not conditional on any previous learning. Now if a click is sounded about a half-second before the puff of air reaches the cornea, we have one of the important conditions for the establishment of a learned connection. The click (or other "neutral" stimulus) is called the *conditioned stimulus* (the "signal"). When this sequence of events—click–puff of air—is repeated a few times, it is usually possible to demonstrate the existence of a newly learned connection, namely,

$$S \longrightarrow R$$
$$\text{click} \qquad \text{blink}$$

This is done by presenting the click by itself, without the puff of air, and noting that the blink response occurs.

Experimental studies have shown that the conditioned blink is not the same as the unconditioned blink (Kimble, 1961). The unconditioned blink is a more rapid response; it occurs in 0.05 to 0.10 second, whereas the signaled blink takes 0.25 to 0.50 second. With suitable methods of measurement, the two are clearly distinguishable as responses. Thus it appears that what is learned may be called an *anticipatory blink* to a signal. Such a blink does not avoid the puff of air; if it did, this would be an instance of S-R learning, which we shall discuss next. But the learned blink anticipates the puff of air; it signals "puff of air to come."

How often does the pairing of signal and unconditioned stimulus have to be repeated in order for a conditioned response to be established? Although there is no single answer to this question, the evidence suggests that a number of repetitions must be used in order to establish a stable response, at least for the eyeblink. Figure 4.1 shows the curves of learning obtained for three groups of subjects differing with respect to "ease of conditioning." These graphs show the frequency of occurrence of the learned response following various numbers of trials in which stimuli were paired. Other instances have been reported, however, of signal learning taking place much more rapidly than this, depending particularly on the strength of the unconditioned stimulus. Signal-response connections have been shown to occur in a very few trials when the signal accompanies a stimulus arousing a strong emotion. This was the case, for example, when the child Albert learned to fear a white rat when a sudden loud sound (produced by striking a metal bar) was made behind his head at the time he was reaching toward the ani-

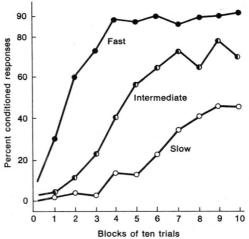

FIGURE 4.1   Learning curves showing the increase in frequency of conditioned eyeblinks in successive blocks of trials, for groups of learners whose rate of conditioning was found to be slow, intermediate, and fast. (Data of K. W. Spence, *Behavior theory and conditioning.* New Haven: Yale University Press, 1956).

mal (Watson and Rayner, 1920). Following this conditioning, the child showed fear whenever the white rat was brought near him.

Conditions of Learning

With the help of these examples, it should not be difficult to state the conditions necessary for signal learning. Evidently, one must deal with conditions that need to be present *within the learner*, as well as with conditions that can be manipulated *in the learning situation*.

CONDITIONS WITHIN THE LEARNER.   In order for signal learning to occur, there must be a natural reflex—typically a reflexive emotional response (startle, fear, anger, pleasure)—on the part of the learner. It must be clear that an *unconditioned stimulus* can evoke such an *unconditioned response*. Further than this, there is much evidence of marked individual differences in the rapidity with which people acquire signal-response connections. Such differences are not markedly related to intelligence (or facility for academic learning). But they *are* significantly related to the level of *anxiety* with which the individual typically faces life's problems and decisions. Many studies have shown that people who tend to be anxious acquire conditioned responses more rapidly than do less anxious people (J. A. Taylor, 1951).

CONDITIONS IN THE LEARNING SITUATION.   The conditions for signal learning that can be externally controlled are *contiguity* and *repetition*.

1. The signaling stimulus and the unconditioned stimulus must be presented in close proximity to each other, in the order named. These necessary time relationships have been tested in situations involving many kinds of signals and responses. Variations have been found to be very small, so that it is reasonable to think that they reflect some stable characteristics of nervous system functioning. Learning occurs dependably when the conditioned stimulus precedes the unconditioned by an interval between 0 and 1.5 seconds, and most readily when the interval is about 0.5 second.
2. As Figure 4.1 shows, repetition of the paired stimuli is also necessary. The amount required, however, may vary considerably depending on the response involved, and on the intensity of the unconditioned stimulus. However, signal learning does not

appear to be an all-or-nothing occurrence. The connection appears to increase in strength (or dependability of occurrence) as the repetitions of paired stimuli increase in number.

Thus the conditions of signal learning are relatively simple to describe and rather easy to control. Besides the eyeblink used in our example, conditioned responses have been established for many behaviors in the human being, including salivation, changes in skin resistance, respiration changes, nausea, and hand withdrawal. Early investigators attempted to establish signal learning with the use of certain simple reflexes like the knee jerk and the pupilary reflex, but these have generally been found to be extremely difficult to condition. Diffuse emotional responses or their components are, in contrast, rather easy to condition. A response falling in this category, for example, is the galvanic skin reflex, which has been used frequently in the study of signal learning. When an electric shock is applied, say, to the individual's hand, physiological processes are set in motion that alter the resistance of the skin to the passage of a weak electric current. This change in resistance can be easily and rather precisely measured by means of simple electrodes attached to the skin and connected with a circuit including a galvanometer. Thus a means is provided for measuring the acquisition of a signal connection. In practice, the subject is seated in a chair and the electrodes are attached. Then the skin resistance (galvanic skin reflex, or GSR) is noted on the galvanometer until a fairly steady base reading is obtained. Signal learning then begins by the presentation of, say, a tone signal followed about half a second later by the shock, evoking the change in skin resistance. These events are repeated at suitable intervals, and the presence of the newly acquired signal connection is detected by a "trial" of the signal tone not paired with shock. The conditioned response can usually be established in such circumstances after only a few repetitions.

Some Other Phenomena of Signal Learning

Some other events that occur in signal learning situations have great importance for an understanding of this form of behavior modification, as well as of other more complex forms dependent upon it. For one thing, there is the phenomenon of *extinction*, a kind of unlearning that results in the disappearance of the previously learned association. There is also *stimulus generalization*, the occurrence of responses to stimuli similar to the signal used to bring about learning. Generalization itself may be reduced so that a much narrower range of stimuli will evoke the response, and this set of events is given the name *discrimination*.

EXTINCTION. Suppose that a signal response of blinking the eye to the sound of a bell has been reliably established. How may it be eliminated? The most dependable way to bring this about is by repeated presentation at suitable intervals of the signal (the bell) *without* the unconditioned stimulus (the puff of air). When these conditioners are put into effect, the signal connection undergoes a progressive weakening; in other words, it appears less and less dependably, until it fails to occur. The rate at which extinction occurs is illustrated in Figure 4.2. After an initial period of extinction, upon presentation of the signal, the conditioned response may appear again. Pavlov called this *spontaneous recovery*. However, the connection is obviously weaker, and may be re-extinguished in a few trials in which the signal is presented alone. Ultimately, under the extinction procedure, the newly learned connection does disappear completely.

Although the conditions for bringing about extinction are

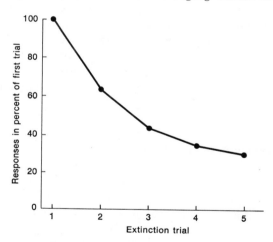

FIGURE 4.2   A typical curve of extinction for the conditioned galvanic skin response (GSR), showing the decrease in percent of response in five extinction trials that followed immediately after the signal learning (Data of C. I. Hovland, "Inhibition of reinforcement" and phenomena of extinction. *Proceedings of the National Academy of Sciences*, 1936, 22, 430–433.

quite straightforward, it is nevertheless a puzzling phenomenon. There are many different theories of extinction (Kimble, 1961, pp. 281–327). Perhaps the best known are, briefly, that (1) an active process of *inhibition*, generated by the act of responding, depresses the strength of the learned association; and (2) extinction is mainly a matter of learning other associations that *interfere* with the initially learned one. Despite the theoretical differences implied in these and other theories, there is general agreement on the conditions under which extinction of signal learning occurs, as well as on extinction's importance as a basic behavioral event.

STIMULUS GENERALIZATION. The conditioned response, once established, may be elicited by signals other than the one used to establish it. The closer the physical resemblance between these other signals and the original one, the stronger the response obtained. Suppose that a galvanic skin response has been conditioned to a tone signal of 1000 cycles per second. It may then also be shown to occur, in somewhat reduced strength, to a tone of 1025 cycles or 975 cycles. The signal connection, in other words, is not a highly precise one. *Generalization* may be shown to other stimuli that resemble the original stimulus, as measured along some physical dimension. Hovland (1937) obtained the results shown in Figure 4.3 when he measured the strength of the GSR to stimulus tones differing from the original signal by increasing amounts of "just noticeable difference" (JND). Evidently, the *gradient of generalization*, as such curves are called, drops off sharply at first and then more gradually as the resemblance between the original stimulus and the "test" stimulus lessens.

STIMULUS-RESPONSE LEARNING

Another fundamental kind of learning, simple to observe and widespread in its occurrence, is here called *stimulus-response learning*. Thorndike called it *trial-and-error learning*, but this is probably not a good descriptive name. It is also called *operant learning*, notably by Skinner (1938). Many writers call it *instrumental learning* (Kimble, 1961), and this name has two advantages: (1) it emphasizes the precise skilled nature of the responses involved, as in "using instruments"; and (2) it implies that the learned connection is instrumental in satisfying some motive. The phrase "stimulus-response learning" is chosen to emphasize two other characteristics. (1) Such

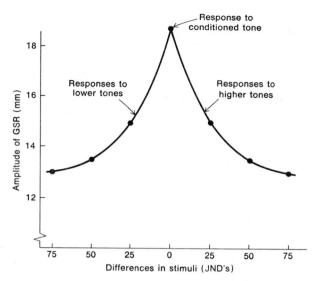

FIGURE 4.3   The stimulus generalization gradient obtained for a conditioned GSR to a tone of 1000 cycles. Decreasing amplitude
of response was found as the stimulus tones used to "test"
the responses were made decreasingly similar to the original
tone. (Data of C. I. Hovland, The generalization of conditioned responses. I. The sensory generalization of conditioned
responses with varying frequencies of tone. *Journal of General Psychology*, 1937, *17*, 125–148).

learning concerns a *single* connection between a stimulus and a
response, not multiple or chained associations, which will be dealt
with later. And (2) the stimulus and the response appear to become
integrally bound together in such learning, in a way that does not
happen with signal learning. A bell really has nothing to do with
eyeblinking, except as a signal for it. But because of the occurrence
of stimulus-response learning, a colored block may become for a
child a thing to be picked up.

It is difficult indeed to find an example of human learning that
might represent stimulus-response learning in relatively pure form.
Many instances that seem at first glance to be suitable examples turn
out on closer inspection to represent the somewhat more complex
forms of chaining or verbal association. Human beings rapidly
acquire a background of prerequisite learning which enters into the
subsequent acquisition of these more complex varieties. Animals
such as white rats and pigeons have frequently been used to study

the characteristics of stimulus-response learning because a less extensive repertoire of previous learning can be assumed for these animals than for human beings.

This difficulty makes it necessary to turn for an example to the behavior of the very young human infant. Although the amount of systematic experimental evidence is very limited for infant learning, it can be assumed with some safety that not much previous learning has occurred. Accordingly, the example to be considered here is the infant's learned response of holding the nursing bottle in the proper position for feeding. Under what conditions does a child learn to perform this act?

At first, of course, there is the stage at which this behavior has not been learned. The parent must hold the bottle tilted at the proper angle in order for feeding to be possible. During the course of feeding, however, the infant will often grasp the bottle in her hands, somewhat unsystematically to be sure. Now suppose the parent begins to release his own hold on the bottle, so that greater pressure is exerted against the child's own hands. So long as the child's hands exert a sufficiently firm grasp in a sufficiently raised position, the feeding continues. Should this muscular tension be relaxed, a point will be reached in the tilt angle of the bottle where no formula reaches the mouth. Then perhaps the parent pushes the bottle upward into position again, and feeding is restored. By gradually "helping" the child hold the bottle properly, and gradually removing the help so that the child's own responses are appropriate, the stimulus-response connection becomes established. Eventually the child, once given the bottle, can reinstate the necessary response. She has then "learned to hold her bottle."

This learning event appears to be not so much a "trial-and-error" procedure as a "successive approximation" procedure. The learning that occurs here, as Skinner says, is a matter of shaping. A set of stimuli, including the sight and feel of the bottle as well as the proprioceptive stimuli from the child's arm and hand muscles, becomes connected with a correct response of holding the bottle in a position from which the formula can be sucked into the mouth. At the same time, a slightly different set of stimuli, involving a slightly different "feel" (when the bottle is lower), results in no food in the mouth. Thus the learning is really a matter of *discrimination* of correct and incorrect stimulation; the learner must discriminate the set of stimuli which produces reward (reinforcement) and the set of stimuli which does not. It is equally true to say that the response of holding the bottle correctly becomes progressively *differentiated*, since the muscles involved in making this response actually provide part of the stimulation which is "correct" or "incorrect."

Conditions of Stimulus-Response Learning

We consider here the nature of conditions necessary for stimulus-response learning (abbreviated as S→R learning). Learning conditions within the learner are distinguished from those outside the learner (in the learning situation).

CONDITIONS WITHIN THE LEARNER. First of all, it is evident that there must be a terminating act which provides reinforcement. In the example given here, it is necessary that the infant suck on the nipple and thereby fill her mouth with food. This produces what Thorndike called a "satisfying state of affairs." In modern usage, taking of food by sucking is the reinforcer that is made contingent upon the performance of holding the bottle.

A single S→R may be established when the terminal reinforcing act does not immediately follow the response, as in the sucking example, but is more remote. This is the more usual case when one is dealing with human behavior. For example, a correctly performed S→R may be followed by a word of praise, "Good!", which is in turn connected with a response that ultimately provides the reinforcement. Thus, meeting this condition does not require that the terminating act be an innate one, such as the ingestion of food. For learning to occur, one needs only to insure that there is such a response, terminating in reinforcement, which can be performed by the learner.

CONDITIONS OF THE LEARNING SITUATION. Turning to the conditions outside the learner, we see that the critical set of events is the occurrence of a *reinforcement contingency*. Reinforcement must take place when the act to be learned occurs, and only when it (rather than some other action) occurs. As for the reinforcement, some theorists hold that this must be something that the learner already does vigorously, whereas others maintain that the act must lead to an external reward, such as food, praise, or relief of pain. It is not possible here to consider the essential nature of reinforcement, as discussed, for example, by Kimble (1961) and Hilgard and Bower (1975). But the fact of reinforcement, which makes the learning of any new S→R connection dependent upon the directly following consequences, is widely accepted. In the example of the infant and her bottle, the S→R learning will not occur if the bottle is empty, and the sucking and swallowing of liquid does not occur (unless, of course, some other reinforcer is provided). Modern learning theorists call this condition the *empirical law of effect.*

Contiguity has an important part to play in the establishment of an S→R connection. The shorter the time elapsing between the occurrence of the learned response and the occurrence of reinforcement, the more rapidly learning will take place. If the infant had to wait, say, five seconds between the time she tilted the bottle correctly and the time food arrived in her mouth, it would be more difficult for her to learn than if this interval were only a second. This relationship between *ease of learning* and *delay of reinforcement* has been well established in laboratory studies of S→R learning (Kimble, 1961, pp. 140–156).

Repetition of the stimulus situation is also a necessary condition for the occurrence of stimulus-response learning. As Thorndike's findings (1898) demonstrate, the amount of repetition needed may vary from a single trial to many, depending on the difficulty of the discriminations involved, and the degree to which they conform with responding that is either innately determined or previously learned. The function served by repetition, therefore, appears to be one of *selection* of stimuli to be discriminated, as a number of learning theorists, notably Estes (1959) assume. In successive repetitions of the learning situation, particular samples of the total stimulus situation (including, of course, its kinesthetic components) are associated with particular responses. Some of these are more successful than others in producing reinforcement; the successful ones therefore are selected and the unsuccessful ones drop out of the picture. The correct behavior is gradually *shaped* by means of this selective process. According to this conception, a total learned connection is really composed of several individual S→R's, and learning is a matter of gradual recruitment of the "bundle" of individual connections that lead to reinforcement, rather than to a strengthening of each individual one. This view of S→R learning is similar to that originally enunciated by E. R. Guthrie (1935).

Other Phenomena of Stimulus-Response Learning

EXTINCTION. Just as there is a phenomenon of "unlearning" for signal learning, there is a comparable event in S→R learning, also called *extinction.* In both cases, these events result in the disappearance of a previously learned connection, and it is understandable on these grounds that the two forms of unlearning should be given the same name. But the conditions under which they occur are *not* the same.

Extinction of a learned S→R occurs when the reinforcement that follows the learned response is omitted. Under these circumstances, the association gradually decreases its likelihood of occurrence when the stimulus situation is presented, until it dies away. It may be noted that extinction is not a matter of omitting an unconditioned stimulus (like a puff of air to the cornea, in signal learning), but of removing the reinforcing state of affairs. The latter can be done in various ways. For example, extinction of the infant's S→R connection of holding the bottle may be brought about, as has been said, by omitting the milk. It may also be accomplished by making sure that the infant is not hungry when presented with the bottle (this might happen if she were fed by the parent before being allowed to hold the bottle). Under such circumstances, little or no reinforcement would follow the learned response of bottle holding, and it would undergo extinction.

GENERALIZATION.   The generalization of the learned connection to stimuli that resemble the set used in learning is another characteristic shared by S→R learning and signal learning. Guttman and Kalish (1956) established S→R learning in which pigeons pecked at a transparent plate which transmitted light of a given color. Then the birds were tested with this color and a range of other colors with wavelengths differing from the original color. As expected, the frequency with which pecking occurred to a color decreased regularly as the physical resemblance between it and the original hue decreased.

The Basic Forms of Learning in Everyday Life

Responding to signals and executing simple motor responses are no more than a small portion of the capabilities that human beings can and do learn. Perhaps the phenomena they exhibit and the conditions of their learning can help us understand *associative learning* as a basic process. However, to complete our account, we shall describe a few examples of these forms of learning as they occur in everyday life and in the school.

SOME EXAMPLES OF SIGNAL LEARNING.   Signal learning occurs in the lives of all of us. Sometimes it happens because of environmental accidents rather than as a result of planning by parents or teachers. We learn to respond to many kinds of signals, such as automobile horns, alarm clock bells, and certain ejaculatory utterances of other people. Generally speaking, we acquire a connection exhibiting a diffuse, imprecise, "emotional" response to such signals, because they are repeated together with other (unconditioned) stimuli that generate these responses initially and innately.

A number of children's fears are doubtless acquired by means of signal learning. Children may avoid certain locations, animals, or even people because there has been a pairing (whether adventitious or otherwise) of the stimuli they present with some unconditioned stimulus such as a frightening noise. It seems likely that pleasant emotions can also be aroused in essentially the same way, through previous pairings with particular persons or situations. Possibly the young child's favorite teddy bear or blanket may become a signal for pleasant feelings, just as may particular scenes or melodies at a somewhat later stage of the individual's development.

SOME EXAMPLES OF STIMULUS-RESPONSE LEARNING. S→R learning has considerable usefulness. It is a kind of learning that includes such things as reaching and grasping for toys or other objects, smiling at the proper people, positioning the body and limbs, and vocalizing utterances. As the child acquires a larger and larger repertory of these somewhat isolated S→R's, they begin to form into longer chains, and it becomes increasingly difficult to isolate "pure" examples of this kind of learning. Finding such examples of this kind of learning in adults is a practically impossible task.

Stimulus-response learning is undoubtedly the main variety involved in the initial learning of words by children. An initial utterance like "nha-nha," overheard by a parent, may be "shaped" into a connection that yields the response "ma-ma" by suitable use of the procedure of differential reinforcement. A part of this procedure involves getting the child to respond to the proper external stimulus, which may be "ma-ma" spoken by the parent. Another part requires the discrimination of kinesthetic responses from the child's own vocal and facial muscles. Naturally, deaf children have a difficult time making the required discriminations and so learning the desired S→R. As is well known, language training for deaf children typically takes the form of providing stimuli these children *can* discriminate. The teacher may, for example, position the child's mouth and tongue so that something approaching the proper articulation will emerge. In addition, the auditory cues available to normal children may be replaced by visual ones, displayed on an oscilloscope. Under such circumstances, a deaf child can acquire the S→R's, based on suitably precise discriminations, which produce understandable speech.

If one were to attempt a generalization, one might reasonably conclude that S→R learning is almost always involved in the learning of *voluntary motor acts*, including utterances of speech. Simple learned motor acts may be readily identified in young children, and perhaps come as close as any human behavior does to being pure cases of stimulus-response learning.

Reinforcement and the Learning of Receptive Behaviors

Since much school learning requires verbal communication directed toward the learner, one of the important events in instruction is the adoption by the learner of a *receptivity set* toward such communications. While adult learners normally adopt a set for receptivity as a matter of course, this cannot be said of many children. Accordingly, a good deal of the efforts of a kindergarten or prekindergarten teacher may well be devoted to guiding the learning of receptive behaviors in children. The child must learn to attend to verbal requests, to follow verbal directions. These are examples of what may be called "receptive sets." Even though the effects of its learning are quite general, and bring about behavior that precedes the learning of many other things, a receptive set is learned under the same conditions as other more specific acts.

The conditions that pertain to the learning of receptive behaviors are those of S→R learning. In particular, a proper selection of the conditions of reinforcement is involved. According to Skinner (1968, pp. 145–168), the *contingencies of reinforcement* must be suitably arranged so that the reinforcement is made *contingent upon* the occurrence of the behavior to be learned. In simple terms, this means that learning conditions must be so arranged that some reinforcing activity follows closely the occurrence of the desired receptive behavior. Many specific techniques may be designed to conform to this general pattern, and thus to bring about changes in the direction of increased receptivity. These techniques are often called, as a class, *contingency management*; and their effects are spoken of as *behavior modification*. Some examples of the application of the reinforcement principle to the learning of receptive behaviors follow.

INCREASING THE "SPAN OF ATTENTION." The young child may be highly inattentive and may follow the verbal directions of the teacher for only a few minutes at a time. The suggested conditions for learning are to follow each period of attention by reinforcement (perhaps initially a tangible reward), making sure that such reinforcement is given only for instances of attention which gradually become longer, and withheld when the span lapses to shorter intervals.

INVOLVEMENT IN LEARNING TASKS.   Children are sometimes unwilling to become involved in learning tasks; that is, they are unreceptive to the verbal communications that are an essential part of the learning situation. Receptive behavior may be established, according to reinforcement principles, by first choosing a task the child likes to do and insuring that appropriate verbal directions precede it. As the application of reinforcement is continued, the teacher may then expand the preferred activity to include another that is not originally one that the child likes to do. For example, if the child likes to paste circles on construction paper, this activity may be preceded by a suitable communication and expanded to include identifying particular sizes or colors before pasting.

FOLLOWING DIRECTIONS.   The preschool or kindergarten child may not follow directions well or consistently. Again, the idea of reinforcement can provide an important clue for the arrangement of learning conditions. One must begin with a task that is short and requires brief directions. Preferably, such a task has a specific starting and ending point. It is a task, in other words, for which the child *can* successfully follow directions. Working from this base, the teacher gradually expands the length of the task and the variety of directions required, making sure that there are definite "checkpoints" at each step along the way, and that the terminal part of the task is such that the child experiences both success and satisfaction in its completion.

These few examples show that working with reinforcement contingencies to establish receptive behaviors is something that requires a great deal of patience. But even more important is careful attention to the *sequence* of events that reflects the correct contingencies. The reinforcing state of affairs must *follow* the to-be-learned behavior; not precede it. The reinforcement must also have a great deal of *consistency*; that is, it must occur when the desired behavior appears and be omitted when the desired behavior does not appear.

Behavior modification using the principle of reinforcement contingency is a powerful tool for the management of learning. Of course, its applicability is not confined to young children. Liking to read good books, being receptive to music and art, acquiring effective study habits, all may pose problems for students of any age and represent behavior modifications potentially attainable by proper application of reinforcement techniques (see Skinner, 1968, pp. 145–168). Such techniques have also been of particular help in changing the behavior of "emotionally disturbed" children in classrooms in which routines of reinforcement were carefully planned and executed (Hewett, 1968). Still another important field of application is in the training of mentally retarded children (Orlando and Bijou, 1960).

CHAINING

Chaining is the connection of a set of individual S→R's in sequence. Some sequences, such as turning on a television set or a washing machine, are made up of motor responses. Other sequences are entirely verbal, for example, the greeting "How have you been?" or the pledge of allegiance to the flag. For the acquisition of sequences that are nonverbal, the term *chaining* will be used. The subvariety involving verbal behavior deserves a separate description as *verbal association*, or *verbal sequence learning*.

E. R. Guthrie (1935) tells the story of a girl who had acquired the habit of dropping her coat on the floor when she entered the house. Her annoyed mother had often scolded her and required her to go back and pick up the coat. But this was quite ineffective in overcoming the unwanted behavior. The mother, however, discovered an effective procedure. She made the girl go out of the house with her coat on, then come in, and hang it up properly. This illustration shows the importance of correct sequencing of the events in a chain. The original chain troubling the mother had the following sequence: enter house → drop coat → see mother → mother says, "Pick up coat" → pick up coat → hang up coat. What had to be established was a shorter chain with quite a different sequence: enter house → keep coat on → approach closet → hang up coat. The mother displayed some useful wisdom when she realized that the second chain could not be learned by simply adding links to the first one. What was necessary was the institution of the desired chain with correct links from start to finish.

The Conditions for Chaining

The conditions necessary to bring about chaining can now be described. There are, as usual, some conditions that exist within the learner, and others that are external to the learner.

CONDITIONS WITHIN THE LEARNER.   Of utmost importance to the acquiring of chains is the requirement that each individual stimulus-response connection be *previously learned*. One cannot expect a chain such as opening a door with a key to be learned in an optimal way unless the learner is already able to carry out the S→R's that constitute the links. The learner must be able to (1) identify the key's upright position, (2) insert it into the lock fully, (3) turn it clockwise fully, and (4) push the door open. If a novice (a child, perhaps) complains that he cannot unlock the door after being shown how, one immediately suspects that he has not fully mastered one of these links. Similarly, the chain learned in starting the motor of a car requires the previous learning of the individual links. Failure to learn on a single occasion usually indicates that one or more links have not been previously learned (pressing the accelerator as soon as the motor "takes hold" is an example).

CONDITIONS IN THE SITUATION.   Several conditions in the situation are important to chain learning.

Assuming that the links are known, the first condition for the establishment of a chain is getting the learner to *reinstate them* one after the other *in the proper order*. Two different approaches to this sequencing are possible:

1. One can begin with the terminal act and work backward, as T. F. Gilbert (1962) suggests. This insures that the link one is trying to connect at any given point in the chain will always be introduced in the correct order. To connect link 4 with link 3, one waits for the occurrence of link 3 and then immediately follows it with link 4 (the act leading to reinforcement); then one observes the occurrence of link 2, and follows it with links 3 and 4; and so on. This *progressive part* method, it may be noted, follows the procedure of S→R learning *for each successive link*.
2. A *prompting* method may be used, in which additional external cues are employed to insure the reinstatement of the links in the proper order, beginning from the start of the chain.

Both these methods work. Whether one is more effective

than the other, in some or all circumstances, is a question awaiting further evidence.

A second condition is the familiar one of *contiguity*. The individual links in the chain must be executed in close succession if the chain is to be established. The smoothly executed chain pertaining to unlocking a door, for example, requires that the insertion of the key be followed by turning it to the right. Some of the stimuli for the second of these links arise out of the responses made in the first. Should there be a delay between the two links, the stimuli for the second connection will not be like those of the performance aimed for, and the chain may be learned with difficulty. This does not mean, of course, that it is not possible to learn chains that have delays deliberately built into them. Such instances may certainly be acquired; for example, one learns to delay until the coin has dropped fully into a slot machine before operating the lever.

A third condition relates to the *repetition* variable. Presumably, if all other conditions were fully met, repetition would be unnecessary. The chain would tend to form on the first occasion. Practically speaking, however, it is difficult to insure that all the conditions have been fully met. The individual links may be only partially learned, the prompting may be not fully effective, or some delays may creep into the execution of the chain. Given these practical circumstances, repetition of the sequence has the function of "smoothing out" the rough spots, and some practice is almost always desirable for this reason.

The fourth, and final, condition of *reinforcement* is present in the learning of chains. The terminal link must provide reinforcement—the food pellet is obtained, the engine is started, the door is opened. Should the final link cease to be a reinforcer, extinction will occur, and the chain as a whole will then disappear. It has been found that the reinforcement needs to be immediate in order for chain learning to occur most readily. The introduction of a delay in reinforcement markedly increases the difficulty of learning.

The Uses of Chains

Although of widespread occurrence among the human being's activities, chains are of essentially humble nature. In the early grades of school, a number of important chainlike skills must be learned. Buttoning, fastening, tying, using a pencil, erasing, and using scissors fall into this category. At a slightly more complex level are the chains involved in printing and writing, which are of considerable importance as components of more elaborate activities to be acquired in the school. Throwing balls, catching balls, kicking balls, and many other fundamental athletic skills are also acquired as chains in the early years of the individual's life.

In the later years of school, varieties of additional chains must be learned. Sometimes these take the form of *procedures,* complex and lengthy chains that often incorporate simpler chains as components. Students may learn in science courses to carry out weighing procedures, liquid-pouring procedures, and many other measurement procedures. Later still they may learn to adjust and use a variety of scientific instruments, including microscopes, voltmeters, centrifuges—each of them requiring the learning of procedural chains. Vocational students are likely to have to learn a large number of procedures as basic tasks of the occupation they plan to enter. Students of art may learn procedures such as "brush techniques," students of music the complex procedures of playing an instrument.

The individual motor chains that are learned, many early in life, become components of more complex, purposeful activities called *motor skills,* which are the subject of Chapter 9. Chains of motor responses become the components of motor skills, often as "part-skills." The latter are combined into organized motor performances which learning and continued practice invest with characteristics of smoothness and precise timing.

VERBAL ASSOCIATION

If it is true that people are capable of a tremendous variety of performances with the use of their legs, arms, and hands, it is also even more strikingly true that their vocalizations show an enormous versatility. Although the individual sounds human beings can make are limited in number, the patterns that can be constructed from these sounds are virtually limitless. Such patterns, at least the simplest ones, are learned as chains. But the tremendous variety of these chains as well as the subtlety of resemblances and differences among them make verbal behavior a subject of special interest from a learning standpoint. Here we shall deal with only the most elementary kind of verbal behavior, the learning of verbal associations and verbal sequences. Chapter 8 will describe the learning of the more highly meaningful forms of verbal learning, such as propositions, as *verbal information learning.*

Probably the simplest verbal chains are illustrated in the activity of *naming.* A youngster is told while being shown a three-dimensional object, "This shape is called a tetrahedron." If conditions are otherwise right, the next time he sees this particular object, he will be able to say that it is a tetrahedron. But these other conditions are important. It is fairly easy to identify some conditions which would insure that the learner would *not* be able to say "tetrahedron." To mention two of the most obvious, (1) he may not have discriminated the object as a stimulus, and (2) he may not have learned to say its name.

The act of naming a specific object like a tetrahedron seems likely to be a chain of at least two links. The first of these links is an observing response, an S→R that connects the appearance of the object with some responses involved in observing the triangular character of its sides, and that at the same time serves to distinguish it from other three-dimensional objects of roughly the same size and color. The second link is the S→R connection that enables the individual to stimulate himself to say "tetrahedron" (that is, to say it is as a voluntary response, in the manner of stimulus-response learning). As a diagram, a simple act of naming is represented by this kind of chain:

$$S \longrightarrow R \qquad \sim \qquad s \longrightarrow R$$

object   observing   tetrahedron   "tetrahedron."

The small *s* in the diagram stands for the internal representation of the object resulting from its observation.

Verbal Sequences

Chains of verbal associates may be longer than two links. Relatively brief verbal sequence of previously discriminated words can readily be learned as chains in a single presentation.

Verbal chains may be very long indeed, if we think of the memorization of digits twenty-eight places beyond the decimal point, or, for that matter, of the verbatim learning of verses of poetry or books of the Bible. Are there some limitations on how long a chain can be "taken in" or learned as a single event? So far as the evidence from experiments goes (Jensen, 1962; G. A. Miller, 1956), it appears that a chain of about seven links (plus or minus two) represents the limit of what can be learned as a single event. This figure describes the *immediate memory span*. Chains longer than this must be broken up into parts in order for learning to occur most efficiently. However, it may be noted also that the length of the span of immediate memory increases when the material is familiar, and has been organized by previous learning.

If presented with an entire verse of poetry to learn, the learner may "break it up" into various pieces, and put the pieces together in various ways. On the whole, the evidence suggests that under many circumstances the most efficient procedure is what is called the *progressive part* method, in which the learner adds a new part (like a line of the poem) as he continues to rehearse the older parts (McGeoch and Irion, 1952). On the first try, the learner may attempt to say line 1; on the next, lines 1 and 2; on the next, lines 1, 2, and 3; and so on. Such a procedure not only insures that parts are chosen which are within the span of immediate memory, but also allows for the continued practice of earlier learned parts which are subject to forgetting through interference.

In the case of lengthy verbal chains, some aspects of the sequence may have been previously learned, as well as the individual links. The English language displays some remarkably predictable sequences, as is illustrated by the completion of such phrases as "Boy meets ———," and "Now is the ———." The predictability of such sequences means that the ordering of English words has in many cases been learned previously (see G. A. Miller, 1951). Longer chains may be taken in as a "chunk" under such circumstances. Another implication is that the learning of many prose sequences has already been partially accomplished, not only in terms of the discrimination of links but also in terms of their order.

Conditions of Learning
Verbal Sequences

It should now be possible to state in more formal terms the important conditions for the establishment of the capability of reinstating verbal associates and verbal chains.

CONDITIONS WITHIN THE LEARNER. The previous discussion leads to the following summary of the conditions for optimal learning.

1. Each link of the chain to be acquired must have been previously learned as an S→R. This means, of course, that the verbal unit must have been discriminated as a stimulus from other units resembling it in a physical sense. Also implied is that this unit should be discriminated as the response portion of the connection; in other words, it should be a highly familiar response (Underwood and Schulz, 1960).
2. Mediating connections between each verbal unit and the next must have been previously learned. The greater the learner's available supply of these "coding" connections, the more rapidly

will learning take place. Evidence clearly shows (Noble, 1963) that verbal associates are learned more readily, the greater the number of verbal "free associates" there are to the syllables or words being chained. But verbal "codes" are not the only mediators usually available. Visual images or auditory images (as in rhymes) may also serve this function extremely well.

CONDITIONS OF THE LEARNING SITUATION.   When conditions within the learner are satisfied, the learning of a verbal chain is a fairly simple matter.

1. The verbal units must be presented in the proper sequence. Various methods may be employed, the two most common being presenting the entire chain to be read from left to right, or presenting the units in the chain one after another. This latter method has been extensively used in laboratory studies of verbal sequence learning.
2. The learner must actively make the responses required by the chain. The importance of this condition for verbal chains, as well as for other kinds of chains, is that the responses generate internal stimuli which become a part of the succeeding links in each case.
3. As is true for nonverbal chains, learning is aided by the use of external stimuli that furnish cues for order. Such an extra cue is provided, for example, by mnemonic devices that may have been previously learned. Students of neuroanatomy sometimes learn the names of the cranial nerves in order by learning the rhyme "On old Olympus' towering top . . . ," the first letters of which cue the order of the nerves: olfactory, optic, oculomotor, and so on. Pronounced poetic meter serves such a function for chains of medium length, as in "The cur'few tolls' the knell' of par'ting day'." Other kinds of "prompting" stimuli may also be used.
4. For words that have not previously been learned in a sequence, the limit of verbal chain length that can be apprehended as a single event (for previously unchained material) appears to be seven plus or minus two. In other words, the individual's *span of immediate memory* determines the length of a chain that can be learned all at once. There is no limit, apparently, to the length of a verbal chain that can be learned part by part, for people have memorized entire books verbatim. For long chains, the *progressive part* method has usually been shown to be most efficient one.
5. *Confirmation of correct responses* must be provided for in the learning situation. This is often done by showing the learners

a printed form of the entire verbal chain immediately after they have tried to reproduce it, or of each link of the chain following each response. In the learning of sequences of nonsense syllables, the *anticipation method* is often employed, in which learners attempt to make each response in the chain within a limited time period (for example, two seconds), after which the printed representation of that response is exposed to them. If they have responded correctly, this exposure enables them to confirm the link by matching what they have just said with what they now see.

The Effects of Interference

One of the most important phenomena that occurs in the learning of verbal associates and sequences is *interference*. Many experimental studies of such learning have led to the inference that the linking of one verbal unit with another (1) tends to reduce the retention of another such linking that has *preceded* it in time, and (2) reduces the probability that a *subsequent* linking will be retained (Underwood, 1964). In the first case, the interference works "backward" on something previously learned, and so is called *retroactive;* in the second, the interference works forward on something yet to be learned, and is termed *proactive.*

Suppose that one is to learn a verbal chain of twelve links, beginning CAT RED SIT LAM TIN ROW, and that each one of these links has been well learned as an individual word. If one were to require the learning of chains involving two words at a time, such as CAT-RED, or RED-SIT, it is obvious that each chain could be learned immediately on a single occasion. Yet when the twelve words are put together as a chain, and exposed one after another, they probably cannot be learned with perfect accuracy on a single ocasion. Why it this so? The most probable explanation is that in the process of connecting a particular link, other links (both previous and subsequent ones) become *harder to remember* because of interference.

If one has learned CAT RED SIT, in the chain of twelve links used in our illustration, these links will be available in memory when one is trying to recall TIN (as a later part of the chain), and the recall of TIN will to some extent be made less likely. Similarly, once TIN has been learned, it will be available in memory when CAT, RED, or SIT are being recalled; and this in turn will reduce the likelihood of recall of each of those words in the chain. The longer the verbal chain, the greater will be the effects of interference on any link.

Another condition of importance to the establishment of verbal sequences is one which overcomes interference by making the items highly *distinctive*. For example, it is known that a highly unusual word occurring, say, in the fourth position of a ten-item sequence will be recalled in this position better than most other items in the sequence. An example of an unusual unit in a five-unit sequence is as follows: PAL BOY CAT 8 SIR. This factor of distinctiveness may also partially account for the better retention of items at the beginning and at the end of a sequence. Rhythm and meter in a verbal sequence may also have the effect of increasing distinctiveness, making poetry generally easier to remember than the same amount of prose.

Meaningful Verbal Learning

While the learning of verbal sequences, including those containing meaningful words, may be usefully conceived as a process of "chaining," it appears doubtful that this conception is capable of encompassing the whole of what is meant by verbal learning. When students "learn" a chapter in their history text, for example, one does not expect them to demonstrate this learning by a verbatim oral reproduction of the text. Instead, one may expect them to be able to reproduce in the proper order the "ideas" that are contained in the text. Is such a performance achieved solely by the processes of association and chaining, or are some other processes at work? There are several reasons for believing that the learning of meaningful propositions (or verbal information, as we call it in Chapter 8) requires internal processing that is different from, and may be more complex than, verbal chaining. Some of the major reasons follow.

1. Learning the substance (that is, the "ideas") of meaningful verbal material is accomplished more rapidly than learning the same material as verbal chains to be reproduced verbatim (Briggs and Reed, 1943; Jones and English, 1926).
2. The retention of ideas, as contrasted with the verbatim reproduction of meaningful passages of prose, shows considerable superiority in recall (English, Welborn, and Killian, 1934).
3. The effects of interference, which are prominently involved in the retention of nonmeaningful material, have in a number of studies failed to appear as influences on the retention of meaningful passages (Ausubel and Blake, 1958; Hall, 1955; E. B. Newman, 1939).
4. The system of memory for meaningful material permits the re-

trieval of information that was not directly stored in it, rather than being confined to what was specifically learned (Bartlett, 1932; Tulving, 1972).

Such evidence has led a number of learning theorists to hold that verbal chaining is entirely inadequate to account for the learning of meaningful material. The former may be considered an example of *episodic memory*, whereas the latter is *semantic memory* (Tulving, 1972). Chapter 8 is devoted to a description of conditions affecting meaningful verbal learning, which we call *verbal information learning*.

Some Educational Implications

Human performances that involve the use of learned verbal chains can be found in everyday life, both in and out of school. Children *do* sometimes learn the sequence of letters in the alphabet, whether or not this is considered good pedagogical practice. Students memorize formulas, or key numbers like the square roots of 2 and 3, and occasionally much longer numbers. Children are often expected to learn the Lord's Prayer, the first verse of "The Star Spangled Banner," the Pledge of Allegiance, and a number of other verses, sayings, or quotations. Students often have to memorize the school cheer, and may, of course, learn many lines as amateur actors. But all these tasks seem to lack an essentiality, an urgency, when considered in terms of the larger goals of education. The sequence of the alphabet, after all, is not involved in learning to read. Formulas can easily be looked up. And although "The Star Spangled Banner" may be of some use in social gatherings, it can gradually "sink in" by being heard many times through mechanical amplifiers. Although few educators would be inclined to say memorization is bad, it is generally thought to be unimportant. Perhaps it is a matter of priority. Students must acquire knowledge and the ability to think, and these goals are heavily emphasized in today's curricula.

It was not always thus in American schools. Half a century ago there was much verbal memorization—the alphabet, the multiplication table, numerical quantities and formulas, poetry, prose writings like the Gettysburg Address, the Preamble to the Constitution, and so on. Students practiced reciting the verbal passages they had learned; and declamation contests rewarded oratorical skill. Verbal memorization is still emphasized today, we are told, in schools in many parts of the world, particularly in Asia and to some extent in Europe.

Is there an educational value to the memorization of verbal sequences? What considerations should enter into a determination of priority for instruction of this sort? The answer to these questions lies in a recognition of the most important usage for recalled verbal phrases, sentences, or passages. The time saved by recalling a formula rather than looking it up is not that important. The major use of recalled verbal sequences is in the area of language itself— specifically, in the construction of verbal utterances that communicate ideas. The question is, What degree of skill is it important for students to have in expressing their ideas in oral form, whether in simple conversation, in informal conference, or in lectures and speeches? To what extent are we interested in providing students with skills of communication and persuasion?

It is no accident that some of the most renowned American orators of previous generations knew such literature as the Bible and the writings of Shakespeare to the extent that they could repeat whole passages verbatim. These and other literary sources are fundamental to our language. People who are skilled in oral communication are able to recall words, phrases, or entire passages of flowing English, and to weave them into their own vocal utterances in highly effective ways. They are able to do this not simply because they have *read* these classics of English literature, but because they have *memorized* them. In the terms used in the present chapter, they have learned many varieties of verbal sequences, and can recall them readily. They are able to utilize at will such phrases as *dedicated to the proposition that all men are created equal* or *a tide in the affairs of men* or *seeking the bubble reputation* or *the slings and arrows of outrageous fortune* or *in the course of human events* or *I shall not want*, or *with what measure ye mete, it shall be measured unto you*.

Naturally, such memorized verbal sequences may also become a source of clichés in both writing and speaking. Phrases such as *stark naked, utterly exhausted, starry-eyed wonder, justifiable wrath*, and *global diplomacy*, since they have been encountered so frequently in reading material and in everyday speech, become memorized portions of the individual's language repertoire. An orator may sometimes deliberately exploit the appeal such clichés have for her audience. But a skillful speaker is one who has also learned to "play the changes" on such familiar materials, so that the overly familiar is avoided. And it is even more important for the writer to avoid excessive use of such phrases, even though they form an important part of his background.

In sum, then, the most direct and obvious employment for memorized verbal sequences is in the construction of created language, particularly in oral speech. The construction of effective original speech does not depend simply on an understanding of rules for grammatical expression. It requires the ready recall of a large fund of verbal sequences that can be woven into novel passages of spoken English in a countless variety of patterns.

GENERAL REFERENCES

SIGNAL LEARNING
Kimble, G. A. *Hilgard and Marquis' "Conditioning and learning."* New York: Appleton, 1961.
Mowrer, O. H. *Learning theory and behavior.* New York: Wiley, 1960.
Pavlov, I. P. *Conditioned reflexes.* (Transl. by G. V. Anrep.) London: Oxford University Press, 1927. (Also in paperback, New York: Dover, 1960.)

STIMULUS-RESPONSE LEARNING
Kimble, G. A. See above.
Mowrer, O. H. See above.
Skinner, B. F. *Contingencies of reinforcement: A theoretical analysis.* New York: Appleton, 1969.
Staats, A. W. *Human learning.* New York: Holt, Rinehart and Winston, 1964.

CHAINING MOTOR RESPONSES
Gilbert, T. F. Mathetics: The technology of education. *Journal of Mathematics,* 1962, *1,* 7–73.
Keller, F. S. and Schoenfeld, W. N. *Principles of psychology.* New York: Appleton, 1950. Chap. 7.

CHAINING VERBAL ASSOCIATES
Cofer, C. N. (Ed.) *Verbal learning and verbal behavior.* New York: McGraw-Hill, 1961.
Cofer, C. N., and Musgrave, B. S. (Eds.) *Verbal behavior and learning: Problems and processes.* New York: McGraw-Hill, 1963.
Deese, J., and Hulse, S. H. *The psychology of learning.* 3rd ed. New York: McGraw-Hill, 1967. Chaps. 8, 9.
Dixon, T. R., and Horton, D. L. (Eds.) *Verbal behavior and general behavior theory.* Englewood Cliffs, N.J.: Prentice-Hall, 1968.
McGeoch, J. A., and Irion, A. L. *The psychology of human Learning,* 2nd ed. New York: McKay, 1952.
Underwood, B. J., and Schulz, R. W. *Meaningfulness and verbal learning.* Philadelphia: Lippincott, 1960.

5

INTELLECTUAL SKILLS: DISCRIMINATIONS, CONCRETE CONCEPTS

The learned associations which have been described in the previous chapter may be put together in a sequential fashion to generate chains and verbal sequences. These and the chains constructued from them may also be the objects of further learning, as we shall see in the present chapter. First, we should point out that *sets* of associations (or sets of chains) may become increasingly differentiated, in the sense that the individual members become more readily distinguishable from one another. Through learning, an initially undifferentiated stimulus object may come to be responded to in ways that distinguish its parts or its dimensions or its characteristics. Second, once these fundamental distinctions have been made, another learning possibility becomes available to the learner: he may acquire the capability of responding to stimulus objects as members of a common class or category.

Suppose an individual has learned a simple S→R association to the stimulus provided by a door key. We have already seen that this link may be combined with others to form a chain, such as using the key to open a door. But there are other ways of responding to a key, and also to collections of keys. To be considered here are the learning of capabilities that may be briefly described as follows:

1. The individual is given a set of three keys, one for each door in his office. Initially the keys all look and feel alike. Soon, though, the individual can tell them apart by the number of notches and the depth of the first notch.
2. The individual responds to a specific collection of keys as door keys and to another collection as padlock keys. He is able to identify an entirely new key as belonging to one of these categories.

Both of these occurrences begin with stimulation provided by collections of stimulus objects or events. However, these are two rather different kinds of capabilities, the first being somewhat simpler than the second. In the first kind of performance, the individual becomes capable of distinguishing one key from another, or from several others. He makes different responses to the different members of a particular collection. This is called *discrimination*, or when several distinctions are involved (as in the example given) *multiple discrimination*. In the second type, the learner is able to respond in a single way to a collection of objects as class; this class extends beyond the members that were originally present. This second kind of learning is called *concept learning*. Notice that in the second example, the learner is able to distinguish keys also, only he now is distinguishing *classes* of keys (that is, he has learned two different concepts) rather than merely distinguishing a specific key from others (discrimination). Both these forms of learning are of considerable importance in a practical sense. As will be seen, the second kind is really dependent on the prior learning of the first, and there is a marked contrast in the versatility of behavior produced by learning of the second kind as opposed to the first.

This chapter, then, deals with two different kinds of learning that may occur when an individual is confronted with a set of stimulus objects. In some circumstances of discrimination learning, the learner may have to acquire a response which differentiates (by name or otherwise) the stimulus features of a single member of a set from those of other members. Or she may learn to distinguish several different members of a set, making a different response to each. Having previously learned to make these distinctions, the learner may be required to acquire the capability of responding to the set of stimuli as a class, and distinguishing members of the class from nonmembers; this is what is meant by "learning a concept." Of course, the learner may be required to respond to a stimulus set in *both* these ways on different occasions, and this response is perfectly possible.

LEARNING DISCRIMINATIONS

Acquiring discriminations is obviously an undertaking of great importance in everyday life and in school learning. Young children must learn at a very early age to distinguish among the parts of their environment: colors, brightnesses, shapes, sizes, textures, distances, loudnesses, and pitches. Adults, too, are constantly called upon to acquire new discriminations of stimulus objects, such as the locations of doors or streets, the distinctions among newly encountered faces, the taste of wines. As for learning in the school, the student is confronted early with the necessity of learning discrimination among printed colors, shapes, letters, numerals, and among the sounds of speech. Considerably later on, students learn distinctions, perhaps, among the microfeatures of body tissue, or among the aparent brightnesses and sizes of stars. E. J. Gibson (1969) describes the relevance of *perceptual learning,* conceived as a matter of increasing differentiation of parts of the environment, for the early years of the child's learning. Discrimination learning leads to perceptual differentiation, she points out, within five media: objects, space, events, representations, and symbols. The child's earliest learned perceptions pertain to objects and space, while discrimination learning of events comes a bit later, as the child becomes able to manipulate objects and to move about. Still later, and much emphasized in early school grades, is the learning of discriminations of representations (pictures) and symbols. Thus, it is important to realize that many discriminations of a basic sort have already been acquired when the child first goes to school.

Discrimination learning is often concerned with the *distinctive features* of stimulus objects. Thus the child learns to respond differentially to the characteristics that serve to distinguish objects from one another: shapes, sizes, colors, textures, and so on. Similarly, the child learns to distinguish phonemes, the smallest units of speech, by means of such distinctive features (here, technically named) as grave-acute, lax-diffuse, vocalic-nonvocalic. The young schoolchild learns to discriminate the distinctive features which will be needed to distinguish pictured or drawn representations, and also letters.

The discrimination learning engaged in by children when learning to differentiate printed letters provides an instructive example of the process. Suppose the children first learn to make the response "gee" to the printed letter g. In its simplest form, this may be S→R learning of the following sort:

$$S \longrightarrow R$$
printed g   oral "gee"

The response connection thus learned is of no particular significance for the learning of the discrimination—it is simply a response different from others that the children might make. The critical learning is that of using this response for g, and *not* for a or p or q. Thus, the learning has to involve reinforcement when the response "gee" is made to the letter g, and an absence of reinforcement when this response is made to other letters. The children must learn to indicate by their response that they can distinguish the critical features of g (a loop above the line, a tail on the right, which extends below the line and curves inwards) from the features which are "not g."

Consider another example—the discrimination of a circle and an ellipse—which young children may be asked to learn (without their names). Initially, two figures may be presented on a set of cards, some containing two circles, others two ellipses, and still others a circle and an ellipse. In the procedure of learning, the children are asked to say whether the two figures are "the same" or "different"; or they may be asked to say "Yes" or "No" to whether the figures are alike. As a response is made to each card, the children are told whether it is correct or incorrect (by a nod of the head, the statement "Right," or some other signal). As the trials proceed, the learners obviously increase their probability of being "right" and their confidence in their answers. They have acquired the discrimination when it becomes evident that they "see" the difference in the figures without appreciable error. This performance may then be checked with a *matching* task, in which the children select one of the figures from a set containing both circles and ellipses, by matching it with whichever shape has been designated in the directions.

Discrimination learning of this sort commonly takes the form of presenting a single letter (such as g) along with other letters, one at a time, in mixed order. The learner is asked to respond to the g's by saying "gee," and to make no response to the other letters. Alternatively, pairs of letters may be presented, one a g and the other a different letter, and the child asked to point to the g. The child who has learned to say the names of several letters may be asked to name each of them when they are presented sucessively in a mixed order. At this stage, of course, the child may be learning *multiple discriminations,* or several discriminations at once. All of these methods of presentation are examples of *contrast practice.* The learner is given an indication of being "right" when an appropriate response to a letter is made, and "wrong" when an incorrect response occurs. By means of such differential reinforcement, the learner comes to respond correctly to the differential features of the letters.

Pupils are asked to learn different names for printed letters so that they can make consistent distinctive responses to these letters on a page. In some forms of early instruction, children are asked to learn the sounds of letters as responses (g as "guh") rather than their names, since these sounds will later be involved in oral reading. There may be some advantage for later learning in acquiring responses which "sound" letters rather than "name" them. The important thing to be noted, however, is that what is being learned at this stage is *not* the names of the letters (which the child may well have learned previously as oral responses), but the *discriminations* among their physical appearances.

Interference in Discrimination Learning

When multiple discriminations are learned, it is apparent that the task of discriminating the stimuli one from the other increases in difficulty as more stimuli become involved. When g is presented alone, the discrimination task is not very demanding, but when g is presented along with y, the chances of confusion are increased; and this trend continues when the even more similar letter p is added. The possibilities of confusion in the appearance of p and g, d and b, m and n are well known to teachers of young children. As a set of stimuli, all of these letters must be distinguished from each other by multiple discrimination. A learning technique is sometimes used to magnify the differences among the letters when they are initially being learned, for example, by empasizing the left and right positions of the "tail" on the letters *d* and *b*. Another technique, again designed to make stimulus differences more prominent, is to have children feel cut-out letters; this provides additional tactual and kinesthetic cues to their differences.

A major change in the multiple-discrimination as opposed to the single-discrimination situation is that great potential for *interference* exists in the former. That is to say, the similarities between stimuli tend to favor the occurrence of *confusion errors*, increasing the difficulty of learning. No sooner has the learner acquired the discrimination which permits different responses to be made to *p* and *b*, than he must further learn to distinguish *d* and *g*. The occurrence of interference shows up when he attempts to recall any of these.

Learning is thus made more difficult when a multiple set of discriminations is being learned. One solution (a practical one, which may or may not be the best) is to proceed to learn the single discriminations one by one and then to provide additional practice one by one, using a mixed-up order of presentation. The question of how many single discriminations to learn before undertaking recall and repetition is one that has not received a clear answer from laboratory experimentation. Likely to work well for this purpose is "progressive part" learning, in which new discriminations are introduced while old ones are reviewed (see McGeoch and Irion, 1952). Another approach is to initially exaggerate the differences among the stimuli and in successive practice trials to gradually reduce these differences to those that are normal. The most efficient technique for multiple discrimination of stimuli such as the set of letters may turn out to be one which incorporates both these approaches.

CONDITIONS OF LEARNING DISCRIMINATIONS

The various examples described should make possible a formulation of some propositions regarding the conditions necessary for learning discriminations.

Conditions Within the Learner

One condition that must exist within the learner is the ability to recall and reinstate the different response chains necessary to exhibit the discrimination. If this is a matter of "knowing the name" of an object or object-quality, this requirement appears not to be an overly demanding one. The S→R, or response chain, is learned in the manner described in the previous chapter, as a verbal label or as some other kind of response. When discriminations are learned to multiple stimuli, of course, the learner must be able to exhibit as many different responses as there are differences in stimuli.

Conditions in the Learning Situation

A discrimination is usually established by the selective reinforcement of correct versus incorrect responses to the stimulus (an object or object-quality). For example, if young children are learning to distinguish *closed* and *open* plane figures (curves), positive reinforcement is provided when they are shown sets of figures both closed and open, and distinguish them correctly. This may be done in various ways. (1) The children may be asked to identify closed figures, and then shown pairs (closed and open) in which they point to the correct one; (2) a large set of figures, closed and open, may be shown, in which the children must point to either the closed or open ones; or (3) closed and open figures may be shown one by one, and the children asked to say "closed" or "open." In any of these situations, it is understood that differential reinforcement will be employed, that is, some indication will be given that correct and incorrect responses have been made in each trial.

Procedures such as these have the purpose of permitting a *selection* of the correct stimulus features to be made. Initially, the learner may respond to some stimulus features which are correct and to others which are incorrect. The child, for example, may be responding at first to large versus small gaps in the figure, rather than to continuity versus discontinuity of the curve. As additional trials are given, the responses to incorrect aspects of the stimulus are progressively subject to *extinction*, and the correct discrimination becomes established. When correct responses are made by the child, their correctness is confirmed by a teacher; when the responses are incorrect, such confirmation is omitted.

When multiple discriminations are learned, the learning task becomes more difficult because of confusions among the stimuli to be discriminated. In other words, there tends to be *interference*. Consequently, a greater amount of contrast practice is required so that the responses to "incorrect" stimulus features will be suitably extinguished. Although the different responses learned in multiple discriminations are commonly *names* for the objects differentiated, they need not be. The sender of Morse code learns a set of key-tapping patterns to differentiate the individual letters of the message to be transmitted. The student of the clarinet learns to distinguish a set of printed notes by means of a set of fingering responses, each of which bears a specific relationship to a particular note. The operator of a panel controlling industrial or other machinery may have to have a number of different key-pressing responses to distinguish the various signals received. In all these instances there are strong tendencies to interference among the individual response chains; this interference is overcome by the use of contrast practice.

Educational Implications of Discrimination Learning

Discrimination learning is deceptively simple, and the need for it may be overlooked. The discriminations most of us are able to exhibit have been acquired early in life and without deliberate intent. We tend to think that everyone is able to "see" (that is, discriminate) the difference between green and yellow, red and pink, pointed and curved, rough and smooth. It is common, therefore, to *assume* that the discriminations needed for further learning are already available to the learner. But the need for discrimination learning is often made apparent when we encounter new kinds of stimuli to be incorporated in learning—stimuli which are not common in the sense of having been previously encountered. Thus, learners who tackle a foreign language may be confronted with sounds they have not heard before—the umlauted "u" in German, or the uvular "r" in French. The student who looks through a microscope for the first time may similarly encounter a new field of view, which contains many features to be discriminated. The student of music may face the task of discriminating tonal differences not previously attended to.

Multiple discriminations are frequently required in the learning that takes place in schools. Young children must learn distinguishing features for a great variety of things and events in their environment; rocks, birds, stars, flowers, and coins are a few examples. Children must learn to make different responses to many kinds of printed symbols, including letters, numerals, words, and other signs. Students acquire a multitude of discriminations of the stimulus features involved in the objects encountered during education —in gases, liquids, solids, parts of the earth and universe, animals, plants, music, works of art. All their lives, people must learn new discriminations of novel objects, symbols, faces. Besides being a widespread type of learning outcome, discrimination also plays an important role in other more complex learning activities which are yet to be described.

LEARNING CONCRETE CONCEPTS

One way the individual can learn to respond to collections of things is by distinguishing among them. Another way, even more important as a human capability, is by putting things into a class and responding to any instance of the class as a member of that class. In a sense this latter learning seems just the opposite of the first kind. But it is more than that, because it incorporates the first kind as one of its preconditions. This latter learning, which makes it possible for the individual to respond to things or events as a class, results in the kind of learning outcome called a *concept*.

At this point, it is important to note that the term "concept" has several meanings. Obviously, it will not be possible to deal with them all at the same time, and it would doubtless be a mistake to try to do so. First, we should consider the most fundamental meaning of the term "concept," which is exhibited in individual behavior by responding to object-qualities such as those implied by the names *red*, *double*, *circular*, and *smooth* or by common objects such as *cat*, *chair*, *tree*, and *house*. It is customary to refer to these as *concrete* concepts, since they can be denoted by being pointed out; in other words, they are *concepts by observation*. Later on, it will be possible to describe *concepts by definition*; these are abstract in the sense that they involve relations. Some examples are physical concepts of mass and temperature, language concepts of subject and object, mathematical concepts of square root and prime number. Further descriptions of defined concepts will be undertaken in the next chapter.

An Example of a Concrete Concept

The topic introduced here is the learning of concepts that are concrete in the sense that they depend upon direct observation. Suppose one were to show a seven-year-old child a set of three hollow blocks on a tabletop. Two of these blocks are identical for practical purposes, but the other is different. The child is told that a small piece of candy is under one of the blocks, but not under the others. She is to try to "guess" where the candy is, and lift one or more blocks to get it. (We may call the blocks A, A, and B.) Unknown to the child, the experimenter follows the rule of always placing the candy under the *odd* block, the one that is unlike the other two. Initially, of course, the child really does guess, and the association $S_B \rightarrow R_{lift}$ is reinforced. Now the experimenter places a new set of hollow blocks, of different appearance, C, C, and D, on the table, with the candy under D. (Of course, the spatial placement of the blocks is unsystematic in all cases.) Now the child, after one or more errors, chooses block D, and the association is reinforced. Other combinations may be tried, such as BBA, DDC, BBC, FEF. Eventually, it is found that the child *chooses the odd one*. Once this happens, she is able to perform the task without error for *any* set of blocks, such as XXY, with which she has had no specific previous experience. It may then be said that the child is *using a concept*, or that she is behaving conceptually.

In order for such a statement about the child's behavior to be valid, certain things must be true. First, it must be known that her behavior could not have been learned as a simple $S \rightarrow R$ connection, or as a chain of such connections. If one used only a single set of blocks, like AAB, the child could learn to choose the odd one on the basis of its appearance alone (B), as an $S \rightarrow R$ association. Similarly, if one placed the blocks in the same spatial order, so that the odd one was always on the extreme right, the child could learn a simple stimulus-response association to a particular location as the stimulus. In order to state that the child is using a concept, one must demonstrate that the performance is impossible on the basis of simpler forms of learning. This can be done, as in the example given, by presenting the child with novel stimulus objects in novel positions. If she responds correctly, it may be justifiably said that the child "knows what the *odd one* is," or that she knows the concept *odd*.

The example illustrates a way that individuals have of responding to collections of things, which is different from multiple discrimination. In this case the collections of objects may vary widely in appearance. Individuals naturally must distinguish among them. But what is important is that people respond to them in terms of some *common abstract property*. In a real sense, people *classify* them.

What the child does in this situation with the blocks may be inferred to be something like the following. She may initially say to herself, "Oh, it's B." Having found that this doesn't work when CC and D are presented, she may say to herself, "It's the one on the right" or "It's the blue one." But none of these responses is successful; they are unreinforced and become extinguished. Eventually, she says to herself, "It's the odd one," and this works every time. Does she *actually* say these things to herself? It is difficult to obtain evidence that proves this. But so far as the ultimately correct performance is concerned, the child behaves *as if* she says to herself, "It's the odd one." To be able to state that the child uses a concept, one has only to demonstrate that such an "as if" clause is true.

Returning to our example of concept use in the seven-year-old, it is of considerable interest to ask whether she has to go through this trial-and-error procedure in order to demonstrate knowledge of the concept *odd*. The answer is, of course, no. It is much easier to bring about the performance required by saying to the child, "Choose the odd one!" For an average seven-year-old, this instruction should bring about the correct performance immediately. What is shown by the use of this new verbal condition, naturally, is that the seven-year-old has not really *learned* the concept in the block situation. She knew it all the time, and an external verbal cue was sufficient to reinstate the correct behavior.

The trial-and-error exercise is often used by psychologists who study concept use in order to make a detailed analysis of the process. It is not a good example of how concepts are usually learned, but only of how they *may* be learned. But it is nevertheless instructive. Suppose the seven-year-old were a child who knew no English, so that the word "odd" could not serve as an S→R connection. Naturally, the instruction "Choose the odd one" would not enable her to perform the task correctly. In order to find out whether she knew the concept, one would have to use an exercise. The same sort of trial-and-error exercise might be used if one wished to determine whether an animal could use such a concept as *odd*. Harlow (1949) has used similar procedures to demonstrate that monkeys can respond correctly to tasks requiring the concept *odd*.

From Discrimination Learning to Concept Learning

It has often been shown that discriminations are prerequisite to the learning of concepts. The nature of concept learning and its relation to the discrimination learning which precedes it is suggested by the stages depicted in Figure 5.1.

Assume that learning begins with the discrimination of a straight line, to be distinguished from lines which are not straight, (curved). The learner first masters the discrimination shown as Stage 1, so that he responds positively to the straight line, negatively (or in some different fashion) to the curved line. Stage 2 then intro-

STAGE 1: DISCRIMINATION

Straight   Curved

STAGE 2: GENERALIZATION

STAGE 3: VARIATION IN IRRELEVANT DIMENSIONS

FIGURE 5.1   Stages of learning beginning with a discrimination and leading to the learning of a concept.

duces the same straight line, paired with various curved lines; none
of these are straight, but they differ in a number of ways. Another
way to say this is that the curved lines vary in their irrelevant dimensions (such as amount of curvature and orientation). Contrast practice is continued under these conditions until the learner shows
convincingly that he discriminates "straight" from "not straight."
Thus there is *generalization* of the original discrimination learning.
Varied contrast practice is again continued in Stage 3. In this stage,
there is variation in the irrelevant dimensions of the nonstraight
lines and also in the irrelevant dimensions (orientation, thickness,
etc.) of the straight lines. Once the learning of this stage has been
mastered, there is convincing proof that the learner has "abstracted"
the relevant object-quality. He has acquired the *concept* of line
straightness.

     To make a final check on the learning of the concept, it is
customary to choose a brand-new example, which has not been
used during learning. A new straight line may be drawn, with a dif-

ferent, nonstraight line. We say that the concept has been acquired when the learner can identify such a *novel instance*. Note that what the learner is doing is placing this new instance into the category "straight." In other words, he is classifying it.

Verbal Instructions in Concept Learning

The meaning of concrete concept is illustrated by the examples we have given. But the description of concept learning is not yet complete. A concept may be acquired by means of the contrast practice procedure, employing a succession of instances varying in their irrelevant dimensions. But this procedure is not necessarily typical when the learner can be guided by language.

Suppose that a child capable of using language does not know the concept *edge*. Assume it is desired that he exhibit the capability of identifying an edge by name, and more importantly, of identifying any one of a class of things called edges in novel situations. How can such learning come about?

The first step might be for the child to acquire the word as a self-generated S→R connection, so that when the instructor says "edge" and then asks that the word be repeated, the pupil says "edge." Next the pupil will learn to say the word "edge" to that part of an object, and to refrain from saying "edge" to other parts which are not edges, such as a *side*, a *top*, or a *corner*. This is the generalization stage, previously described. The important event in each case is a firm and precise attainment of *edge* discriminations, even when other dimensions of the object are varied. Now greater variety is introduced into the situation. Edge is learned as a feature of a flat-surfaced object such as a piece of paper, involving distinctions between *edge* and *surface* and *corner*; again with reference to a drawn two-dimensional figure, which may show *shading* as well as clear edges.

How many situations need to be used to assure a sufficient number of variations in which edge is distinguished from features that are "not edge"? There appears to be no known answer to this question. But it is important to conduct the learning within stimulus situations that *represent the actual range of the concept being learned*; otherwise the concept that emerges will be incomplete in some sense. Concepts that are *inadequate in range* are frequently learned by all of us, owing to the peculiarities of the situations we have encountered. For example, a young child who has seen only one or two bears may have an inadequate concept of this class of animals. A concept which is inadequate in this sense, however, is *not incorrect*, and may in fact be perfectly adequate for many purposes. Extension of the range of a concept can readily be brought about by additional learning occasions.

When the learner is able to say "edge" to several different specific stimulus situations, it is reasonable to suppose that the concept has been learned. The instructor might confirm the learning by using a verbal commmunication, presenting three of the stimuli at once (the three-dimensional object, the paper, the drawing). She might say, "Each of these has an edge. What is this? (An edge.) And what is this? (An edge.) And what is this? (An edge.)" Finally she takes one more step, and shows the pupil a new object or drawing with which the word "edge" has not previously been associated. The instructor says, "Where is the edge?" The pupil points to it. A concept has been acquired!

It is not entirely clear whether the use of the final new example is necessary for the learning, or whether it is merely a test of what has already been learned. Quite probably, the former is the case. At any rate, the instructor will probably wish to make a more reliable determination that concept learning has really happened by asking the student to respond to one or two additional examples, each a novel one.

What is the role of the verbal label, the word "edge," in this set of events? Obviously, it provides an important shortcut to the learning of a concept. Without it, one would have to conduct a greater number of trial-and-error trials in order to insure that edges and nonedges were responded to correctly. When the word is known, however, it can be used to *cue* the correct responses to stimulus to recall, which makes it relatively easy to structure the situation required for learning.

Thus it may be seen that the learning of a concept is not *necessarily* a verbal matter, since concepts can be learned in other ways by animals as well as by human beings. But using verbal cues makes concept learning a relatively *easy* task for human beings who have already mastered the prerequisites. The verbalization described here, however, needs to be carefully distinguished from the verbalizing that presents a definition. As an example of the latter, an edge might be defined as "a region of abrupt change in intensity of the pattern of light waves reflected to the eye from a surface." It should not be supposed that this such verbal definition would be very effective in bringing about the learning of a concept. (Learning of concepts does sometimes occur this way in highly sophisticated adults, but that is another story.) The learner must instead begin with concrete situations, to which he may bring a common verbal associate. When this condition obtains, using the word as an "instruction" is a convenient way of generating the proper conditions for concept learning.

Adults learn new concepts in much the same way. Suppose, for example, an adult who is studying physiology must learn the concept of *striated muscle*. In such a case one assumes that the basic learning of the words has already been accomplished. But the verbal chains that connect several instances of observed tissue samples (actual or pictured) to the response "striated muscle" must be established. Furthermore, a number of multiple discriminations must probably also be acquired; the individual must learn to distinguish muscle tissue from other forms and to distinguish striated from smooth and heart muscle. Once these differences have been mastered, the basic instructional conditions for concept learning can be carried out. That is, various instances of striated muscle can be shown at one time (or in quick succession) and identified by the student, who should then be ready to classify a new example of striated muscle as a member of the concept class.

Is this all the adult must learn about a concept in order to be said to "know" it? The answer is yes, so long as the word "know" means nothing more than to use the new entity as a concept. Of course, an adult will probably go on to learn more about striated muscle in the form of rules (to be discussed in the next chapter). How striated muscles work, where they occur in the body, their embryological development, and many other things may also be learned. But these additional learnings will be useless except as sheer verbalizations, unless the learner first knows the concept by reference to a *class of concrete situations*. It may be noted that this observation about concepts has profound implications for educational practice. For example, the fundamental reason for laboratory work in science instruction is to give such concrete examples. Concepts may be aroused by verbal means, as we have seen. In human beings, their learning is almost always verbally mediated. But to be accurate tools for thinking about and dealing with the real world, concepts must be referable to actual stimulus situations. These provide concepts with an "operational" meaning that can come in no other way.

Seven-year-old children show marked differences from four-year-olds in acquiring concepts, presumably because the younger

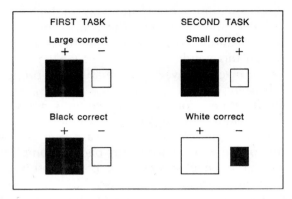

FIGURE 5.2   Two examples of discrimination reversal problems learned by children of two different age groups (four and seven). After learning the first task, the children were shifted to the second (reversed) task. (Kendler, H. H., and Kendler, T. S., Effect of verbalization on reversal shifts in children. *Science*, 1961, *141*, 1619–1620.)

ones have not yet acquired the words that make concept learning an easy matter (Kendler and Kendler, 1961). This has been shown by giving children of two age groups a task like that illustrated in Figure 5.2. In the first task, the children were asked to choose between two exposed squares, one large and one small. Although the relative position of the squares was varied, the "large" one was always correct, and the child received a marble for choosing it. Once this task had been learned, each child was given a second task in which the "small " square was now correct. (Another group of children first responded to "black" as correct, and then were shifted to "white.") The seven-year-olds took an average of eight trials to make this shift, whereas the four-year-olds required twenty-three. It seems probable that the older children in this study were able to use the concept *opposite* quite readily, whereas the younger children had difficulty with it and tended to continue responding to the situation by learning anew a reverse discrimination. The preavailability of language has been shown in other studies to make considerable difference in children's acquiring of concepts.

The Conditions of Concept Learning

It is now possible to summarize in a more formal way the conditions for the learning of concrete concepts.

CONDITIONS WITHIN THE LEARNER. Prerequisites to the learning of concepts are capabilities that have previously been established as discriminations. These must be recalled by learners at the time they undertake concept learning. When verbal instructions are employed, verbal labels must have previously been learned as associates to the stimulus features that represent the concept. The learning of the concept is usually arrived at through the intermediate stage of generalization of the basic discrimination, in which distinctions are established between the relevant and irrelevant stimulus dimensions (see Figure 5.1).

CONDITIONS WITHIN THE SITUATION. In human learners, the situational conditions for learning concepts are largely embodied in a set of *verbal cues*. To have animals learn concepts usually requires a slow and complex procedure that accomplishes the same effects as verbal instructions do with human beings (Gagné, 1964).

1. The specific stimulus object, or stimulus dimension, is presented as an instance along with a noninstance (a different object or dimension). The learner identifies the dimension by name. In terms of the example used here, the instructor asks "What is this?" or "Show me the edge." The learner's response confirms the presence of the discrimination.
2. In the generalization stage, the instructor introduces the instance along with various noninstances. Again, the identification of the discriminated feature (such as the edge) is asked for and obtained in each case.
3. Now the stimulus feature which is to become the concept is itself varied, and presented along with various noninstances. The new capability may be verified by asking for the identification of several additional instances of the class, again using stimulus objects not previously been employed in learning. If these are successfully identified, one may conclude that a new concept has been learned.
4. The condition of *reinforcement* is present in the concept-learning situation. The learner's correct responses to edge and nonedge must be confirmed if the concept is to be learned. *Contiguity* also appears important to concept learning, as illustrated by the contiguous presentation of several instances involving the same discrimination. The absence of contiguity may well be the factor mainly responsible for the slowness of concept learning done in a trial-and-error fashion. When all the specific instances on which the concept depend are "lively" in memory at the

same time, concept acquisition is rapid. As for *repetition*, it does not appear to be necessary when other conditions are optimal. The provision of one or more new examples may merely serve the purpose of "testing" the presence of the concept. There is no available evidence whether these additional instances aid in concept retention, although this may be true.

Generalizing with Concepts

The possession of the capability generated in the learner when a concept is acquired is distinguished from all other forms of learning so far described by the characteristic of *generalizability*. Having acquired the concept *edge*, the individual is able to generalize this concept to different stimulus situations that have not played a part in the learning. He can immediately and unhesitatingly identify an edge on a roof, a cliff, an automobile fender, a lampshade, or any of a great variety of stimulus situations. (Of course, this assumes that the initial situations used to exhibit the concept were sufficiently representative of the total class covered by the concept.) If he has learned the concept *raise*, he will be able to recognize this class of event in such diverse circumstances as the raising of an arm, a flag or a window. *The effect of concept learning is to free the individual from control by specific stimuli.* This kind of learning, then, is obviously of tremendous importance for most kinds of intellectual activity engaged in by human beings. We read in terms of concepts, we communicate with concepts, we think with concepts.

It is not surprising, then, that the "test" for the presence of concepts is a matter of demonstrating that generalizing can occur. Regardless of what stimuli have been used for learning, the acquisition of the concept *odd* or *edge* or *raise* is tested by presenting a stimulus situation that was not involved in the learning. There must be a demonstration that the learner can generalize the concept to a variety of specific instances of the class that have not been used in learning. Otherwise, the learning may not be a concept, but merely a collection of specific chains.

The generalizing capability provided by concept learning goes far beyond the *stimulus generalization* that is a fundamental property of S→R learning. Of course, this latter property is still present in the connections used to establish or to arouse the concept. But it is limited by the physical resemblances of objects or events. Generalizing by means of concepts, in contrast, is not limited by physical resemblances. When using a concept, the individual experiences no difficulty in identifying the *edge* in a large round swimming pool or in a tiny letter on a printed page. The property held in common by such widely different stimulus situations cannot be described in terms of the resemblances of physical stimulation. An *edge*, in other words, is an abstraction from all the specific situations in which it occurs. This is apparently what some writers mean when they refer to concepts as "relationships of stimuli."

The world experienced by human beings is largely organized by means of concepts. We think of our environment, as well as ourselves, primarily in terms of concepts of objects, places, and events. We communicate with other people, and they communicate with us, to an overwhelming degree by means of concepts. There are concepts of things and places, like *chairs, tables, trees, lawns, houses, automobiles, top, bottom, side, corner.* Things in conceptual form are the nouns of sentences. Then there are concepts of relations, which generally are represented by verbs, such as *go, stay, take, put, raise, lower, sit, accept, deliver, reject.* Because of the accidental character of their experiences with them, children sometimes acquire these words as concepts in a trial-and-error fashion. But a new concept such as that represented by a technical term may readily be taught in the more systematic manner just described.

An Example—Letter and Phoneme Identification

An example of concept learning of considerable educational importance, and illustrative of many of the characteristics previously discussed, is learning to identify printed letters and syllables as parts of words.

As pointed out in the early portion of this chapter, one prerequisite learning is that of acquiring discriminations such as $d=$ "duh," $b=$"buh," $k=$"kuh." Once such discriminations have been learned, a firm foundation has been laid for the acquiring of letter-sound concepts. The distinction is that letters must now be identified as corresponding to an entire *class* of acoustic stimuli, depending upon their context within a syllable or word. In terms of actual response characteristics, the flat "a" is pronounced with considerable difference in the words "frantic" and "stagger"; yet as a concept to be acquired for the purpose of reading or listening, it is still a member of the class of letter *a*. In the word "dumb," the "d" has a good deal of force behind it, with the tongue far back; in "dirt," however, the "d" is much closer to a "t" in sound. But both sounds are members of the class *d*. For each printed letter there is a class of *phonemes*.

Following the learning of basic discriminations, the child who is learning to read must learn to identify phonemes by recognizing a single printed letter for each letter-sound contained in the class. Thus, phonemes constitute an educationally important concept. The acquisition of these concepts takes place under learning conditions comparable to those for other concepts. The different instances of the class must be presented and each identified (recognized) as belonging to a single class of printed letters. For example, the sound of "d" in "dirt" must lead to recognition of "d," and the sound of "d" in "dumb" must lead to the same recognition; the sound of "b" in "book" must be identified as b, as also the sound of "b" in "table." The conditions for learning, then, may be described as consisting of the presentation of a sufficient variety of positive and negative instances of the phoneme class, accompanied by suitable provisions for reinforcement.

It seems that difficulties in learning to pronounce printed words may sometimes result from an unsystematic sequence of learning events. The systematic sequence is (1) learn to identify the letters, as *d*—"duh," and so on; (2) learn to put letters together in longer chains, sometimes called "blending," as in "buh"–"a"–"tuh" for "bat"; (3) learn to pronounce the entire printed word as "bat." At this third stage, however, the concepts called phonemes are of particular importance. The children must recognize the printed *t*, for example, as a member of the phoneme class "t" which has a particular sound in this context. By so doing, they are enabled to match the letter combination *at* to a familiar sound in their oral repertoire. Similarly, having also recognized the phoneme *b*, they are enabled to match the entire printed word to the word "bat" in their oral vocabulary. Thus children read the word. Letter discriminations are obviously a necessary prerequisite in such a sequence; but they are not enough. Phoneme concepts must also be learned before word reading can occur successfully.

Some Educational Implications

It would be difficult to overemphasize the importance of concept learning for formal education. The acquisition of concepts is what makes instruction possible. One cannot take the time to present even a small fraction of all the specific situations in which students may encounter an edge or an odd one or a cell or a striated muscle.

But if the use of a few examples can help learners to acquire these concepts, one may expect that generalizing will occur to the whole of the learners' experience. Students are freed from the control of specific stimuli in their environment and can thereafter learn by means of *verbal instruction*, presented orally or in printed form. They can also communicate their intentions, actions, and thoughts to other people—again because the specific words employed arouse concepts in their hearers that function just as their own do.

Young children arrive in kindergarten with many concepts learned and many not yet learned. They probably have already acquired concepts for a number of common objects in the environment, such as chairs and floors and ceilings and streets and flowers and animals and trees. Most probably they know such place concepts as *above, below, on top of, underneath, next to, middle*. Similarly, the youngsters will doubtless respond conceptually to words like *start* and *stop, go* and *come, sit* and *stand*. But the children still need to learn many other concepts which will form the basis of much of their later learning. They may not yet know what *the one before* means, or *the next one* or *double* or *like* and *unlike*. Kindergarten children probably have not yet learned to conceptualize word sounds as printed letter combinations as a basis for reading and writing. They may not be able to use number names for quantities (whether or not they can recite a verbal chain such as "one, two, three") but will need to learn these foundations of arithmetic. In fact, it would be valuable to know with some confidence what concepts the typical kindergarten child does not yet have or what concepts he needs to learn first. The problem is clearly an important one.

As the student progresses in school, he continues to acquire concepts. Once the fundamental skill of reading has been acquired, concepts can often be introduced by means of instruction with accompanying pictures or diagrams. In mathematics this is fairly easy because the stimulus situations that must be responded to with concepts are usually marks on a printed page; adding can be represented by + and subtracting by −. Languages can also be represented in print, so that the concepts pertaining to language structure (subject, verb, and so on) are learned in response to printed sentences such as "John's hat is on the table." But in other subjects, there may be greater difficulty in presenting the fundamental situations to be conceptualized, and pictures and diagrams are often employed. Thus, at some stage of science learning, the concept *fulcrum* may be introduced with the presentation of several diagrams depicting levers; or the concept *cell* may be presented by means of an idealized diagram. Most difficult of all are likely to be abstract concepts like *family* and *legislature*, of the type that makes up the disciplines of the social sciences.

The great value of concepts as means for thinking and communicating is that they have *concrete references*. The importance of this characteristic cannot be overemphasized. But since concepts are learned by the human being via language, there is often a danger of losing sight of this concreteness. Learning can become oververbalized, which means that the concepts learned are highly inadequate in their references to actual situations. The learner "does not really know the meaning of the word," even though he can use it correctly in a sentence. For example, the verbal information obtained by reading that striated muscles are made up of bundles of long narrow cells is unlikely to provide a student of physiology or anatomy an adequate concept of striated muscles. The danger of verbal superficiality, and the necessity for avoiding it, has been recognized in several educational doctrines. "Learning by doing" is one of these. Another recognizes the importance of the laboratory and the demonstration in science teaching. The concepts of science deal with the real world and therefore must be based on "operations" that are equally concrete.

Besides having concrete references, concepts possess the additional property of freeing thought and expression from the domination of the physical environment. As will be seen in the next chapter, concepts in their generalized form may be linked together in various ways to form principles. "Water boils" is a simple sentence recalling two different concepts to the individual who has already acquired them. But the linking of these concepts results in the conveying of information, that is, *knowledge* in propositional form. The tremendous variety of knowledge imparted by means of verbal communication is, of course, a fundamental fact of education. Once concepts have been mastered, the individual is ready to learn an amount of knowledge that is virtually without limit.

GENERAL REFERENCES

DISCRIMINATION LEARNING
Gibson, E. J. *Principles of perceptual learning and development.* New York: Appleton, 1969.
Riley, D. A. *Discrimination learning.* Englewood Cliffs, N. J.: Prentice-Hall, 1968.
Vanderplas, J. M. Perception and learning. In M. H. Marx (Ed.), *Learning: Interactions.* New York. Macmillan, 1970.

CONCEPT LEARNING

Bourne, L. E., Jr. *Human conceptual behavior.* Boston: Allyn and Bacon, 1966.

Glaser, R. Concept learning and concept teaching. In R. M. Gagné and W. J. Gephart (Eds.), *Learning research and school subjects.* Itasca, Ill.: Peacock, 1968.

Harlow, H. F., and Harlow, M. K. Learning to think. *Scientific American,* 1949, *181,* 36–39.

Trabasso, T., and Bower, G. H. *Attention in learning.* New York: Wiley, 1968.

CHILDREN'S CONCEPTS

Flavell, J. H. *The developmental psychology of Jean Piaget.* New York: Van Nostrand, 1963.

Lovell, K. *The growth of basic mathematical and scientific concepts in children.* New York: Philosophical Library, 1961.

Piaget, J. *The construction of reality in the child.* New York: Basic Books, 1954. (For other works of Piaget, see references in Flavell.)

Sigel, I. E., and Hooper, F. H. *Logical thinking in children.* New York: Holt, Rinehart and Winston, 1968.

6

INTELLECTUAL SKILLS: DEFINED CONCEPTS AND RULES

Some concepts can be learned by direct interaction with the learner's environment, while others must be learned by the use of language. The latter kind of concepts are really rules for classifying objects and events.

This chapter deals with the learning of concepts and rules, varieties of intellectual skills highly representative of human intellectual capabilities. To some readers it may seem, at last, that the types of behavior being described are those with which formal instruction most typically concerns itself, and this is probably the case. It should be emphasized, however, that these forms of learning build upon learnings that have preceded them. Although the learning of defined concepts and rules may well represent some frequent goals of a formal schooling process, it would be mistaken to believe that these goals can be reached by simply ignoring all other forms of learning or by pushing the latter into a trash can of unimportant events. The varieties of learning described here are possible only because they have been preceded by the acquisition of a set of simpler prerequisite capabilities.

Many concepts cannot be learned in the manner described in the previous chapter, that is, as concrete concepts. Instead, they must be learned by *definition* and, accordingly, may be called *defined concepts*. Sometimes they are called abstract, in order to distinguish them from the concrete variety. For example, the concept *diagonal* is a defined concept, not a concrete concept. The statement "A diagonal is a line connecting opposite corners of a quadrilateral" represents a relation (connect) between the two concepts "line" and "opposite corners of a quadrilateral." Another example is the concept *pivot*, which may be defined as the relation, "pointed end of a shaft on which an object turns." In this instance, it may be seen that the defined concept is composed of other concrete concepts, including "pointed end," "shaft," and "turns." This is not always the case, of course; a defined concept may be composed of one or more concepts which are themselves defined rather than concrete.

The inclusive subject of this chapter is the *learning of rules*. The defined concept is, in a formal sense, one type of rule. The relation expressed by a defined concept may be used, as its name implies, to enable the learner to identify the relation and distinguish it from others: The concept of *uncle* is distinguished from *aunt*, or the concept of *mass* from *weight*. Rules are also used for other purposes. They operate to guide the individual's behavior in meeting a host of particular problems. The rule that is symbolized in mathematics as $a+b=b+a$ guides the individual's behavior in selecting a combination of seven objects and two objects as being equivalent to a combination of two objects and seven objects; or four objects and five objects as equivalent to five and four. It is not necessary to learn each individual combination of numbers in a rote fashion as verbal chains. Instead, the rule is applied to whatever combination of numbers is being dealt with at the moment. Students learn to apply a *rule*, and their behavior may be said to be *rule-governed*.

The ability of human beings to respond to an enormous variety of situations and to operate effectively—despite almost infinite variety in the stimulation they receive—makes it at once apparent that rules are probably the major organizing factor, and quite possibly the primary one, in intellectual functioning. The S→R connection, once proposed as the unit of mental organization, has now been virtually replaced by the rule in the theoretical formulations of many psychologists. Even those who still favor the connection as a fundamental entity of neural functioning are forced to concede that the preponderance of observed human behavior occurring in natural situations is rule-governed. When a young child constructs the imperfect sentence "Daddy, in" to express her intention that her father enter the house, she is applying a rule—perhaps an inadequate one by adult standards, but a rule nonetheless. One knows this not from observing the single instance of the child calling her father but from additional observations that indicate the child can construct the same kind of sentences for her mother, her dog, or other people. The stimuli in these other situations are all different and may actually not have occurred previously in the child's life. Yet her sentence-constructing behavior can be seen to be *regular*, or rule-governed.

DEFINED CONCEPTS

A defined concept is a rule that classifies objects or events. The set of *prime numbers* is classified by the definition of any number divisible only by the number one and by a number with the same value as itself. A *circle* is a closed plane curve on which every point is equidistant from a fixed point. A *jungle* is an area of land overgrown with masses of vegetation. A *cousin* is the son or daughter of an aunt or uncle. These concepts require verbal definitions if they are to be learned in an adequate form.

It may be noted that some of these examples, like *circle*, may have been learned previously as concrete concepts. This is not an unusual occurrence. However, the concrete form of a concept such as circle has some inadequacies when compared with its defined form. For instance, the child who has attained the concrete concept of circle might identify plane figures which are not quite circles—that is, the points on their curve might not all be equidistant from a fixed point. Of course, the concrete concept of circle may be perfectly useful in many situations over a period of years. Yet the defined concept is more adequate for even a greater variety of situations.

Some concepts can only be learned in a defined form.

Cousin is an example. One cannot identify instances of the class *cousin* on the basis of their appearance, by picking them out or pointing to them. It is necessary to apply a definition to show that one knows what a cousin is. Exact words do not have to be employed, of course, but the relation between son or daughter and aunt and uncle must be shown in a way that follows the definition. (It is interesting to note that in doing this, aunt and uncle have to be defined first). As one might expect, abstract concepts like *family*, *city*, *transportation*, and *justice* also have to be learned as defined concepts. They have no concrete counterparts, which can be identified by their appearance. These abstractions must be understood and communicated by means of the statement of a *classifying* rule, which is also called a *definition*.

Definition

Definitions are statements that express rules for classifying. An individual who has acquired a defined concept has learned this kind of a rule, and is able to apply it to any instance of the class. Notice that it is not essential that the individual learn the rule *statement* itself (that is, the definition) in order to show us that he has learned the concept. The definition merely represents the classifying rule he has learned.

In the simplest case, a definition represents one or more objects (which may be called *thing-concepts*) and a relation (or *relational concept*). Consider the definition of *saucer*: a dish (thing-concept) for holding (relational concept) a cup (thing-concept). While this is the basic form, most definitions are more complex. They are modified primarily by additional descriptions of the features of the thing-concepts they contain. The definition of *bottle*, for example, might begin with a container (thing-concept) for holding (relational concept) liquid (thing-concept). For increased adequacy, the definition must contain additional modifiers so that it becomes "a rigid container with a round narrow neck and no handle, made to hold liquid."

This analysis shows us that when *objects* are defined, their definitions have four essential parts:

1. A thing-concept which is the superordinate class (as "dish" is superordinate to "saucer," "container" to "bottle")

2. A set of characteristics or features of this superordinate concept ("rigid," "narrow-necked," etc.)
3. A relational concept which tells what the object does or is used for ("holding")
4. Another thing-concept which is the object of this verb ("cup," "liquid")

In some accounts of concepts, all of these parts are considered "relevant features" (for example, Klausmeier, 1971). There seems to be some usefulness, however, in the distinction between "features" (1 and 2) and "function" (3 and 4).

Definitions of concepts which are themselves *relations* have somewhat different components. Such definitions appear to require the use of a near-synonym, usually a simpler and more familiar relational concept, such as that expressed by a verb. Defining the relation homogenize, for example, begins with the familiar verb "break up." A liquid (such as milk) is homogenized by "breaking up" its particles into uniform size. The relational concept *swaddle* appears to require "wrap" in its definition, followed by the modifiers "completely or almost completely." Thus, the typical components of a definition for a relational concept are these:

1. A relational concept which is familiar to the learner, and a near-synonym ("break up," "wrap")
2. A thing-concept which is the object of this relational term ("liquid," or a concept as general as "thing")
3. Modifier words, such as adverbs or prepositional phrases, which function as the characteristic of the relation (and are thus comparable to the adjectives that represent the characteristics of thing-concepts). Examples are "into uniform size," and "completely or almost completely."

Defined concepts, whether they are things or relations, must apparently be represented by definitions composed of other concepts. These latter components are already familiar to the learner, that is, they have been previously learned. Unless the definitions are to be completely circular, this means that some concepts must originally be learned *without* definitions. As we have seen, *concrete concepts* are learned on the basis of encounters with class instances that can be directly sensed by the learner. If the concept of a *pentagon* must be learned from a definition containing the concepts "straight" and "side," the latter are likely to have been learned as concrete concepts at some earlier time. Or if *tabulate* is to be learned as a concept by definition, the familiar relational concept "list" presumably has been acquired previously, and quite possibly as a concrete concept.

Concepts as Classifying Rules

Defined concepts are rules for classifying. When learners have acquired such a concept, they are able to follow the definition in actually classifying some object or some relation. (Remember that this does not necessarily mean that they can state the definition). If learners have acquired the concept *hackney*, one expects that they will be able to follow the definition in showing that this means a trotting horse used chiefly for driving. In an ideal sense, learners will be able to identify instances of horses (perhaps in pictures) which are trotting and used for driving, as opposed to other animals that are not trotting and not used for driving. Of course, when the assumption can reasonably be made that they know the meaning of component concepts, learners may satisfactorily use words to identify the concepts "horse," "trotting," and "used for driving." It is important to note, however, that acceptance of these verbal statements as evidence that learners have acquired a defined concept *does* involve an assumption. In essence, the evidence that the concept has been learned derives from a *demonstration* that the definition can be used to classify instances.

Consider another example. Suppose that learners must acquire the concept *courtesy*, represented by the definition "well-mannered behavior indicating respect for others." One way to determine whether such a concept has been acquired would be to present learners with instances of behavior (either shown in pictures or described). Some of these behaviors would be well mannered, some not; some would indicate respect for others, while others would not. The conclusion that learners could *classify* these instances in accordance with the definition would be shown by their identifying instances which are "well-mannered" and which "show respect for others," and their rejection of instances which could not be so classified. Again, it would be possible to ask learners to use verbal responses, by asking them to "tell why" they had classified each instance. This would be a convenient method, but it obviously requires the assumption that learners know the meaning of the words they use. One might be more inclined to accept this assumption, and therefore the evidence that the concept has been learned, in a twelve-year-old student than in a six-year-old.

LEARNING DEFINED CONCEPTS

Defined concepts are usually learned by means of their definitions. In contrast to concrete concepts, defined concepts cannot be readily acquired simply by the presentation of a variety of instances and noninstances whose characteristics can be directly perceived by the learner. Instead, the component concepts of the definition are typically communicated to the learner. Thus, the verbal statement that represents the defined concept (that is, the definition) may be communicated to the learner. This means that the learner is reminded by these verbal cues, of the *thing-concepts* and the *relational concepts* which comprise the new concept to be learned, and is able immediately to "grasp" the meaning of the new concept.

By this means, it is fairly easy for a suitably prepared learner to acquire a new concept. Suppose one communicated the concept *caliche* (a concept unknown to many Americans, used in a speech by President Lyndon Johnson) by means of the statement "a crust of calcium carbonate which forms on the top of soil in arid regions." Obviously, this verbal communication is an adequate means by which an adult learner can acquire this new concept. The statement of the definition provides memorial cues for previously learned concepts such as "crust," "calcium carbonate," and "forms."

At the same time, it is apparent that the learner *cannot* acquire the concept by means of these verbal cues if he does not know the referential meaning of the component concepts. If he does not know the concept "calcium carbonate," the *caliche* concept will not be learned in adequate form. If he does not know the concept "arid," the new concept cannot be adequately formed. And, of course, if he does not know the relational concepts "form," and "on top of," the newly defined concept will not be learned.

External and Internal Conditions for Defined Concept Learning

The typical conditions for learning a defined concept can be seen as comprising both internal and external events.

CONDITIONS WITHIN THE LEARNER.   The learners must have access in their working memory to the component concepts represented in the definition of the to-be-learned concept. These are (1) the "thing-concepts" (nouns), which are the subject and object of the verb, and (2) the "relational concept," which is represented by the verb. As noted previously, the latter relation may be either "has the characteristics of" or "functions to" or both. These component concepts are simply the basic requirements. Of course, as definitional concepts become more complex, the meaning of modifier words such as adjectives and adverbs must also be known.

One other internal condition needs to be noted, and is often assumed. Learners who are to respond adequately to a verbal statement must have previously acquired the intellectual skill (rule) of representing the *syntax* of such a statement to themselves. That is to say, they must be able to distinguish the subject (the "actor") from the verb (the "relation") and both from the object. This very fundamental language skill is usually learned during the early years.

CONDITIONS IN THE LEARNING SITUATION. Externally, the conditions for learning a defined concept usually consist in the presentation of the definition in oral or printed form. The learner is confronted with a statement such as "A roof is the outside cover of a building." Such a proposition calls upon the learner's syntax skills of language understanding to maintain the proper order of the component concepts. The words themselves are *cues* to make these component concepts re-accessible in one's working memory. Thus one is able to acquire a concept that has not been previously learned. We know the concept has been acquired when the learner can demonstrate what a roof is, perhaps by drawing a building and indicating the part called "roof."

RULES

A defined concept is a particular kind of rule, a rule that classifies. Thus a rule must be an internal state which governs one's behavior, and enables one to demonstrate a relationship. A rule must be more than the verbal statement by which it is represented, for instance, the proposition "Things equal to the same things are equal to each other." It must be something that accounts for regularity of behavior in the face of virtually infinite variations in specific stimulation. *A rule, then, is an inferred capability that enables the individual to respond to a class of stimulus situations with a class of performances,* such performances being predictably related to the stimuli by a specific class of relations.

An illustration follows: an individual responds to a class of stimulus situations (2+3, 3+4, 7+5) with a class of performances (adding 3+2, 4+3, 5+7) that are predictably related to the stimuli by a relation that may be expressed as "independence of order."

The rule that governs this behavior may be represented by the statement "Adding the class of numbers *a* to the class of numbers *b* is independent of the order in which *a* and *b* are combined." We as external observers may *represent* the rule by this verbal statement. In fact, we *must* represent it in some way if we are going to talk about it. However, we do not know how the individual being observed would represent the rule, and at this point we are not concerned with that question. We can observe that a rule is being *applied* when the individual responds regularly to a large class of specific situations.

Consider another illustration: pronouncing English words with long "a" or short "a." Children learn to pronounce printed words like "mate," "dame," "sane," with a long "a" and words like "mat," "ram," and "fan" with a short "a." If their behavior is rule-governed, this may be demonstrated by asking them to pronounce a word new to them, such as "concentrate," or even a novel pseudoword such as "jate" or "raf." When the children respond to these situations correctly, one may say that they are exhibiting a class of performances (pronouncing the medial letter *a*) to a class of stimuli (various *a* and *ae* combinations of printed letters), which are related to each other by a class of relations (long when e follows, short when e does not follow the intervening consonant).

Typically, a rule is composed of several concepts. In the example just given, there is the concept "long 'a,'" the concept "e at end of syllable," and the relational concept "follows." An individual possesses the rule as a capability can be observed to identify these component concepts and also to demonstrate that they relate to one another in the particular manner of the rule. In accordance with the theoretical position taken here, the individual must have learned these component concepts as prerequisites to learning the rule. Assuming that these concepts have been acquired, learning a rule becomes a matter of learning their correct *sequence*—it is the e that follows the a, not the other way around.

Rules are obviously of many types, insofar as their content is concerned. They may be defined concepts, serving the purpose of distinguishing among different ideas; and they may be capabilities which enable the individual to respond to specific situations by applying classes of relations. In language learning, the individual acquires rules for pronouncing, for spelling, for punctuating, for constructing ordered sentences. In mathematics, all number operations require the learning of rules. In science, the individual learns many rules in the form of defined concepts, such as those for force, mass, density, and energy, and many others that relate these concepts, such as $F = ma$. Evidently, rules may vary in such properties as abstractness and complexity, although the dimensions of these characteristics have not been specified.

Rules and Verbalizations

One of the essential distinctions that must be made is between a rule as *an inferred capability* and the representation of a rule as *a verbal statement* (or a *verbal proposition*). The process of communicating rules, or describing them as learned capabilities, requires that one use words and other symbols to represent the rules. But the term "rule" should not mean the same thing as its representation as a verbal proposition.

When a student is able to state the proposition that represents the rule, one does not usually assume that he has, in fact, learned the rule. For example, a student may be able to state the verbal proposition "A millimeter is four hundredths of an inch," but his statement of this rule is unlikely to be taken as convincing evidence that he "knows the rule." To determine whether the rule, rather than merely its verbal statement, has been learned, one must find out whether the student can (1) identify the component concepts, namely, *inch* and *four hundredths*, and (2) show the relation between these concepts that constitutes a millimeter. There are various ways of doing this, but all of them appear to reduce to the act of *demonstrating* what a millimeter is. The student might be shown a scale of inches divided into hundredths and asked, "If each of these major divisions is an inch, show me how to determine how many millimeters an inch contains." The expected performance would be for the student to identify the "four hundredths," and by counting, obtain the number twenty-five.

While "knowing the verbal statement" does not necessarily mean "understanding the rule," it is important to recognize that verbal statements usually are crucial in the process of *learning* a new rule. Once a child has learned to use language, the process of learning is vastly facilitated by the use of verbal statements as *cues* to the learning of new defined concepts and rules. Adult learning, in many spheres, is largely carried on by the use of verbal statements read in textbooks or other written materials. A student reading for the first time that "a gene is an element of the germ plasm that transmits hereditary characteristics" is able to learn a great deal from this verbal statement, particularly if its component concepts (*germ plasm, transmits,* and so on) have been previously learned.

Thus, the communicative function of such verbal statements and their role in learning need to be affirmed without question, even though the student's recall of them as verbalizations is inadequate evidence that the rule has been learned.

RULE LEARNING

It will be most useful to begin our description of rule learning with examples of some very simple rules that might be learned by a child, and later show how such rules can grow in complexity.

Examples of Rule Learning

A young child may be told "Round things roll." Such a statement represents two different concepts: (1) *round things* and (2) *roll*. Under what circumstances might it be expected that learning has occurred from such a statement? What are the conditions under which one can be pretty certain that the child has learned the rule that round things roll?

It seems fairly evident that if learning the rule is expected, the child must already know the concepts *round things* and *roll*. If the concept *round* has not already been acquired, the child may end up learning a more restricted rule, such as *Balls roll*, and therefore be unable to show that a half-dollar or a saucer will roll. Accordingly, if the rule is to be acquired in its fullest sense, the learner must know the concept *round* in its full sense, as it applies to a variety of objects, including discs and cylinders as well as spheres such as balls.

Similarly, the concept of the event *roll* should have been previously acquired. Naturally, rolling must be distinguished from such events as *sliding* and *tumbling*. The concept of *rolling* may be considerably more difficult to learn than *round*, since the stimulus events of rotating about an axis may not be easy to discriminate from other events involving the motion of bodies. But again, the child must have acquired the concept *roll* to adequately face the task of learning the rule and not just a partial rule.

With these prerequisites, the remainder of the learning situation is provided by a representative set of stimulus objects and by a set of verbal instructions to which the learner responds. The stimulus objects might include an inclined plane and a set of unfamiliar blocks, some of which are round and some not. The instructions might go like this: "I want you to answer the question, What kinds of things roll? . . . You remember what 'roll' means *(demonstrate with one round object)*. . . . Some of these objects are *round*. Can you point them out? . . . *(Learner responds)*. . . . Do all *round* things roll? *(Learner answers 'Yes')*. . . . Show me. . . . *(Learner responds by rolling two or three round objects)*. . . . Good! . . . What kinds of things roll? *(Learner responds, 'Round things roll')*. . . . Right!" With the completion of this exercise, it is reasonable to conclude that the rule has been learned. However, to test this, a new and different set of blocks may be presented to the student, who is asked to answer the question, Which of these will roll?

To many adults, this instruction may seem elaborate and detailed, but it surely will not have this appearance to a kindergarten teacher. Why does one not simply say to the children, "Round things roll; remember that"? There are two major reasons. First, the children may not recall the concepts *round* and *roll* at the time they are presented in the sentence. Special pains must be taken to be sure that these concepts are highly accessible at the moment the rule is stated. The second reason is to insure that the children do not simply learn the words "Round things roll" as a verbal chain. This, of course, is very easy for them to do, since the statement is a short chain and they already know the links. But the purpose of the instruction in this case is not the learning of a verbal sequence; rather, it is the learning of a *rule*. Consequently, the children must be asked to exhibit terminal responses possibly only if they can, in fact, put together the concepts *round* and *roll*. Knowing the rule means being able to demonstrate that round things roll, not simply to say the words.

Adults often have to learn principles that are structurally more complex than this. A student of biology, for example, may encounter the rule (which might be equally well termed a defined concept): *Metamorphosis occurs when the larva of an insect turns into a pupa.* It seems quite evident that in this case, too, in order to learn the principle, the adult must not only have learned the relatively well-known concepts *insect* and *turn into* but also the less familiar concepts *larva* and *pupa*. One may suppose that the adult who has the intention to do so can learn the new rule entirely from the verbal statement. To do this properly, the learner might think of an actual example or two of insect larvae turning into pupae, that is, exhibiting metamorphosis. It may be noted, though, that this new rule is more likely to be learned adequately if the adult has seen metamorphosis in the laboratory or museum, on a field trip, or in a picture. For one cannot be sure that an adult who is confronted with the verbal proposition, "Metamorphosis occurs when the larva of an insect turns into a pupa" will, in fact, learn it as a rule, although this may be the assignment. Just as the child can learn this statement as a verbal proposition, so too can the adult.

For adults, then, the external conditions of learning rules are often reduced to verbal statements in textbooks or lectures. Provided that the component concepts have been previously learned, verbal instruction *can* be sufficient, although it may not be. The test, of course, is to provide an instance that requires students to *demonstrate*. The test must probe for the rule, not simply for the sequence. A test that says "Metamorphosis occurs when the _____ of an insect turns into a _____" (or something equivalent) is commonly employed. Notice, though, that such a test makes the assumption that learners are able to identify the concepts involved. In contrast, a test that presents pictures of an insect in various stages of development, including the larva and pupa, and requires students to "show what is meant by metamorphosis" (or something equivalent) will be able to determine whether the rule has been learned.

As these examples indicate, rules having the simplest formal structure are composed of two concepts. Often these can be thought of as having the form, "If A, then B" (Gagné, 1964). Although the two-concept rule may be simplest, it is probably not as typical or frequent as the three-concept rule, which is the form of many defined concepts as well. An example is the rule, *A pint doubled is a quart*. This statement verbally represents the three concepts *pint, quart,* and *doubled*. It is interesting to note another typical characteristic, namely, that two of these are thing-concepts while one is a relational concept. Berlyne (1965, p. 114) refers to such three-concept rules as transformational chains, and distinguishes their components as situational thoughts and transformational thoughts.

Rules can become much longer than those illustrated so far. The simple rule *birds fly* can be expanded to *birds fly south in the winter,* which contains four concepts rather than two. Classifying rules (defined concepts) can sometimes become quite lengthy, as in the following examples: (1) *Forgetting is a decrease in performance from the level exhibited immediately following the learning which has produced that performance, occurring after a time interval during which no practice has occurred.* (2) *Mass is that property of an object which determines how much acceleration will be imparted to the object by the action of a given force.* Usually such rules are stated verbally at the end of a sequence of instruction rather than at the beginning. To learn them typically requires breaking them up into simpler parts, which are finally put together as a total rule.

Conditions of Rule Learning

The conditions of rule learning that derive from these examples may now be drawn together.

CONDITIONS WITHIN THE LEARNER.   The prerequisite for acquiring the chains of concepts that constitute rules is knowing the concepts. *A pint doubled is a quart* is easily learned as a rule when the learner has already learned *all three* concepts involved. There is, of course, a "partial" learning of a rule that may result when the individual knows only some of the component concepts. Should a learner know all the concepts except *doubled,* some kind of rule could still be learned, but it would be an inadequate one.

As previously emphasized, knowing the concepts means being able to identify any members of the class. It is only when such prerequisite concepts have been mastered that a rule can be learned with full adequacy. Otherwise, there is the danger that the conceptual chain or some of its parts will be learned merely as items of verbal information, without the full meaning that inheres in a well-established rule. Unfortunately, inadequate rules *can* be learned. It is a challenge for instruction to avoid these, and it is a challenge for measurement techniques to distinguish them from adequate ones.

CONDITIONS IN THE LEARNING SITUATION.   The major external conditions of rule learning are embodied in *verbal instructions.* The sample instructions used with "Round things roll" will be useful to recall here.

1. The conditions of rule learning often begin with a statement of the general nature of the *performance expected when learning is complete.* In the example, the instructor says, "I want you to answer the question, What kinds of things roll?" Why does he say this? Isn't he simply stating the rule, giving it away, so to speak? The main reason for making such a statement, which learners "hold in mind" during learning, appears to be this: it provides learners with a means for obtaining immediate reinforcement when they have reached the terminal act. Having this statement for a model, they will be able to know when they have *finished learning* and, in many cases, when they have acquired the correct rule. Since rules may be long chains, learners may need a conveniently retained reference to tell when the end is reached. The instructor, though, cannot be said to be "telling the rule." He is not stating the rule itself, but only the kind of performance that will demonstrate the attainment of the rule.

2. Verbal instructions continue by *invoking recall of the component concepts*. The instructor says, "You remember what 'roll' means. . . . You remember what 'round' means." In many cases, the recall of these concepts is stimulated entirely by verbal means. In others (as in the example previously given), the class of stimuli that represent the concept may also be shown; students may be asked to recall the *roll* event by identifying one and the *round* thing by picking out one. Pictures, of course, may be used for this purpose as well.

3. Verbal cues are next given for the rule as a whole. In our simple example, the verbal statement "Round things roll" accomplishes this purpose. However, it should be noted that these verbal cues to the rule need not be an exact statement of the entire rule; they are so in this example only because the rule is such a short one. If the rule were from elementary geometry, for example, "An angle is formed by the intersection of two rays," the verbal cues might be contained in such statements as "Here are two rays. They intersect. We have an angle." Such statements do not correspond exactly to an acceptable verbal definition. Yet they function as well or better in providing verbal cues to stimulate the learning of the rule.

4. Finally, a verbal question asks the students to demonstrate the rule. The instructor says, "Show me." The exact form is not of great importance as long as it truly requires the students to demonstrate the rule in its full sense. Students may also be required to state the rule verbally, as when the instructor asks, "What kinds of things roll?" But such a verbal statement is not essential to the learning of the rule, nor does it prove the students have learned the rule. Then why is it done? Probably for a very practical reason: the instructor wants the students to be able to talk about the rule later on, and so he teaches them the right words to say. This ability is undoubtedly useful, but it is important to note that this kind of information learning is an unessential part of rule learning.

5. The presence of some familiar learning conditions may be recognized in rule learning. *Reinforcement* is provided when the rule is demonstrated in its complete form. The instructor may say "Right!" Even prior to this, the students may receive reinforcement by noting the match between their terminal act and what they have been told is their learning objective. If it means the repeated application of the rule to examples immediately following learning *repetition* has not been shown to be an important condition for this kind of learning (Gagné and Bassler, 1963). However, when repetition takes the form of *spaced review* (Reynolds and Glaser, 1964), it is likely to have a marked effect in enhancing retention.

EVENTS OF INSTRUCTION.   The conditions for learning rules that are in the situation, then, are incorporated into a sequence of instructional events. Perhaps it will be worthwhile here to recapitulate that sequence (see Gagné, 1963), since it may be considered to represent the steps for instruction of rules, whether practiced by a teacher, a film, or textbook:

Step 1: Inform the learner about the form of the performance to be expected when learning is completed.

Step 2: Question the learner in a way that requires the reinstatement (recall) of the previously learned concepts that make up the rule.

Step 3: Use verbal statements as cues that will lead the learner to put the (new) rule together with its concepts in their proper order.

Step 4: By means of a question, ask the learner to demonstrate one or more concrete instances of the rule, and provide feedback as to correctness in each case.

Step 5: (optional, but useful for later instruction): By a suitable question, require the learner to make a verbal statement to the rule.

Step 6: Provide for "spaced review" a day or more following learning, to aid retention of the newly learned rule. Present new instances for recall and demonstration of the rule.

LEARNING HIERARCHIES

Although it is useful to discuss the learning of a single rule, most rules are not learned in isolation, except perhaps by the young child. Instead, the school student or the adult typically learns related sets of rules pertaining to a larger topic. What is learned is an *organized set of intellectual skills.* The individual rules that compose such a set may have demonstrable relations to each other in a logical sense. They are also related to each other in the *psychological* sense that the learning of some are prerequisite to the learning of others, just as concepts are prerequisite to the learning of rules. Here our interest centers on the psychological organization of intellectual skills, and not on the logical organization of verbal information which may be involved in their learning.

The psychological organization of intellectual skills may be represented as a *learning hierarchy,* often composed largely of rules. As previously shown, two or more concepts may be prerequisite to (and in this sense subordinate to) the learning of a single rule. Similarly, two or more rules may be prerequisite to the learning of a superordinate rule. Once the latter is learned, it may combine with another rule, and so on. The entire set of rules, organized in this way, forms a learning hierarchy that describes an *on-the-average* efficient route to the attainment of an organized set of intellectual skills which represents "understanding" of a topic.

An Example of a Learning Hierarchy

Many subjects taught in schools have an organization that can readily be expressed as a learning hierarchy. The rule, or set of rules, that is the learning objective may be shown to be composed of *prerequisite* rules and concepts. The learning of the intellectual skills which are the "target" of instruction is a matter of *combining* these prerequisite skills, which have been previously learned. (They may have been *just previously* learned or recalled from learning that took place a while ago).

An example of such a learning hierarchy, applicable to a topic in physics, is shown in Figure 6.1. The intellectual skill of demonstrating the calculation of horizontal and vertical components of forces using vector diagrams, is seen to depend on the prerequisite learning of several subordinate rules. In order to acquire the target skill the student must previously have learned to (1) use rules to verify the conditions for equilibrium, (2) represent the magnitude and directions of forces as parts of triangles, and (3) employ trigonometric rules to represent the relationships in a right triangle (sine, cosine, tangent, etc.). If these three sets of subordinate rules have been learned and can be made accessible in the learner's working memory, the learning of the target skill (shown at the top of the hierarchy) can proceed without a hitch. If these subordinate rules are not known, however, the learning of the target skill is not possible. Of course, this "strong" statement is not intended to exclude the possibility that the three subordinate rules and the target skill may be learned "all at once" or on a single occasion by the learner. The important point is that the component skills (rules) are indeed prerequisites, and must be available to the learner when the target skill is "put together."

Each of the subordinate rules may be analyzed to reveal other subordinate rules or concepts which are prerequisites to its learning. For example, as Figure 6.1 shows, the skill of representing magnitudes and directions of forces as parts of triangles requires that the learner know the prerequisite concepts that identify the parts (angles, sides) of triangles, and that the learner also know how to identify the magnitudes and directions of forces (as these may be

VECTOR RESOLUTION OF FORCES

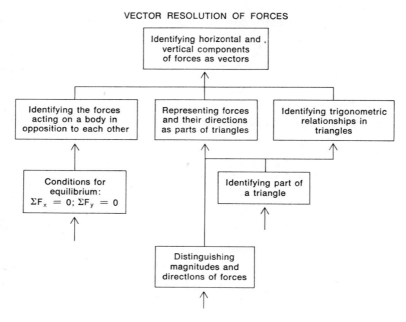

FIGURE 6.1   A learning hierarchy showing the analysis of a rule to be learned (top box) into prerequisite components, which are subordinate rules and concepts.

represented verbally or pictorially). Still other "lower-order" skills, such as the identification of right triangles, the distinguishing of vertical and horizontal directions, are not shown in Figure 6.1, but could surely be identified as underlying those that are illustrated.

   Many other topics learned in school have the character of organized sets of intellectual skills, and may be represented as learning hierarchies. The rules of syntax and punctuation in English obviously can be depicted in learning hierarchy form. All sciences, as well as mathematics, are composed of sets of rules that build upon each other. In the social sciences, the total structure is often a looser one, but individual topics—classifying family relationships, comparing and contrasting systems of government, formulating predictions of social trends—can be viewed as examples of intellectual skills having a hierarchical character. A variety of learning hierarchies can be used to represent the learning of a foreign language: beginning with the elementary concepts of word-sounds and proceeding through the complex rules governing the generation of communicative speech. Some additional examples of learning hierarchies are given by Gagné and Briggs (1974).

Cumulative Learning

Since learning hierarchies indicate some requirements for *prior learning*, when any new intellectual skill is to be learned, they imply certain conclusions about *readiness* for learning. Developmental readiness for learning any new intellectual skill is conceived as the presence of certain relevant subordinate intellectual skills. The individual who is to engage in problem solving to acquire a new higher-order rule must have first acquired some other simpler rules. These in turn depend for their acquisition on the recall of other learned entities, rules, or perhaps concepts. As we have seen in previous chapters, concepts in their turn depend for their learning on the recall of other prerequisites, the discriminations which are specifically related to them. The learning history of the individual is *cumulative* in character. The discriminations that are learned form a basis on which concepts are built. Concepts contribute positive transfer to the learning of rules; and the latter support the learning of more complex rules and the capabilities of problem solving.

Learning has the specific effect of establishing the capabilities necessary for the performance of any intellectual task. It also has cumulative effects. When a particular rule is learned, for example, the individual establishes a capability that can transfer to the learning not only of a single more complex rule but also to several others. As a specific instance, learning rules regarding the factoring of numbers up to one hundred may be shown to contribute to the learning of the higher-order rules involved in adding fractions. The factoring rules are also prerequisite to other mathematical tasks, such as completing ratios and simplifying equations. When learning of the latter tasks is undertaken, these subordinate rules of number factors do not have to be learned all over again. They are already available in the learner's memory. Learning is cumulative, then, because particular intellectual skills are transferable to a number of higher-order skills and to a variety of problems to be solved. As individuals develop, they continually increase their store of intellectual skills. This means that the possibilities of transfer to the learning of higher-order capabilities multiply as each new intellectual skill is learned. These cumulative effects of learning are the basis for observed increases of intellectual "power" in developing human beings.

An Example of Cumulative Learning

The effects of cumulative learning may be illustrated in a task of liquid conservation, similar to that used by Piaget (Piaget and

Inhelder, 1964) and by other investigators interested in studying aspects of his theory. The task to be performed is illustrated in Figure 6.2. When the liquid in a container shaped like A is poured into a container B (top row), many children below age seven are inclined to say that the taller container has more liquid. In another variant of the task, children at this age level tend to say that the volume in the shallower container (second row), exhibiting a larger surface area, is "more." Thus a few children at age seven are "conservers" in this task, while most are "nonconservers." To Piaget, these differences in performance reflect a critical point in intellectual development, marking the difference between a "pre-operational" phase of thought and a "concrete operational" phase. The logical operation particularly relevant to such a task is considered to be the *multiplying of relations* (recognizing that an increase in height may be compensated by a decrease in width). Such operations are dependent on others that appear at an earlier stage of development, particularly reversibility (carrying out an inverse operation).

From the standpoint of a cumulative learning theory, performance of this conservation task may be accomplished when the individual has acquired the specific intellectual skills that are relevant to it. The set of intellectual skills required may be derived in

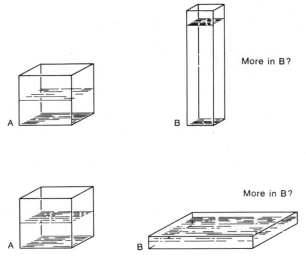

FIGURE 6.2   Two tasks of "conservation of liquid" in rectangular containers. (From R. M. Gagné, Contributions of learning to human development. *Psychological Review*, 1968, *75*, Figure 2, p. 183. Copyright 1968 by the American Psychological Association and reproduced by permission.)

the manner described in the previous section, to yield a learning hierarchy shown in Figure 6.3.

It may be noted, first of all, that this particular hierarchy has been derived under the assumption that the children to be tested are uninstructed in mathematical concepts of volume, specifically in the relation volume equals height times width times length. Obiously, one *could* construct a learning hierarchy that proposed that children learn this exact mathematical relation in order to perform the final task. This possibility was not followed in the present instance in order that fewer assumptions about prior learning could be made.

According to Figure 6.3, reading from the top down, the child needs to have learned the rule that volume of liquid in rectangular containers is determined by length, width, and height. Volume will be changed if any of these is altered. Proceeding one step further in the analysis, we find three rules about compensatory changes in two dimensions when the third dimension remains constant. (The fact that Piaget considers compensatory multiplying of relations essential to this task is noteworthy.) If the width of a liquid remains the same in two different containers, the two can have the same volume if a change in height in one is compensated by a change in length in the other.

In order to learn these complex rules, Figure 6.3 says, a child must have learned three other rules relating to change in only one dimension at a time. For example, if height is increased while width and length remain constant, volume will increase. The learning of these rules is in turn supported by the prior learning of other rules. One is that volume of a container is produced by accumulating "slices" of the same shape and area. A second is that volume can be projected from area in any direction, up or down, to the front or back, to the right or left. Following these rules, one can identify considerably simpler rules, such as those comparing areas of rectangles by compensatory action of length and width, and the idea that length and width determine area. One who chooses to trace the hierarchy still further downward encounters the concepts of rectangle, length, width, and an even simpler one, the concept of length of a line.

In its right-hand branch, the hierarchy describes the intellectual skills dealing with liquids in containers. Included here are rules having to do with changes in shape of liquid in containers, and liquid volume as cumulative slices of area. This branch is necessary because at the level of higher-order rules, the child must distinguish the volume of the liquid from that of the container. It is notable

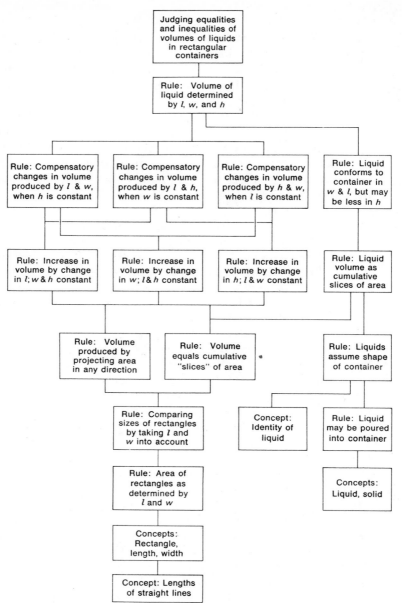

FIGURE 6.3   A learning hierarchy which shows the cumulative learning of intellectual skills leading to the task of judging equalities and inequalities of liquid volume in rectangular containers. (From R. M. Gagné, Contributions of learning to human development. *Psychological Review,* 1968, *75,* Figure 3, p. 184. Copyright 1968 by the American Psychological Association and reproduced by permission.)

that this branch also includes the concept of liquid "identity"—that is, matching a liquid poured from one container to another as "the same liquid." This concept of identity is generally considered to be arrived at very early in the intellectual development of the child.

The cumulative learning theory proposes a conception of "what is learned" (or "what develops") which differs from Piaget's theory. The latter states that performing conservation tasks depends on the development of logical processes such as "reversibility," "seriation," and "compensation." The proposal of the cumulative learning theory, in contrast, is that development results from the learning of relatively specific intellectual skills having to do with liquids, containers, volumes, areas, lengths, and heights. Specifically, it is supposed that the child does not acquire a general ability of "compensatory multiplying of relations" all at once, at some particular stage of development. Instead, the specific intellectual skill of "identifying equal volumes given compensatory changes in length and width, height remaining constant," is acquired through learning. In addition, and at approximately the same time, the child may acquire a number of other intellectual skills such as those shown in Figure 6.3. If the necessary specific capabilities are learned, perhaps by being taught in some systematic fashion, the child will be able to perform the conservation task.

Do the intellectual capabilities of the child remain this specific? Of course not. That well-known property of learning, *transfer of learning*, occurs. Suppose that a child has learned to judge equalities of liquids in rectangular containers. Suppose, further, that one then undertook to have her learn to judge volumes of liquids in cylindrical containers. Presumably, such learning could be based upon another learning hierarchy, which would have certain skills in common with that of Figure 6.3, but would also have some new ones dealing with areas of circles and volumes of cylinders. Having learned to judge volumes in *both* kinds of containers, a learner would then have some intellectual skills of great value for *generalizing* to still other problems. One might, for example, have her try the entirely new problem of judging volumes of liquids in irregularly shaped containers. Since she would already know how to equate volumes in rectangular and in cylindrical containers, we would expect that these skills would transfer to the new problem, dealing with shapes that were partly and roughly rectangular and partly and roughly cylindrical. Transfer of previously learned skills to the entirely new problem seems highly predictable.

Once learners have acquired a repertoire of learned specific skills, their performance of conservation-type problems is likely to become progressively easier, because an increasing number of these subordinate skills will exhibit transfer of learning to any new conservation task devised. Thus the specific intellectual skills learners acquire provide the basis for the formation of skills of increasing generalizability, of the sort described in the next chapter as *cognitive strategies*. At some stage in their development, one might then choose to speak of children as "conservers," or to say that they possess the learned capabilities which make possible the solution of novel conservation problems, regardless of their specific composition.

The conception of cumulative learning, then, is that any type of intellectual skill, although learned as a relatively specific entity, will generalize through the mechanism of learning transfer to the learning of many other skills and to the solving of many previously unencountered problems. Readiness for new learning is thus a stage of development, to be sure. But the readiness stage of development for any learner depends first upon what relevant prerequisite skills have already been learned, and, second, upon what capabilities have yet to be acquired in order to meet the learner's particular objective. Stated simply, the stage of developmental readiness of any learner is determined by what he already knows and by how much he has yet to learn in order to achieve some particular learning goal.

SOME EDUCATIONAL IMPLICATIONS

The learning of *rules* is obviously of vast educational importance, if only because of the fact that rules make up the bulk of what is learned in the school. An important component of rules is the kind of learned entities typically referred to as *defined concepts*. While the distinction between rules and defined concepts needs to be maintained, we are concerned here to emphasize that these two entities, considered as human capabilities, are formally alike. In the case of the defined concept, the individual is using a rule in order to *identify* something that embodies a relation; in the case of another kind of rule, the individual may be concerned with demonstrating the relation itself. But in both cases one is dealing with a sequence of subordinate entities that in the simplest instance contain the components concrete concept → relation → concrete concept. An example is *A latch* (concrete concept) *closes* (relational concept) *a window* (concrete concept). The entire range of the category *rule*, then, includes defined concepts, rules that pertain to language (such as pronouncing ie as "ee"), rules that have the character of scientific principles (such as $F = ma$), and even very complex rules (such as those for the division of fractions). As will be seen in the next chapter, the category also encompasses a very important variety of rule applicable to the learner's own behavior, which is called a *cognitive strategy*.

The performance of which learners are capable when they learn a rule is called *rule-governed behavior*. Unlike simpler categories of performance, rule-governed behavior exhibits the learners' capability of responding to entire *classes* of stimuli with *classes* of responses. For example, drivers are able to respond to *any* red signal light by bringing to a stop by *any* means *any* vehicle they are driving. It would be an entirely inadequate description of such behavior to say that these individuals had learned the S→R connection $S_{red} \longrightarrow R_{stop}$. They may, of course, also have learned this connection, but their behavior goes far beyond what such a capability would make possible. Their behavior in making classes of response to classes of stimuli is regular and, therefore, is called rule-governed.

Another distinction of great relevance to education, emphasized in this chapter, is that between the *rule* (the inferred capability that makes possible the regular performance) and the *verbal representation* of the rule (often called a *proposition*). The individual may learn a rule without learning the proposition, although the human adult often learns both, because the proposition may be used as a cue to the learning of the rule. The learner may also be able to demonstrate the rule without being able to verbalize the proposition or to recall it as a verbal statement. Many examples of this latter state of affairs may be given. The individual who correctly doubles the consonants in words ending in *ing* probably can not recall the verbal statement of the rule, although she may originally have learned it as a verbal proposition. The rule continues to be present as a capability, but the verbal statement is gone from her memory.

However, the important role of verbal statements in the learning of new rules must be recognized. Much adult learning is accomplished by reading printed verbal statements in textbooks and other materials. Such verbal statements communicate the to-be-learned rule and often constitute the first step in its learning, particularly when the component concepts have previously been learned. Reading that "hydrogen is a univalent element" may make possible little learning (except that of a verbal chain) if the student has not previously learned the component concepts *univalent* and *element*. If these have been learned, however, such a statement becomes an effective communication for learning a new rule. When followed by an action that demonstrates the learner's application of the rule to one or more specific situations, the learning of a new rule can be inferred to have taken place.

Much school learning is a matter of learning rules, including rules that define. Typically, the learning of a topic or part of a course of study can be viewed as a *hierarchy* in which the most complex rules (representing "target" objectives) require the learning of simpler rules as prerequisites to efficient attainment. These simpler rules in turn imply the learning of still simpler ones, including defined concepts, which in their turn may rest upon previously learned concrete concepts. While such an analysis can theoretically be carried to the point of revealing underlying discriminations, chains, and even simpler associations, it is not often useful to do so, since students usually are assumed to have already acquired such intellectual skills, perhaps in the earliest grades. Accordingly, learning hierarchies most often represent an ordered set of rules and concepts which the student needs to learn in order to achieve an understanding of the topic to be acquired.

Learning hierarchies imply that learning has a *cumulative* character, in which the acquisition of specific rules establishes the possibility of transfer of learning to a number of more complex, "higher-order" rules. Because of this property of transfer, each newly learned intellectual skill increases the intellectual power of the individual in a manifold sense. The specific rules that are learned make possible the learning of other more complex rules that are increasingly general in their applicability. Human intellectual development may be conceived as resulting from the learning of many specific intellectual skills which enter into the learning of other more complex and more general intellectual skills. Cumulative learning ultimately results in the establishment of capabilities that make it possible for the individual to solve a great variety of novel problems.

GENERAL REFERENCES

LEARNING DEFINED CONCEPTS

Bourne, L. E., Jr. *Human conceptual behavior.* Boston: Allyn and Bacon, 1966.

Glaser, R. Concept learning and concept teaching. In R. M. Gagné and W. J. Gephart (Eds.), *Learning research and school subjects.* Itasca, Ill.: Peacock, 1968.

Johnson, D. M. *A Systematic introduction to the psychology of thinking.* New York: Harper & Row, 1972. Chaps. 2, 3.
Klausmeier, H. J., Ghatala, E. S., and Frayer, D. A. *Conceptual learning and development: A cognitive view.* New York: Academic Press, 1974.
Mowrer, O. H. *Learning theory and the symbolic precesses.* New York: Wiley, 1960. Chaps. 4, 5, 6, 7.

RULE LEARNING

Berlyne, D. E. *Structure and direction in thinking.* New York: Wiley, 1965.
Bruner, J. S., Goodnow, J. J., and Austin, G. A. *A study of thinking.* New York: Wiley, 1956.
Gagné, R. M., and Briggs, L. J. *Principles of instructional design.* New York: Holt, Rinehart and Winston, 1974. Chap. 6.
Johnson, D. M. (See above.) Chaps. 4, 7.

PROBLEM SOLVING: COGNITIVE STRATEGIES

One of the major reasons for learning rules is to use them in solving problems. The activity of problem solving is thus a natural extension of rule learning, in which the most important part of the process takes place *within the learner*. The solving of a problem may be guided by a greater or lesser amount of verbal communication as part of instruction. However, the components which appear to make problem solving possible are the rules that have previously been learned. Problem solving may be viewed as a process by which the learner discovers a combination of previously learned rules which can be applied to achieve a solution for a novel situation.

Problem solving is not simply a matter of applying previously learned rules, however. It is also a process that yields new learning.

The learners are placed in a problem situation, or find themselves in one. They recall previously acquired rules in the attempt to find a "solution." In carrying out such a thinking process, the learners may try a number of hypotheses and test their applicability. When they find a particular combination of rules that fit the situation, they have not only "solved the problem" but have also learned something new. One newly learned entity is a "higher-order rule," which enables individuals to solve other problems of a similar type. The other aspect of new learning may be ways of solving problems in general—in other words, *cognitive strategies* which can guide the learners' own thinking behavior.

The sequence of events involved in problem solving is often referred to in the writings of Dewey (1910). The initial event is the *presentation of the problem*, which may be done by a verbal statement or some other means. The learner then *defines the problem*, or distinguishes the essential features of the situation. As a third step, the learner *formulates hypotheses* which may be applicable to a solution. Finally, *verification* of the hypothesis or successive ones is attempted, until the learner finds one that achieves the solution. Relating these steps to our previous discussion, it may be noted that only the first step is an external event; the rest are internal. The hypotheses that are formed are new rules; the successful one will be learned when its application has been tested and confirmed (see Gagné, 1964). In addition, in carrying out the steps, the learner practices using some cognitive strategies that govern his own thinking behavior.

This chapter is concerned with a description of both the external and internal events in problem solving. The phrase "problem solving" is used throughout to refer to the finding of solutions to *novel problems*, and should be carefully distinguished from the routine substitution of numerical values in mathematical expressions of the same type—a kind of "drill." We will see that problem solving depends upon previously learned *rules*. It also depends upon a type of intellectual skill governing the individual's own thinking processes: a *cognitive strategy*. First we shall examine the application of rules in problem solving. Later we shall introduce the cognitive strategy and describe several examples of this type of human capability, including its usefulness in problem solving.

APPLYING RULES IN PROBLEM SOLVING

Situations that require problem solving are of great variety, yet they appear to have several formal characteristics in common. Someone may have the problem of parking her car in a spot that is close to work, but at the same time free of parking restrictions. A student may have the problem of figuring out why the moon has phases. A scientist may have a problem of accounting for a discrepancy in the predicted and measured velocity of a nuclear particle. A fiction writer may have a problem of conveying a representation of sloth-fulness in describing the actions of one character. All these situa-tions imply the existence of problems that are to be brought to some successful termination by thinking. All these problems are solved by the use of *rules*, simple or complex. Rules are the stuff of thinking.

One might be tempted to conclude, therefore, that problem solving is a set of events in which human beings *use rules to achieve some goal*. This is quite true; yet it is not the whole story. The results of using rules in problem solving are not confined to achieving a goal, satisfying as that may be to the thinker. When problem solu-tion is achieved, something is also *learned*, in the sense that the individual's capability is more or less permanently changed. What emerges from problem solving is a *higher-order rule*, which be-comes a part of the individual's repertory. The same class of situa-tion, when encountered again, may be responded to with great facility by means of recall, and is no longer looked on as a "prob-lem." Problem solving, then, must definitely be considered a form of learning.

Some Examples of Problem Solving

At some point in the study of modern algebra, students may be asked to demonstrate that the following statement, in which a and b are rational numbers, is true:

$$(a+b)21 = a \cdot 21 + b \cdot 21$$

If the students have acquired certain rules previously, they are able to do this in the following steps:

Step 1: $(a+b)21 = 21(a+b)$; by the commutative property of mul-tiplication
Step 2: $(a+b)21 = 21 \cdot a + 21 \cdot b$; by the distributive property
Step 3: $(a+b)21 = a \cdot 21 + b \cdot 21$; by the commutative property

Of course, it is possible to instruct the students to take these specific steps, thus acquiring a rather lengthy verbal chain. But the intention here is to illustrate the instance in which they are not in-structed by display of the steps (either in a text or on a chalkboard).

Rather, they are simply given the *problem:* "Show that this statement is true: $(a+b)21 = a \cdot 21 + b \cdot 21$." The learners' problem is one of selecting and using certain number rules which they have previously learned, in an order that will make it possible to arrive at a logically correct solution.

In considering this example of a set of events as problem solving, the reader should bear in mind that it is the *first encounter* of the students with this problem that is being discussed here. Once these operations have been performed, of course, they may be repeated many times with any numbers belonging to the class concerned. Most adults naturally carry out these operations very rapidly, and in fact would be inclined to accept the given statement as true by inspection. But young students who meet this problem for the first time have no such recalled experience to fall back upon. All they know is that numbers can be manipulated in accordance with certain rules. To young learners the situation is a brand new one, and they must *supply* the steps in thinking that will achieve a solution. The most notable things about the problem situation, from the standpoint of such children, are two. First, instructions inform the learners of what they want to achieve, namely, a statement in which the product of two numbers is equal to the sum of two products. Second, the children obviously have to be able to recall from previous learning some particular rules.

As a second example, let us turn to a problem of a fairly simple and concrete sort, used for the experimental study of problem solving. Here the students are presented with a set of square figures made from arrangements of wooden matches, examples of which are shown in Figure 7.1. In each case, the students are given the problem of transforming one pattern of matches into another in a stated number of moves. The object is for them to be able to make such transformations for a variety of match patterns they have never seen before, not simply to remember the particular patterns on which they have practiced. In the studies performed with such problems (Katona, 1940), the following results were obtained:

1. The least effective method of establishing the desired capability was showing the learner how to solve several problems by actually moving the matches until the learner could recall the correct moves.
2. Of considerably greater effectiveness was a method in which the learner was instructed in a *verbal proposition*. (Two different propositions were used, one called "arithmetic," which stated that the matches with double functions should be changed to

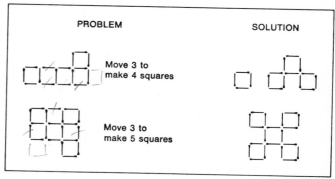

FIGURE 7.1   Two matchstick problems, with their solutions. (Katona, G. *Organizing and memorizing.* New York: Columbia University Press, 1940).

have single functions; the other called "structural," which instructed the learner to proceed by creating holes and loosening the figures. Both statements were about equally effective.)

3. Most effective for solving new problems was a method that proceeded a step at a time to illustrate the changes that would be brought about by using a rule, without stating the rule verbally. Several examples were used to demonstrate the operation of the rule by shading drawings of the squares so as to create "holes" in the original figure. This was called "learning by help," and could equally well be termed "guided discovery." In other words, the performance of the learners subsequent to the presentation of these examples led to the inference that they had *discovered* the rule required for problem solving.

These conclusions throw considerable light on the events of problem solving. As in the previous example, the learners were instructed about the terminal achievement to be expected, the goal of their activity. Again, these results make clear that a higher-order rule is acquired when the problem is solved; and this rule may be immediately generalized to other new situations presenting problems of the same class. Presenting the *solutions* of problems to the learners was markedly ineffective for learning. Undoubtedly the reason is that such presentations did not require the acquisition of the higher-order rule; the solutions could be learned as simple chains. Using verbal cues to stimulate learning, by stating the higher-order rule verbally, brought about problem solving in some learners, but not in others. The most dependable method of instruction used illustrations to stimulate the learners to discover the rule for themselves.

A third example of problem solving is taken from a famous study by Maier (1930). The learner was first brought into a room about eighteen by twenty feet in size, containing only a worktable. Each learner was provided with a set of materials, including some poles, lengths of wire, pieces of chalk, and several clamps. The problem, as told to the learners, was to construct two pendulums so that each would make a chalk mark at a designated point on the floor when swung over it. As shown in Figure 7.2, the correct solution to the pendulum construction problem was achieved by clamping two poles together and wedging them vertically against another pole, which they pressed horizontally against the ceiling. From the horizontal pole was suspended two wires weighted at their lower ends by clamps which held the pieces of chalk at the proper height, so that they marked the floor when the pendulum was swung.

With some of the subjects in this experiment, Maier used an additional set of instructions that seem to have had the function of recalling certain previously learned rules (see Gagné, 1964). These included instruction on (1) how to make a plumb line by using a clamp, a pencil, and string; (2) how to make a long pole out of two short ones, using a clamp; and (3) how to hold an object up against a wall with two poles, by wedging them tightly. Another group of

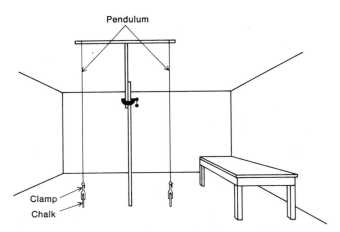

FIGURE 7.2   The solution to Maier's pendulum problem. (Maier, N. R. F. Reasoning in humans: I. On direction. *Journal of Comparative Psychology, 1930, 10,* 115–143).

subjects received an additional instruction to the effect that the problem would be simple if one "could just hang the pendulums from a nail in the ceiling." (Nails were not among the materials provided.)

The results of this study showed that the added instructions which fostered recall brought about solution in a greater proportion of learners than did the simpler instructions stating the problem. The final additional set, which Maier called *direction*, improved the probabilities of solution still more. The proportion of college students solving the pendulum problem under each of these three conditions were 0 out of 15 (with statement of problem), 1 out of 18 (with added instructions), and 4 out of 10 (with instructions plus direction).

It is evident that the verbal instructions used in this experimental situation fulfilled a number of different functions. Briefly stated, these were as follows:

1. They informed the learner about the nature of the expected performance. In other words, they defined the learner's goal—two pendulums that could make chalk marks on the floor.
2. They were deliberately used to bring about the recall of certain subordinate rules.
3. They were employed to "channel," or "guide," the learner's thinking. They did this by emphasizing what was *not* a good direction for thought (for example, the table was not to be used in the construction, and no nails were available) as well as what *was* a good direction (hanging pendulums from the ceiling).

Although the pendulum problem seems simple when one knows the solution, this appearance is deceptive, since none of the college students was able to solve this problem when only the "problem-stating" instructions were given. To increase the probability of solution, additional resources were needed. These came from within the learner in the form of recalled rules applicable to the problem. They also came from the external situation in the form of verbal cues employed to guide thinking in the proper "direction."

Conditions for Problem Solving

On the basis of these and other examples, it is possible now to make a summary of the conditions of problem solving, recapitulating a number of points.

CONDITIONS WITHIN THE LEARNER.   In order to solve a problem, the learner must be able to recall relevant rules that have been
previously learned. In the pendulum problem, rules of weighting a
length of wire, clamping a marking tool, wedging poles to hold an
object up, and clamping two poles to make a longer one must all
be recalled if the problem is to be solved. For matchstick problems,
some rules governing the construction of multiple patterns need to
be recalled either in "arithmetical" or "structural" terms. For the
mathematical problem, the principles of commutativity and dis-
tributivity must be known and recalled. Thus, so far as the individual
is concerned, a problem is never solved "in a vacuum." Problem
solution always depends upon the learner's previous experience,
specifically on the recall of previously learned rules.

The other important internal set of conditions is the activation and use of the cognitive strategies the learner possesses and
may previously have learned. These strategies are likely to show
themselves as individual differences in the rapidity and ease with
which problems are solved. For example, some individuals may use
strategies of *search* which are more efficient than those possessed
by other people, and thus be able to retrieve the necessary rules
more rapidly. Differences in the *differentiating of concepts* among
individuals may exist, making it possible for one person to distinguish relevant aspects of the stimulus situation and thus to "define
the problem" more readily than another. Also, there is the possibility that the *fluency of hypotheses* may distinguish one individual
from another on the basis of the facility with which rules are combined into hypotheses. Intellectual fluency factors have been emphasized by investigators of "creativity," including C. W. Taylor (1958),
Getzels and Jackson (1962), and Guilford (1967), among others.
Finally, there may be differences in strategies of *matching specific
instances to a general class*, an operation performed by the problem solver in verifying the solution. We shall return to a further discussion of cognitive strategies later in this chapter.

CONDITIONS IN THE LEARNING SITUATION.   The external conditions that support processes of problem solving often consist of
verbal instructions. One function of such instructions is to ask the
questions that stimulate recall of relevant rules. Thus, in the pendulum problem some learners were reminded that they knew the rule
for weighting a string to make a plumb line, and the rule of wedging
sticks together to hold up an object. These rules were readily accessible for recall when the learners entered the problem situation.

Verbal instructions that are externally provided may also be used to "guide" or "channel" thinking in certain directions. (Such guidance may, of course, be provided by the learner in self-instructions). Guidance may vary in amount or completeness, always stopping short of describing the solution. As a minimum, guidance of thinking informs the learner of the goal of the activity, the general form of the solution; this amount of guidance appears to be required if learning is to occur at all. Greater amounts have the effect of limiting the range of hypotheses entertained by the learner in achieving solution. For example, the emphasis given in Maier's "direction" instructions limited consideration to the ceiling as a locus for the hanging of a pendulum, while at the same time excluding hypotheses concerning the use of a nail as a device from which to suspend the pendulum.

Problem Solving and Discovery

As we have seen, one result of problem solving for the learner is the acquiring of a new and more complex rule which combines some simpler rules. The capability thus learned does not differ in a formal sense from the rules learned under conditions described in the previous chapter. What does differ is the *nature and amount of guidance* provided by verbal instructions, which are minimal in problem-solving situations. In rule learning, the instructions include a sentence or question that verbally cues the solution, but in problem solving they do not. For example, one group of learners of matchstick problems was told to "remove the matches that serve a double function," while another group was not given this instruction. The first group may be said to have engaged in rule learning, the second in problem solving. A higher percentage of the second group was successful in achieving the higher-order rule (Katona, 1940, pp. 88, 95); and retention of the rule was also superior in this group.

Problem solving as a method of learning requires that the learners *discover* the higher-order rule without specific help. Presumably, they thus construct the new rule in their own idiosyncratic manners and may or may not be able to verbalize it once constructed. A study by Worthen (1968) compared an instructional method emphasizing discovery with one emphasizing expository presentation in sixteen classes of students in the fifth and sixth grades, who were studying mathematical concepts over a six-week period. This investigation found the expository method resulted in superior recall of rules learned when measured immediately following the learning period. The presentation of problems by means of a discovery method, however, led to greater transfer of the rules acquired. Since the latter is the more important practical outcome, it appears that the encouragement of discovery, under conditions in which problem solving is appropriate to the instructional objectives, can be of great value as a teaching technique. Worthen's study is of considerable significance in view of the uncertainty of interpretation of many studies of "discovery learning" (see Shulman and Keislar, 1966) whose findings are based upon relatively brief topics.

The evidence of experimental studies concerning the use of discovery in problem solving certainly does not demonstrate that higher-order rules *must* be learned by discovery (see Ausubel, 1968, pp. 471–473). In much adult learning, for example, the guidance provided by verbal instructions is so complete that the rule to be learned is stated verbally during the course of learning. The key to achievement of a higher-order rules does not lie solely in the discovery method. Nevertheless, the evidence strongly suggests that achieving a higher-order rule by means of problem solving produces a highly effective capability that is well retained over considerable periods of time. For example, a study by J. T. Guthrie (1967) of problem solving in cryptograms showed a marked advantage of the discovery method of instruction for transfer to a task involving new rules. This finding suggests that exploratory strategies relevant to such new learning may have been engendered by the discovery method.

The discovery method is liable to gross misinterpretation in practical learning situations. Some writers and practitioners have treated problem solving as though it could be achieved with a *minimum* of instructions and prerequisite knowledge of rules. This is obviously an incorrect point of view, as the evidence shows. College students who tried to solve matchstick problems without prerequisite knowledge of rules and without guidance were markedly unsuccessful. Similarly, students who were told only the goal of problem solving for the pendulum problem, without being reminded of subordinate rules and without "direction," were unable to solve the problem. Problem solving, or discovery, is only the final step in a sequence of learning that extends back through the many prerequisite learnings that must have preceded it. To be successful, problem solving must be based on the prior attainment and recall of the rules that are combined in the achievement of the solution, the higher-order rule. Of course, a problem may be set up that is "beyond" the individual learner in the sense that none of the subordinate rules have been acquired. Thus the learner must learn these rules in order to achieve a solution. Under such circumstances a problem may happen to be solved on certain occasions and in particular individuals; but to advocate such an approach as a practical learning method makes no sense.

To summarize, discovery or problem solving involves the combining of previously learned rules into a new higher-order rule, which "solves" the problem and generalizes to an entire class of stimulus situations embodying other problems of the same type. Problem solving occurs when the instructions provided the learner do not include a verbally stated "solution," but require the construction of such a solution "on one's own." When this happens, the individually constructed higher-order rule is effective in generalizing to many situations and is, at the same time, highly resistant to forgetting. But the capability acquired by this means does not appear to differ in a fundamental sense from that acquired when instructions include the statement of a "solution" (unless, of course, the latter is learned simply as a verbal chain). What is learned in either case is a higher-order rule, which is based upon some previously learned simpler rules.

Problem Solving and Creativity

No one can fail to stand in awed admiration of the great intellectual discoveries of history—Newton's laws of motion, Kepler's principles of planetary movement, Einstein's general theory of relativity. Equally awe-inspiring are artistic creations in painting, sculpture, music, and literature, which have also been generated by individual discovery. What do these remarkable achievements of genius have to do with problem solving as described here?

A great scientific discovery or a great work of art is surely the result of problem-solving activity. The solution to a problem, we are told, often comes to thinkers in a "flash of insight," although they may have been turning the problem over in their minds for some time. As problem-solving behavior, these creative acts are based on a tremendous amount of previously acquired knowledge, whether this be of the "public" sort known to science, or of the "private" sort known to the artist. Many creative thinkers testify that they have previously immersed themselves deeply in the subject matter of the problem, often over considerable periods. Indeed, it would be strange if they had not done this. Nothing in such testimony supports the idea that there is anything very different about the problem solving that leads to discoveries of great social import. The act of discovery, even in the relatively predictable sense that it occurs in everyday learning, involves a "sudden insight" which transforms the problem situation into a solution situation. As we have seen, everyday discovery also requires that the learner have previous knowledge of the rules involved in the solution.

But the major discovery, in contrast to the common garden variety, involves a feat of generalizing far beyond what may be expected in the usual learning situation. There is an "inductive leap," a combining of ideas from widely separated knowledge systems, a bold use of analogy that transcends what is usually meant by generalizing within a class of problem situations. An excellent example of such inventiveness is provided by the kinetic theory of gases. What was known, on the one hand, was a set of principles concerning the behavior of gases; the relations among the variables of temperature, pressure, and volume. On the other hand, there were the laws of motion; the effects of force in imparting acceleration to objects of specified mass. The stroke of genius in this case was the hypothesis that the gas was composed of particles (molecules) that had mass and whose reactions to force could, therefore, be considered to obey the laws of motion. From this single new synthesizing idea—this remarkable higher-order rule—the consequences follow that permitted the confirmation of the theory. But the central idea was arrived at by putting together subordinate rules from two widely disparate systems of organized knowledge. A problem of this magnitude had to be solved by combining two sets of rules that originally seemed to have only the remotest connection with each other.

What has learning to do with creative discovery? The most obvious and dependable answer is that discoveries of great social importance have been made by people with a great store of intellectual skills. These persons have acquired many kinds of hierarchies of rules. They have been deeply immersed in the rules of the discipline within which they work and, often, in the rules of other disciplines. How did they learn these rules? Just as everyone else does —by combining sets of subordinate rules—partly, perhaps, with the aid of verbal instruction and partly by making the "small" discoveries involved in the acquiring of the higher-order rules of any particular topic or system of intellectual skills.

Some scholars feel that this relation between learning and Discovery with a capital D is quite incomplete. Kestin (1970), for example, describes learning which involves discovery as a process of "bisociation," following Koestler (1964). In discovering solutions to problems, according to this conception, the learner's thoughts jump from one domain of rules to a second quite different domain, forming a link ("bisociation") between the two that leads to a new understanding. The instructional implication of this view is that in fostering creativity the teacher must create favorable grounds on which bisociations can flourish. Bruner (1966) appears to hold a similar view, in his emphasis on varied and challenging problems as basic elements of a curriculum. Because this method is rich in reinforcement value, the solving of problems by students may well contribute to their love of learning, and "thirst for knowledge." However, it is by no means certain that this kind of learning will predispose the learner to become a "creative" thinker, capable of making a great contribution to science or art. As a method for acquiring the necessary skills and strategies, "practicing discovery" is not necessarily the antecedent variable involved in the production of genius (see Ausubel, 1968, pp. 473–497).

COGNITIVE STRATEGIES

The varieties of intellectual skills we have described in Chapters 5 and 6 constitute some of the most valuable capabilities that individuals learn. They provide the basic structures for the learning that takes place in the school. They are brought to bear on the solving of problems, as we have seen. Yet as learners proceed to learn and store intellectual skills and other capabilities, they are also developing ways to improve their self-regulation of the internal processes associated with learning. In other words, they are learning *how* to learn, *how* to remember, *how* to carry out the reflective and analytic thought that leads to more learning. It is apparent as individuals continue to learn that they become increasingly capable of *self-instruction*, or even of what may be called *independent learning*. Presumably, this is because learners acquire increasingly effective skills to regulate their own internal processes. This new function of control over internal cognitive processes is what distinguishes the capabilities to be discussed in this chapter from the intellectual skills described in the last two chapters.

As our description of the information-processing view of learning has indicated (Chapter 3), the processes of learning are modified and regulated by some internal processes of *executive control*. These internally directed skills are called *cognitive strategies*. They are skills with which learners regulate or modulate their internal processes of (1) attending and selective perceiving; (2) coding for long-term storage; (3) retrieval; and (4) problem solving.

Cognitive strategies are often assigned a high priority as learning outcomes by writers on educational topics. For example, Bruner (1971) acknowledges the basic importance of intellectual skills in school learning, but distinguishes these skills in solving problems from *problem finding*, which requires the location of "incompleteness, anomaly, trouble, inequity, and contradiction" (p. 111). Presumably, both the identification of novel problems and the translation of known rules into a form that can readily be put to use in solving such problems represent the kinds of human capability that deserve to be classified as cognitive strategies. They are ways that individuals use to focus their knowledge and skills on problem situations that may not previously have been encountered. Cognitive strategies are ways of "using one's head."

Cognitive Strategies in Attending

The use of executive control skills in attending to and selectively perceiving particular parts of printed texts has been explored in experimental studies by Rothkopf (1970), Frase (1970), and others.

The general procedure used in these studies is illustrated by one carried out by Rothkopf and Bisbicos (1967). High school students read a passage from a book by Rachel Carson, *The Sea Around Us*, consisting of thirty-six pages. After each three pages, two questions were interspersed with the text. One group of students saw questions which required a numerical quantity or a proper name as an answer. Another group saw questions inquiring about either a common English word or a technical term. After completion of the passage, the retention of information was tested in each of these categories for all students. Retention of numerical quantities and proper names was enhanced in the students who had answered questions during their reading on numerical quantities and proper names (different questions, of course, but in the same categories). Similar results were obtained for the students who had answered questions on English words or technical terms.

This series of experiments suggests that interspersed questions had the effect of *activating a strategy of attending* to facts of a particular category. These investigations appear to demonstrate that learners are able to exercise control over their own attention in learning from a text, by utilizing a cognitive strategy that is available to them and that may previously have been learned. Thus learners are employing an executive control process to direct their own attention and to selectively perceive portions of what they read.

Cognitive Strategies in Encoding

In the learning of word-pairs (COW-BALL, ROCK-BOTTLE) many studies have demonstrated improved learning when the learners are given "elaboration" instructions (for a comprehensive review, see Rohwer, 1975). Often, the elaboration takes the form of sentences which the learner is encouraged to construct by himself and "to himself." Examples might be "The COW chases the bouncing BALL," or "The ROCK breaks the BOTTLE." Substantially improved learning has been shown to result in children and in adults from the use of these "explicit prompts," when the amount of learning is compared with that obtained under simple "memorization" instructions.

Another explicit prompt may be employed when learners are instructed to imagine a mental picture formed by the word-pairs or to use a visual image (Bower and Winzenz, 1970; Paivio and Yuille, 1969). In this case too, studies have revealed enhanced learning in children of various ages and in adults (cf. Rohwer, 1975). In a number of instances, the prompts that learners devise and use themselves have been shown to be more effective than those deliberately given to them as learning and memory aids. Thus these tasks of word association appear to be readily learned when the learners are encouraged to use particular cognitive strategies—sentence-forming strategies or image-forming strategies. Of course, a learner who has practiced using such strategies may be able to easily excel over a naive learner who has not used them, and who may not even be aware of them.

Presumably, such cognitive strategies represent *ways of encoding* word-pairs to be learned. Encoding strategies employed in the learning of concrete concepts have also been studied in the laboratory (Bruner, Goodnow, and Austin, 1956). In this group of studies, learners were asked to identify a classifying concept in sets of cards, each containing drawn figures that could be categorized in various ways—on the basis of shape of figure, color of figure, number of figures, and number of borders. The concept sought, for example, might be the class of cards containing *two yellow rectangles*. Learners were required to arrive at the correct concept by viewing the cards one by one, and stating (initially guessing) whether each did or did not represent the concept. After each identification, the learners were told whether their guess was "right" or "wrong."

Two main strategies were employed by the learners in acquiring the correct concept. In one, the entire set of features on the card first identified as a positive instance was used as the basis for a hypothesis. For example, if the first "correct" card showed three yellow rectangles, this would be the learners' hypothesis. They would then compare subsequent cards with their memory of this initial one, looking for features in common with it and ignoring others. This strategy was called "focusing." Other learners adopted a strategy called "scanning." Using this method, they would choose one feature of a card (such as color) as belonging to the concept being sought. They would then have to change their hypotheses to select a different feature, whenever they encountered a negative instance. At the same time, they would have to remember other features of cards that had been called positive instances, in order to form a new hypothesis. This study found that when learners were put under time pressure, the focusing strategy was more frequently successful than the scanning strategy.

Other kinds of strategies were also adopted by a certain number of learners in this investigation. Some of these strategies were "conservative" in the sense that a wrong choice did not require starting all over again with a new hypothesis. Others were "risky" in the sense that they jumped to a hypothesis before the evidence was complete. The study confirms the idea that various strategies are used in discovering concepts and that particular kinds of strategies tend to be favored by particular people. It also makes clear that concept learning under these conditions may be undertaken with more than one kind of cognitive strategy.

Strategies of Retrieval

Strategies that enable people to retrieve names, dates, and unconnected events from their memories have been known for a long time (Yates, 1966) and are often called *mnemonic systems*. Mental images of "places," such as the parts of a familiar room, have been used by orators as cues to the successive points of their speeches. This practice is described by Cicero. Other "systems" require the association of names or events with certain previously learned coding systems, such as the letters of the alphabet, numerals, or the signs of the Zodiac. Rhyming words and novel images are often prominent features providing cues for the retrieval of masses of information (cf. Paivio, 1971).

Cognitive strategies of this sort appear to be useful for the memorizing and retrieval of special kinds of information, particularly information that is not otherwise related by its meaning or by the meanings it shares with other knowledge. Of course, these strategies make possible the demonstration of amazing feats of memory by professional mnemonists. The average person has little need to remember such disconnected information under most circumstances, unless simply to impress friends. What remains of "mnemonic systems" as techniques of perhaps broader usefulness for retrieval are *visual images*, and *rhyming sounds* (which may possibly be viewed as auditory images).

Cognitive strategies of retrieval have been compared in children and young adults by Salatas and Flavell (1975). The learners were required to learn a list containing words belonging to certain categories (for example, toys, clothes, tools). Upon learning the total list, each learner was asked under three different conditions to recall the words contained in it. In one condition, recall was asked for without mention of the category names (spontaneous use). In another, learners were explicitly asked to use the categories (explicit instructions). And in a third condition, they were asked to recall a word from one category, then a word from another, and so on (flexible use). Young children did not use the categories as retrieval cues spontaneously, although a substantial proportion did use them when asked to do so. Many college students did not use the categories spontaneously, but all did so when explicit instructions were given. Flexible control of the strategies was evident for half the kindergarten children, most third-graders, and all of the college students who participated in the study. The strategy of categorizing thus seems to be available to many learners for retrieval of word lists, and perhaps might be learned as a strategy even by very young children.

It is of some importance to discover what cognitive strategies are available to young children, and how these strategies develop with increasing age (presumably by means of learning). Several retrieval strategies have been studied in elementary school children, including rehearsal (Belmont and Butterfield, 1971) and deliberate restudy of missed items (Masur, McIntyre, and Flavell, 1973).

One more example of remembering strategies in children will be briefly described. A memory task requiring a delayed response to objects (toys) placed under inverted cups was employed to study such strategies in three-year-old children (Wellman, Ritter, and Flavell, 1976). Each child was told a story involving one of the toys, which was then placed under one of four cups arranged in a semicircle on a table. Some children were told to "remember" where the toy was, some simply to "wait." After a delay of forty seconds each child was asked to locate the toy in question. Most children were able to do so with little hesitation. Interest in the study centered on the question of what kinds of strategies the children used for deliberate remembering during the delay period. These were inferred from the children's behavior in deliberately looking at and deliberately touching the "correct" cup. Children who were told to "remember" engaged in these activities more often and for longer durations than did children told to "wait." Evidently many of these young children possess the strategies of visual rehearsal and of tagging (by touching) the cup to be remembered. When faced with the task of remembering, they are capable of using the retrieval strategies available to them.

Cognitive Strategies in Problem Solving

When students practice solving novel problems, they presumably learn not only rules applicable to those problems, but also general ways of accomplishing problem solving. That is to say, they learn ways of exercising control over their own thought processes: how to seek relevant features of the problem, how to keep in mind what has been tried previously, how to weigh the probabilities of their hypotheses, and so on. These capabilities of self-control are the *cognitive strategies* of thinking.

Research investigators who study the learning of cognitive strategies applicable to human problem solving are faced with two major difficulties. The first is *identifying* exactly what these strategies are. Although it is easy enough to understand what they do in exerting control over internal thought processes, it is not at all clear at the present that these strategies can be named appropriately or that the investigator can control the problem situation sufficiently to know which strategies are being engaged by the learner. Are there a great many cognitive strategies of problem solving or only a few? What specific processes of thought do these strategies control or influence? The problem of identifying cognitive strategies differs markedly from that of identifying the intellectual skills described in previous chapters: the concepts and rules applicable to solving problems in specific areas like language and mathematics are quite definite and readily identifiable.

The second difficulty experienced in the investigation of cognitive strategies is demonstrating their *generalizability* or *transfer*. If a cognitive strategy has been learned in the course of problem solving (rather than only a higher-order rule), one must expect transfer of learning to a variety of other problem-solving situations to be exhibited. It is not sufficient to demonstrate that learning has brought about improvement in solving problems of the same type.

For example, if students have learned and practiced a cognitive strategy tentatively identified as "holding several hypotheses in mind at once" in problems dealing with geometric proofs, it is not sufficient to show that the learners can use this strategy with some new geometric proofs. If a cognitive strategy has been learned or improved by practice, it must then be shown to be capable of transfer to an entirely different domain of problems, such as solving anagrams or finding the roots of simultaneous equations. It is often not an easy matter to arrange conditions so that this transfer can be demonstrated.

Varieties of Strategies of Thinking

Suggestions concerning the identity and nature of cognitive strategies of thinking have come from a variety of sources. They occur in studies designed specifically to study the process of thinking such as those by Bruner, Goodnow, and Austin (1956); in theories of problem solving like those of Newell and Simon (1972) and Wickelgren (1974); in the theory of cognitive development of Piaget (Piaget and Inhelder, 1964); in the studies of human abilities previously mentioned (Guilford, 1967; C. W. Taylor, 1958); and in many other writings which attempt to analyze human thinking.

The development of thinking skills and cognitive strategies has been studied by Crutchfield, Covington, and their associates with the use of a systematic instructional program called *The Productive Thinking Program* (Covington, Crutchfield, Davies, and Olton, 1973; Olton and Crutchfield, 1969; Olton, Wardrop, Covington, Goodwin, Crutchfield, Klausmeier, and Ronda, 1967). This program consists of sixteen cartoon booklets containing lessons centered on "mystery" problems, presented in story form, which students attempt to solve. As students work individually on a lesson, each is called upon to generate ideas, to look for and evaluate the meaning of discrepancies, to ask questions, and to practice other strategies of thought. The strategies identified and practiced in these series include the following: (1) generating new and unusual ideas (divergent thinking), (2) avoiding premature judgments, (3) breaking mental sets to look at a problem differently, (4) clarifying the essentials of a problem, and (5) attending to relevant facts and conditions of the problem. In addition, these investigators consider that evidence obtained in the use of this program implies the existence of a "master thinking skill" that governs the management of other skills and strategies. Such a "master" strategy, for example, would be used by the learner to determine, at a particular point in problem solving, whether the best course would be to develop new hypotheses or, in contrast, to examine critically those already developed.

In connection with his analysis of a variety of verbal, mathematical, and other problems, Wickelgren's theory (1974) of problem solving includes procedures which fall into the category of general strategies of problem solving. This sophisticated analysis emphasizes first the strategy of drawing inferences, by which is meant making transformations of the goal of the problem or of the "givens." Additional strategies are (1) classifying action sequences, as opposed to randomly choosing them; (2) defining an "evaluation function" over all states involved in problem solution, and choosing actions at any given state with an evaluation closer to the goal (called "hill climbing"); (3) breaking up a problem into parts, thus making it possible to solve a set of simpler problems; (4) identifying contradictions which prove that the goal cannot be obtained from the given; and (5) working backwards from the goals to new statements which imply the goal statement. The applicability of these strategies to chess problems, to algebraic and geometric problems, and to such "brain twisters" as Nim and the Tower of Hanoi are explicated in detail by Wickelgren. It is evident that the learning of such strategies and their practice in connection with such problems (often characterized as "puzzles") would provide the learner with powerful tools for their successful solutions. Presumably, these strategies would also have more general applicability to the solution of problems occurring in everyday life, even though the latter usually have structures that are formally simpler.

Transferring Cognitive Strategies

Perhaps the most important question about cognitive strategies is not whether they can be learned as specific ways of approaching problems, but whether as human capabilities they can be shown to generalize to new problem-solving situations. Can the learner, by practice in solving problems or in particular strategies of thinking, become a better problem solver? Can the efficiency and quality of the learner's thought be improved by instruction systematically designed to bring about such a goal? Can strategies be learned which will make someone a better thinker about every kind of problem— personal problems, social problems, environmental problems, political problems, as well as mathematical and logico-verbal problems?

No one disagrees with the educational goal of making people better thinkers. If there is disagreement, it concerns the feasibility of this goal. At one end of this spectrum are those who tend to believe that basic capacities for original thinking are inborn, although they must be influenced by environmental events which provide the motivation and the occasion for productive thought. At the other extreme are those who think that it should be easy to teach students how to think and, over a period of time, to turn them into excellent problem solvers. Those who hold the latter view tend to look at school learning as being simply perverse. Why is education not *concentrated* on teaching students to think, as a matter of highest priority? Such a view can be simplistic, however. Students must have a firmament of basic skills and of knowledge which makes up the content of their thinking: one cannot think "in a vacuum." Once this premise is admitted, it becomes apparent that much time and effort of school instruction must be expended in giving students the foundations on which their thinking can be based. Thus the time spent on teaching knowledge and intellectual skills does not necessarily imply that problem-solving strategies are being neglected.

CHILDREN'S LEARNING AND TRANSFER.   An experimental study by Wittrock (1967) exemplifies the conditions necessary to demonstrate that learned cognitive strategies are *generalizable*, that is, capable of transfer to new and unfamiliar tasks. Second-grade children were individually set the task of matching pictures shown in slides on the basis of common concepts. Matching was sometimes to be based upon color concepts (blue, green, yellow, and red); sometimes on shape concepts (cat, circle, diamond, and house); sometimes on size (large or small); and in other instances on number (one, two, three, or four). The children learned to match cards containing these concepts with those shown in slides, by hanging the cards on four hooks in front of them. Two different strategies were taught to two groups of children. In the "nonreplacement strategy," the children removed cards which were incorrect matches from the hooks and turned them face down (this effectively eliminated them as incorrect matches on subsequent trials). In the "replacement strategy," children were not instructed to turn the incorrect cards face down, and many used these cards again for matching.

The results of this study showed clearly that the nonreplacement strategy to superior performance not only on the concepts used in learning but also on the matching of entirely new concepts. These latter tasks of new learning were presented to the same children without any "strategy" instructions. Thus evidence was clearly obtained that strategies of concept learning acquired in one situation could be transferred and used to advantage in another situation involving entirely new concept learning.

Another example of the transfer of cognitive strategies is provided by a study using *The Productive Thinking Program* (Covington et al., 1973) with fifth-grade children in schools in Racine, Wisconsin (Olton et al., 1967). These children learned various strategies of thinking by working through the sixteen lessons in this program, each of which presents a "mystery" in a cartoon text. The learning of various strategies and their transfer to successively presented new mystery problems was shown by tests of performance which included (1) number of ideas, (2) quality of ideas, (3) number of puzzling facts noted, (4) number of inventions suggested, and (5) number of available elements used in solution. Performance scores indicated significant gains in these aspects of productive thinking, and these gains transferred from one problem situation to another. Some tendency was shown for performance in problem solving to increase progressively as the children gained more experience with the mystery tasks. This suggests that the children's cognitive strategies were progressively improving throughout the length of the program.

Some Challenging Questions

There is some evidence, then, that cognitive strategies applicable to thinking and problem solving can be learned, and that when learned they exhibit transfer to new problem situations. The latter effect, of course, is supposed to occur if cognitive strategies are real.

At the same time, it cannot be said that a great many studies provide firm evidence for cognitive strategies of thinking or for the large generalizing effects they are expected to exhibit. While it is easy to demonstrate that some people solve problems more easily than do others, it has apparently not been easy to show that deliberate attempts to teach cognitive strategies result in consistent and substantial learning and transfer of learning. Regardless of the nearly universal agreement on the educational goal of "teaching students to think," the evidence that this goal can be successfully accomplished when deliberately undertaken is actually quite meager at the present time.

One of the challenging questions to be faced by experimentation in this area is surely that of identifying the nature of cognitive strategies of problem solving. We have seen in previous sections that there are many hypotheses concerning what useful strategies of thinking may be, and that these hypotheses come from different lines of investigation—from studies of intellectual development, individual differences, productive thinking, and problem solving. Perhaps the most useful course of action would be to try the deliberate teaching of these strategies, one by one, in order to find each strategy that can be learned and that shows the evidences of transfer of learning—which would be a convincing test of the reality of the strategy as a learned internal state.

A second question, both puzzling and challenging, is, How long does it take to learn effective cognitive strategies? The kind of puzzle-solving techniques described by Wickelgren (1974), for example, appear to be learnable in a relatively short time. In the initial study of productive thinking by Covington and Crutchfield (1965), children seemed to acquire new strategies after only a small amount of instruction. Yet the fifth-graders in Wisconsin learned the same or similar strategies only gradually and incompletely during sixteen hours of instruction. Many adults have been convinced by their own experiences that strategies of thinking are seldom acquired quickly, but may require years of practice to reach the stage of refinement at which they are transferable to novel problem-solving situations. The question of how rapidly cognitive strategies can be learned, and how much generalizing experience is needed to make them broadly transferable, obviously relates to the matter of direct instruction. If such strategies can be directly taught in a short time, that would be a highly important fact to be taken into account in the design of school curricula. If, in contrast, learning of strategies takes years (because of the variety of learner experiences required), the implications for curriculum design would be quite different. In the latter case, the curriculum must provide for the learning of many other kinds of capabilities during the time that cognitive strategies are gradually being developed and refined.

SOME EDUCATIONAL IMPLICATIONS

Educational programs have the important ultimate purpose of teaching students to solve problems—mathematical and physical problems, health problems, social problems, and problems of personal adjustment. We have seen in this chapter that there are two primary sources of human capability which can contribute to problem solving. First, there are the intellectual skills, the concepts and rules, which form the fundamental structure of the individual's intellectual competence. Rules that have previously been learned are searched for in memory, retrieved and brought to bear upon novel problems.

Problem-solving activity results in the learning of new and more complex "higher-order" rules, which themselves are stored in memory for future application.

Much of the activity of problem solving is internally guided, and "learning by discovery" is typical of this form of human behavior. Accordingly, the teacher's task is mainly one of finding and organizing appropriate problem-solving situations. Problems for students are most effective when they are (1) novel, in the sense of presenting unfamiliar situations, and (2) within the students' capabilities (that is, their previously learned intellectual skills).

The second source of human capability that makes possible problem solving is the internally organized skills that modify the learner's own processes of learning and thinking. These are *cognitive strategies*. In modern information-processing theories of learning and memory, these are called *executive control processes*. They serve to select, modify, and control the processing that is carried out by the learner in attending, perceiving, encoding, retrieving, generalizing, and organizing responses—all of the phases involved in a learning act.

Beyond question it is a high-priority goal of educational programs to bring about improvement and refinement of all useful cognitive strategies. This is what is meant by the aims of making the student a better perceiver, a better learner, a better rememberer, a better generalizer of acquired knowledge, and a more productive and creative thinker. Generations of educators have recognized the value of these educational aims.

Enthusiasm for the goals of teaching students "how to learn" and "how to think" needs to be tempered by considerations of feasibility. How are these deeds to be done? We must be aware of a first note of caution, arising from the fact that as yet we know little, and that with small confidence, about cognitive strategies and how they are learned. We do not yet know how to identify them— much less how to observe or measure them dependably. In general, the best course of action appears to be to insure that students have plenty of opportunities to learn independently, and to be frequently challenged to solve novel problems.

A second caution will also be apparent to readers of this volume. It resides in the fact that there are many kinds of things to learn besides cognitive strategies. Information, intellectual skills, attitudes, and motor skills are all important to the individual, and many of them are essential to survival in our society. Furthermore, these other capabilities are also involved in the learning of new knowledge, new skills, and the solving of new problems. Human thinking cannot proceed without the presence of these capabilities—a person cannot be "brilliant" without a great store of knowledge and skills accessible in his or her working memory. Thus, it is not possible to concentrate education on the single aim of improving cognitive strategies, to the exclusion of other capabilities. Educational programs must possess a balanced emphasis on all kinds of learning outcomes.

These two cautions aside, the aim of producing better learners and better thinkers through educational efforts will remain. It appears at present that systematic research is beginning to throw some light on the nature of cognitive strategies and their operation. Beginning with relatively simple tasks such as learning words and identifying objects, investigators of childrens' learning have been able to show how strategies can be learned, and how they can be used to improve further learning. It seems likely that the "breakthrough" so fervently sought, if indeed it occurs at all, will come through the pursuit of carefully designed studies of human intellectual functioning.

GENERAL REFERENCES

COGNITIVE STRATEGIES
Bruner, J. S., Goodnow, J. J., and Austin, G. A. *A study of thinking*. New York: Wiley, 1956.
Bruner, J. S. *The relevance of education*. New York: Norton, 1971.
Inhelder, B., and Piaget, J. *The Growth of logical thinking from childhood to adolescence*. New York: Basic Books, 1958.
Rohwer, W. D., Jr. Elaboration and learning in childhood and adolescence. In H. W. Reese, Jr., *Advances in child development and behavior*. New York: Academic Press, 1975.

PROBLEM SOLVING
Berlyne, D. E. *Structure and direction in thinking*. New York: Wiley, 1965.
Gagné, R. M. Problem solving. In A. W. Melton (Ed.), *Categories of human learning*. New York: Academic Press, 1964.
Johnson, D. M. *A systematic introduction to the psychology of thinking*. New York: Harper & Row, 1972.
Katona, G. *Organizing and memorizing*. New York: Columbia University Press, 1940.
Newell, A., and Simon, H. A. *Human problem solving*. Englewood Cliffs, N.J.: Prentice-Hall, 1972.
Wertheimer, M. *Productive thinking*. New York: Harper & Row, 1945.
Wickelgren, W. A. *How to solve problems*. San Francisco: Freeman, 1974.

8

VERBAL INFORMATION LEARNING

One of the most familiar categories of learned capabilities is verbal information. From early childhood, we learn a great variety of things we call *names*, *facts*, or *ideas*. We learn large masses of such information throughout our lifetimes. Some is stored in our memories for only a short time, apparently, before it is forgotten. Other items of verbal information are retained for very long times, over the entire span of our lives. Some verbal information seems isolated and unconnected with any other set of facts, such as the name of a person we once met years ago on a trip to a foreign land. Most individual facts, however, appear to have many connections to a variety of other information, so that recalling a single fact leads readily to the recall of others which are associated with it in some way.

Verbal information in the sense used here refers to information that is *verbalizable*. As a human performance, the capability is one of being able to *tell* or *state* a fact or idea in the form of a proposition. We know that learners have acquired and stored an item of verbal information when they can tell us what it is; that is, when they can communicate it in a form which has a subject and a predicate. Thus, verbal information is not learned when learners can simply repeat words; this may be simply an indication that they have learned a verbal chain. Acquiring verbal information means being able to reinstate *propositions*. These may be as complex as the first sentence of the Declaration of Independence, "When in the course of human events . . . ," or as simple as naming an object a "table" in the understood sentence, "(That is a) table."

Although knowing verbal information means being able to state propositions, it is not always the case that information is stored as propositions. As we shall see, various kind of systems are proposed in contemporary theories for the storage of verbal information. After all, the main requirement for a system of storage is that the learner be readily able to gain access to the information so that he can state it in a form which communicates, as propositions do. The storage itself must represent the words and their relationships, and this function can be performed by an image, as well as by other kinds of cognitive structures.

Another essential characteristic of verbal information is that some of the words which compose it have *meaning*. In a fundamental sense, this means that certain words of the proposition must be known as *concepts*, in the sense that these are described in Chapters 5 and 6. We have already seen that a set of words, such as *mountain typewriter baseball,* is not information because the words, while meaningful, do not form a proposition. Consider next the set of pronounceable "words," *senjux glemrik femtol*. These also are not information, for the additional reason that the words themselves convey no meaning; they have not been learned as concepts. An interesting change occurs, however, when a new "word," seeming to have the function of a verb, is substituted, as in the sequence: *senjux glings femtol*. Reading this sequence, we have the impression that it would be meaningful, if only we knew what *glings* meant. Now if we make the substitution of an actual and familiar verb, we have: *senjux breaks femtol*. In this form, it seems reasonable to classify the sequence as a genuine example of verbal information— minimal verbal information perhaps, and surely not highly useful to the learner. It is, however, in propositional form, and contains at least one word (the verb) with a known conceptual meaning. Thus it shares a basic characteristic with a set of words forming a true sentence, such as *boys break windows.*

VARIETIES OF VERBAL INFORMATION

Meaningful information which is learned occurs in varying degrees of complexity, depending upon its propositional structure. It seems useful for purposes of exposition to distinguish information in the form of (1) *names* or *labels,* (2) single propositions or *facts,* and (3) collections of facts organized as *connected discourse.* In addition, the larger interconnected items of information the individual learns and stores are often referred to as *knowledge,* or *bodies of knowledge.* Many experimental studies have been performed to investigate the learning of single words or word-pairs as labels; and consequently many of the conditions affecting the learning of such labels can be identified and illustrated. Considerably fewer studies have been done on the learning and retention of single facts or of longer passages making up connected discourse. Much has still to be learned about how such collections of propositions are best acquired by the learner.

Learning Labels

Labels which are the names for objects or classes of objects are often learned as single events at the time that concept learning occurs. Thus young children may learn the label "dish" at the same time that they acquire the concept *dish.* As we have seen, knowing *dish* as a concept means being able to identify instances of the class. Although such performance is not dependent upon knowing word "dish," this label is usually employed (by the parent or other teacher) as the way of assessing the children's learning of the concept. Thus, in the natural situation, the learning of new labels does not seem a very difficult learning task. The word "dish" is used by the parent on many different and widely spaced occasions when an actual dish is visible; the children soon begin to say "dish" on similar occasions, and the word as a verbal response is reinforced.

Many studies of label learning have required learners to acquire several labels at once, rather than one at a time. Such a learning situation bears some resemblance to the task faced by the individual at a party of strangers who wishes to acquire the names of twenty new acquaintances at once. Obviously, this is a much more difficult task; and the difficulty increases with the number of new labels to be learned (see the discussion of verbal associates in Chapter 4).

In many instances of everyday life, and also in the school, people learn one or perhaps two labels at a time. Kindergarten children, for example, may learn the label "elephant" from seeing the animal in a zoo or in a picture. But rarely are children expected to learn all at the same time, the names of the ten or eleven animals they see. Thus a *contextual distinctiveness* usually prevails when we learn a single label for a newly seen object. However, sometimes children or adults *are* expected to learn ten or twelve labels all together. An example might be the learning of names of different leaves ("oak," "maple," "birch," etc.) in a science lesson for elementary pupils. When a number of labels have to be learned all at once, such learning is likely to be more difficult (or take more time) than would be expected by adding up the difficulties (or times) of single labels.

PAIRED-ASSOCIATE LEARNING.   When one learns to read a foreign language, it is not uncommon to acquire a large number of "translation responses," such as *donner-"give"* or *acheter-"buy."* The traditional prototype for such learning is the *paired associate*, sometimes used in nonsense form such as RIV-GEX. The exposure to the learner of the paired words (or syllables) over a number of practice trials results in acquisition of the performance of stating (or writing) the second member of the pair when only the first is shown. A great deal is known about paired-associate learning, and a great deal more remains to be studied (see Cofer, 1961; Dixon and Horton, 1968). In terms of conditions for acquiring verbal associates, these appear to be the most important findings:

1. Nonsense syllables do not perform the function that Ebbinghaus intended for them, that is, of being equivalently meaningless and unfamiliar. The learning of an association between two verbal elements, whether syllables or words, is markedly affected by previous discrimination learning of both the first member and the second (Goss, 1963).

2. Most investigators agree that the efficient learning of a two-element verbal association requires the use of an *intervening link*, having the function of *mediation* or coding. The increased ease of learning resulting from the deliberate use of well-chosen mediation links is striking (Jenkins, 1963). Such links are usually

implicit ones; that is, they occur inside the learner and do not appear as overt behavior. In the case of the association "give"-*donner,* an effective coding might be "give" → "donate," → *donner.* Many other mediating links are possible.

3. It is difficult to separate the phenomena of learning *single* associates from those of *multiple* associates. The typical paired-associate learning study, after all, uses ten or twelve pairs like RIV-GEX, not just one. Increasing the number of pairs makes each disproportionately harder to learn.

The reason usually given for this heightened difficulty of learning with increasing number of items is *interference.* The learning of label a for object A, b for object B, c for object C, and so on becomes difficult because the associations of labels with objects tend to be confused with each other, or to cancel each other out. Having learned A-a, the individual next attempts to learn B-b; but since B is not completely unlike A, one may tend to learn B-a, or to fail to recall A-a once the new label B-b is learned. When A-a interferes with the learning of B-b, it is called *proactive interference;* the opposite, when learning B-b interferes with the recall of A-a, is called *retroactive interference.* Both of these phenomena take place in the learning of sets of labels of any considerable number. Both have been studied extensively in the psychological laboratory, with the use of paired-associate syllables or words (Keppel, 1968; Postman, 1961).

An example of a study showing the effects of interference in the learning of names is one by E. J. Gibson (1941). Two different sets of drawn figures were constructed, each containing thirteen figures. In one set the figures were similar to each other, while in the other they were highly dissimilar. Six of the figures used in each set are illustrated in Figure 8.1. In both cases these stimuli were first presented to learners one by one, together with their labels (syllables). On subsequent trials, the stimulus was first presented, and after a brief delay during which the learner attempted to supply its "name," the combination of figure and label was again exposed. The labels for highly similar figures required an average of 19.8 repetitions, whereas the set with dissimilar forms were learned with only 8.9 repetitions.

STORING OF LABELS IN MEMORY. The occurrence of interference among labels learned close together in time is a factor that works against rapid learning—a factor to be overcome. What can be said, in contrast, about factors that aid the learning of information in the

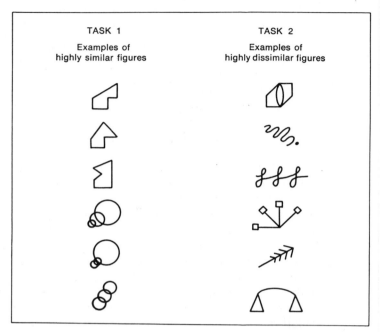

FIGURE 8.1 Examples of figures used in a study of learning verbal (non-sense) names for sets of figures which were highly similar (Task 1) and highly dissimilar (Task 2). (Based on E. J. Gibson, Retroactive inhibition as a function of degree of generalization between tasks. *Journal of Experimental Psychology,* 1941, *28,* 93–115.)

form of labels or names? The answer to this question takes us into the realm of "information-processing" theories of learning. In the terms employed by these theories, the learning of a label is a matter of transforming the memory of the word as it may exist in a temporary form (short-term storage) to the form it takes in long-term memory. This transformation process involves *coding* (or *encoding*). The temporary form of memory for the label is coded for long-term memory into another form, presumably a form that will make the label most readily accessible when the learner wants to recall it.

How does a label get encoded when learned for storage in long-term memory? There are various theories of the organization of such memories. Basically, a label is conceived as being stored as a word having certain distinctive stimulus features. More importantly, though, encoding a label means establishing many associations with other words that are related to it (Bower, 1975). These related associations may be of several types, including superordinate (dog-animal) and subordinate classes (dog-spaniel). Labels are also considered to be stored in relation with the concepts they represent, that is, to their *referents*, the intellectual skills which involve identifying or otherwise using concepts. And not to be overlooked is the possibility that a label may be encoded as an *image* (Paivio, 1971). All of these ways of encoding may be involved in storing the "meaning" of a label. Of course, as a single word, a label may enter into other more complex forms of organizations such as sentences. This will be discussed later.

The coding of names or labels often involves the use of an intervening word association, or *mediating link* (Jenkins, 1963). Thus when newly learned labels have mediating links already in the learner's memory, the process of coding may be both rapid and effective. For example, if the French name is being learned for the English word "give," the word "donate" may serve as a mediating link. As we have noted earlier, the coding would be "give" → "donate" → *donner*.

Other examples of coding links for certain French words are shown in Figure 8.2. Verbal links may be formed by choosing English words, already well known to the learner, that bear some similarity to the French word, and that have some previously learned association with the English associate. Often, a pictorial link of the

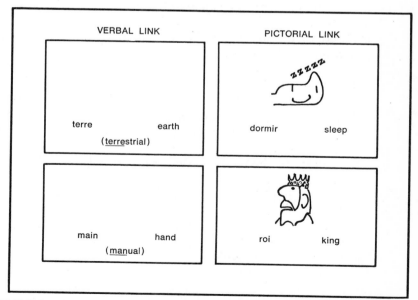

FIGURE 8.2   Some examples of verbal and pictorial links that can mediate English names for French words.

sort indicated in the second column of figure 8.2 works better for most people (see Paivio, 1971). Another method for learning, at least equally effective, is to require the learners to generate their own coding link—a word, an image, or anything they think of that will link the stimulus object with its label.

Another kind of coding of single words (labels) which has been extensively studied is called *clustering*. When asked to learn lists containing as many as sixty nouns, learners tend to recall them in "clusters" of common categories (Bousfield, 1953). The nouns in one list represented the categories of animals, names, professions, and vegetables. Although presented in random order, the items tended to cluster into these categories when recalled by the learner. Other studies (e.g., Watts and Anderson, 1969) have shown that nouns presented in organized categories are learned and stored much more rapidly than lists composed of equally familiar nouns not organized into categories. The process of coding, so far as single names are concerned, can be aided by clustering, or the placing of names into previously learned categories. Obviously, this kind of coding is definitely meaningful, or *semantic*.

Still another kind of meaningful coding of names and labels has been investigated with both children and adults. This coding is called *elaboration*, and is exemplified by placing the word to be remembered in a phrase or a sentence. Rohwer (1966) investigated the learning of word-pairs like COW-BALL, in which the word BALL is to be given as an associate ("label") when the word COW is exposed to the learner. Rohwer compared the following ways of presenting the key words:

No elaboration:	COW	BALL
Conjunction:	The running COW and the bouncing BALL	
Preposition:	The running COW behind the bouncing BALL	
Verb:	The running COW chases the bouncing BALL	

In recall, the word COW was presented and the learner asked to state the associated word BALL. When a phrase using a conjunction was employed, the amount of recall was not increased over the no-elaboration condition. Increased recall was found, however, when a preposition was used; and recall was greatest when a true sentence including a verb was presented. This initial study has been followed by a series which have repeatedly confirmed the substantial advantage for retention of the use of elaborations which include verbs to form whole sentences (see Rohwer, 1975).

From these studies of word coding, we can see that several

fairly definite things are known about the learning of labels. First, learning a single name for an object on a single occasion is quite an easy task, natural for the human memory. Thus, a person who encounters a new object for the first time, and is told its name, not only begins the process of acquiring the concrete concept of which the object is an instance, but also readily learns to associate the object with its name. When several names must be learned for several different objects all at once, the task becomes more difficult. Presumably, this is because confusions tend to occur, attributable to the process of *interference*. A number of ways of overcoming these interference effects may either be suggested to the learner or adopted as self-initiated strategies. Generally, these are ways of making each label increasingly *distinctive* and *meaningful* by associating it with other components of memory, and thus coding it so that it becomes more readily retrievable. Labels may be encoded by being associated with other words which are themselves meaningful, so that they form "mediating links." Coding may also take the form of imagery; the objects themselves, if they are highly distinctive, may aid this process. Labels may also be encoded in other meaningful ways, by clustering into previously acquired categories, or by being deliberately formed into sentences.

Learning Facts

A common form of verbal information that is acquired and stored by a human learner is a *fact*. We readily learn such facts as that a week contains seven days, chlorine is a poisonous gas, Calvin Coolidge declined to run for a second term as President, Caesar described Gaul as having three parts. There are, of course, many kinds of facts. Some are quite specific and concrete, as when we know that "the Statue of Liberty holds a torch in her hand." Others are abstract, as in the saying "Necessity is the mother of invention."

Obviously, facts are composed of words. They may not always be stored in memory as words, or at least this may not be the entire form they take in memory. Presumably, one can store many of the facts shown in a picture as visual images. Yet somehow the words must be stored also, because the means we have of knowing whether a fact has been acquired is for the person to *state* the fact; and this statement requires words. It is reasonable to suppose that memory of facts requires the storage of words, in some linguistic form. Information-processing theories of memory commonly make this assumption (Tulving and Donaldson, 1972).

However, a fact is more than a string of words. Sequences of words which form sentences are learned more rapidly and recalled with much greater facility than are word lists of the same size which are meaningfully unconnected (Briggs and Reed, 1943; English, Welborn, and Killian, 1934). For example, one does not expect a student who is learning facts from a history text to demonstrate this learning by making a verbatim reproduction of parts of the text. Instead, one might expect the learner to be able to reproduce in some ordered fashion the "ideas" contained in the text. The individual words may themselves be associated by means of the various linkings that apply to labels. But beyond this, there is reason to believe that factual information is learned and stored as *meaningful propositions*.

One prominent theory of the learning and retention of meaningful facts is that of Ausubel (1968). He proposes that meaningful new ideas are learned by being *subsumed* in an already existing *cognitive structure* (an interconnected network of knowledge), which in turn has been established by prior learning. For example, if the learner is to acquire a new set of ideas about the principles of Buddhism, these newly incorporated ideas become organized into an already existing structure. An example of such a structure might be the principles of Christianity, or something even more general such as the principles of comparative religion. In the latter case, one would speak of *derivative subsumption* (Buddhism being a specific example of a more general concept); in the former case, of *correlative subsumption* (Buddhism being in this case an extension or modification of previously learned propositions about Christianity).

In considering retention of newly acquired verbal knowledge, Ausubel theorizes that one must consider, first, the availability in pre-existing cognitive structure of specifically relevant *anchoring ideas*. A second factor that affects retention is the distinguishability or *dissociability* of the new ideas from pre-existing cognitive structures. For example, new propositions of Buddhism, not sufficiently distinguishable from those of Christianity, will tend to be lost in retention. Still a third factor influencing retention is the *stability* and *clarity* of anchoring ideas, which act to subsume newly learned verbal propositions.

Ausubel's theory implies that the conditions for learning meaningful verbal material are quite different from those previously described for verbal chains (see Chapter 4). According to this theory, learning will take place in an optimal fashion when several additional conditions are present. First, the learning of specific new propositions will be facilitated by the presentation of *organizers*, verbal propositions that indicate the relevance of the to-be-learned knowledge to the pre-existing cognitive structure. Second, learning will be aided by *progressive differentiation*, meaning that the most general and inclusive ideas are presented first, followed by increasing detail. (It may be noted that this practice is the opposite of that followed by many textbooks.) Third, another helpful condition is called *integrative reconciliation*, the deliberate and explicit pointing out of similarities and differences between the newly presented ideas and those previously learned. Finally, there is *consolidation*, which means insistence on the learner's mastery of currently presented material before new material is introduced. It can readily be seen that these conditions for learning follow from the basic notion that meaningful verbal learning is a matter of subsumption of new propositions into an organized structure that has previously been learned.

ORGANIZATIONAL FACTORS.   The learning and remembering of factual information is often aided by an organization which is different from the facts themselves. Three kinds of organization described by Bower (1972) are (1) *generative rules*, (2) *pegword systems*, and (3) *hierarchical retrieval plans*.

A rule may be used to generate access to facts. For example, the series of numbers 1 4 9 1 6 2 5 3 6 4 9 6 4 8 1 may readily be retrieved by recalling the simple rule that the numbers are the squares of successive whole numbers. Suppose students are asked to remember the following set of geometric figures:

The learners would likely be aided by knowing and using a rule which described the entire set as composed of combinations of three attributes: circle-square, large-small, shaded-unshaded. By generating the whole set according to the rule, learners are able to retrieve the particular facts (descriptions of the four geometric shapes) that they are asked to learn.

Pegword systems have been used for a great many years. A commonly used device for orators at the time of Cicero (described in *De Oratore*) was to associate the succeeding ideas of a speech with various locations within the auditorium in which the speech was to be delivered. Unconnected facts or lists of names can readily be retrieved by using as "pegs" the locations of buildings on a familiar street (Crovitz, 1970) or the items in a familiar room in one's house. Other mnemonic systems use arbitrary lists of words, previously memorized, such as "One is a bun, two is a shoe, three is a tree, four is a door." The words in such a list are meaningfully associated with the facts to be recalled; or sometimes images are formed which incorporate the concepts of the pegword and the fact to be remembered.

A hierarchical scheme for retrieval organizes facts to be learned and remembered in terms of categories of increasing specificity. It is one kind of "cognitive stucture" that might be suggested by Ausubel's theory. One might remember the causes of fire in a garage, for example, by means of a hierarchical scheme such as that illustrated in Figure 8.3.

ORGANIZATION PROVIDED BY TEXTUAL PASSAGES. Besides the organization which may originate within knowledge structures previously acquired by the learner, an organization for factual learning may come from the context in which individual facts are presented to the learner. New facts to be learned are usually presented in a text or oral discourse in a way that suggests organization. An example is the use of a topic sentence to organize a paragraph of text in which a number of different facts are presented. In one study of the effect of topic sentences on fact retention (Gagné, 1968a) five different paragraphs dealing with howler monkeys were shown and read to groups of fourth- and fifth-grade children. One set of paragraphs contained topic sentences, while another set did not. For example, in one set a paragraph containing sentences on play activities of howler monkeys began with the topic sentence, "Howlers have many forms of play." The other type of paragraph included no topic sentence, only another sentence describing a specific play activity. The facts organized by a topic sentence were learned and recalled to a greater extent than were the same facts presented without a topic sentence.

Topic sentences, of course, are only one of many possible kinds of organization which may be employed in the presentation of facts, and which may influence the learning of factual information. Facts may be organized in tabular form: the table exhibits a number of organizational factors. Its title is, in a sense, a topic sentence. The headings of its rows and columns provide clues for generative rules pertaining to the individual facts listed in them. In

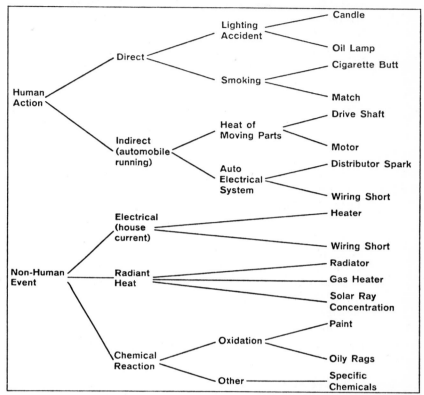

FIGURE 8.3   A hierarchical arrangement of the possible causes of fire in a
garage. (From Gagné, R. M., and Fleishman, E. A. *Psychology
and Human Performance.* Copyright © 1959 by Holt, Rinehart and Winston. Reproduced by permission of Holt,
Rinehart and Winston.)

some instances, the table's format may provide a set of "pegs"
based upon the spatial location of its contents. And the organization of a table is often a hierarchical one, exhibiting superordinate-
subordinate relationships among its items. For all these reasons, the
tabular presentation of factual information may be expected to provide organizing factors which aid the storage and retrieval of factual
information.

Many of these characteristics may likewise be seen when a
graph or diagram is used as an organizing device for presenting
facts. Additionally, a diagram may be recalled as a visual image and
thus provide another advantage for retrieval.

ORGANIZATION BY INSERTED QUESTIONS. Still another way in which organization may be given to factual information is by inserting questions into passages of text. These effects have been studied extensively by Rothkopf (1970) and by Frase (1970), among others, and have been described in Chapter 7. It was found that the performance of students on items they had "practiced" in the inserted questions was substantially better than their performance on items that they had not previously encountered. Thus, the insertion of questions had a definite organizing influence on the facts learned and remembered.

Another and somewhat different effect of the inserted questions was also noted. When given items on which they had no specific practice, students remembered facts in the *categories* suggested by the inserted questions better than those in other categories. The group that had encountered questions on distances, dates, and proper names remembered facts in these categories better than other facts; and results were similar for the students who had seen questions on common words and technical terms. In other studies, this "general" effect of inserted questions has been found to occur when the questions are given *after* successively presented textual passages, but not when they are inserted *before* the passages. There may thus be more than one way in which inserted questions exert their organizing effects on the learning of facts.

Learning Connected Discourse

Students who are given a text to study, such as a chapter in a book on American history, are not usually expected to learn and remember only the specific facts contained in the chapter. One expects instead that they will learn and recall the *main themes* or *main ideas* and a sufficient number of facts to exemplify or elaborate these ideas. For example, a chapter dealing with the economic aspects of the Depression of 1929–1938 might describe the financial speculation in the stock market, business failures and their causes, bank failures, unemployment, and the government actions of the "New Deal." These and other main themes are what students may be expected to remember. The learners might also recall names of specific stocks or of banks or of governmental officials, in order to demonstrate that they can provide instances of knowledge, rather than "mere verbalizations." (It is not suggested here that such information learning is the major aim of instruction in America history —only an essential first step.)

Few systematic studies of how people learn the main themes, and the subordinate details, of passages of connected discourse have been done. Our knowledge of what is learned from such passages and how it is learned and stored in memory is not yet very extensive.

As might be expected, when passages of connected discourse are recalled for "meaning" or "ideas" rather than for verbatim facts, achievement in remembering is greatly superior (Welborn and English, 1937). A number of studies have indicated that learners tend to remember best the "ideas" or "main themes" of a passage of text by reading it once (Henderson, 1903–1904; Sharp, 1899). There are, however, certain distortions in these ideas, which Bartlett (1932) has described as condensations and generalizations of the original meanings. In addition, Bartlett found that certain new meanings were constructed and thus introduced into the recalled version of the learned passage.

How do such passages of connected discourse become organized (encoded) in long-term memory? Is the organization dependent upon certain words, particular propositions, or upon a logically connected structure of propositions? At present, there are no clear answers to these questions. Cofer (1941) found that major words of sentences (those which maintained their basic meaning) tended to be recalled with fewer errors than minor words (conjunctions, modifiers). When essential propositions of a passage are examined in retention, these are usually found to be recalled better than unessential items (E. B. Newman, 1939). A recent study (Crothers, 1972) found that subordinate themes, in the sense of logically connected ideas, were recalled about as often as superordinate themes. However, a study in which college students recalled ideas after hearing passages read, Meyer and McConkie (1973) showed that the more comprehensive (and abstract) ideas were better recalled than were the more specific ideas. The mode of memory organization for such passages remains an interesting puzzle, which additional research will ultimately solve.

CONDITIONS OF LEARNING—
VERBAL INFORMATION

The human individual, who is sometimes a student, sometimes not, obviously learns and remembers a great deal of verbal information. Somewhat arbitrarily perhaps, one can divide the learning of information into the categories of labels (or names), facts, and connected main themes. However, some general principles of learning appear to run through these categories, and these shared principles can be viewed as optimal conditions for learning. As is true for other categories of learning outcomes, learning conditions are conveniently seen as partly internal to the learner and partly external.

Internal Conditions

What internal conditions of the learner favor learning and retention of verbal information? What factors of internal disposition have been shown or suggested to support the coding, storage, and retrieval of information?

A PRE-EXISTING SET OF ORGANIZED KNOWLEDGE. Some previously learned information, interconnected in some manner, needs to be present in the learner's memory. This pre-existing knowledge is what Ausubel calls a "cognitive structure," into which newly learned information is subsumed. Among information-processing theories of memory, there are several concepts of this organized information as stored in the long-term memory. Computer simulation models initially attempted to account for the learning of paired associates, and proposed a network of associations which formed a discrimination net (Simon and Feigenbaum, 1964). A memory model proposed by Quillian (1968) proposes that all factual information is stored as either a "unit" or as a "property"; the *unit* is the representation of an object or event, whereas the *property* represents a predication (such as is implied by a verb or adjective).

Contemporary views of the nature of storage of organized information usually begin with the assumption that *propositions*—including both the concepts they contain and the subject-predicate relation—are stored in long-term memory. This is the case with theories of memory proposed by investigators who favor computer-simulation models, such as J. R. Anderson and Bower (1973); Kintsch (1972); and Rumelhart, Lindsay, and Norman (1972). There are, of course, differences among these theories which are of such detail that they cannot be described here. For present purposes, though, it is important to note that theories which attempt to account for verbal information learning find it necessary to assume that propositions are stored. This means two things for the conditions of learning: (1) new verbal information, in the form of facts or larger units, is learned by being incorporated into a larger network of propositions; and (2) when information is retrieved, the learner has access to propositions, not simply to isolated words.

ENCODING STRATEGIES.   If verbal information is stored in long-term memory in propositional form or in some other organized fashion, this must mean that it is encoded that way. Thus, the learner must have available some methods of information processing (encoding) that transform the perceived stimulation into the form of an "organized network." Generally, this means that the learner has available some *rules* for forming concepts and propositions. Additionally, the learner generates images as a way of storing concepts or relations (Collins and Quillian, 1972; Paivio, 1971). The process of encoding occurs on a number of levels, depending upon what intentions the learner has for later recall of the information (Craik and Lockhart, 1972).

However encoding is done, its most important function is to make the learned information memorable, as well as transferable to situations the learner will later encounter. Effective encoding must therefore provide cues for later retrieval (Thomson and Tulving, 1970). In part, this means that the encoding structure (the image, the tabular format, or whatever) must provide *distinctive* cues. In part also, it means that there must be "deep processing" of the information, in which a variety of relationships are established between the newly learned and the pre-existing knowledge. The effects of such processing are to make greater ease of retrieval possible.

External Conditions

The external conditions for learning, as we have seen in Chapter 3, are the environmental events that lend support to the internal processes of learning. The critical events for verbal information learning, therefore, are evidently those that activate and maintain the processes of encoding, storage, and retrieval.

PROVIDING A MEANINGFUL CONTEXT.   The external situation for learning new verbal information needs to "make contact" with the organized knowledge that is already in the learner's memory. If names or labels are to be learned, associating them with others that are already learned is known to be effective. Or, the new labels may be "clustered" into more inclusive categories that have been previously acquired. Labels may also be more effectively learned and remembered if they are made a part of sentences, and stored as propositions, as the work of Rohwer (1970a) demonstrates. The sentences may be provided, or the suggestion made that the learner form some of her own. Another suggestion would be that the individual form images relating the new label with others that have already been learned.

Whatever method is used to activate internal processes, the function served by these external events is obviously to transform a nonmeaningful stimulus (a to-be-learned label) into one that is associated with meaningful information already available to the learner. Thus the new label is effectively encoded, stored in long-term memory, and can be more readily retrieved when needed.

Sometimes, to be sure, labels need to be memorized or learned verbatim, and no harm to the learner results from doing so. Usually, the names of the days of the week and the names of numerals and many other labels are learned this way, being simply "committed to memory." Useful jingles or rhymes, such as "Thirty days hath September . . . ," may also be acquired by children without elaborate attempts to provide related meanings. But these instances are the exceptions, not the rule. Most new learning of labels is greatly enhanced by provision of a large meaningful context.

Placing the newly learned *fact* within a context of meaning is likewise a condition for its optimal learning. A single fact about the atmosphere of Mars is more readily learned and retrieved if it is presented in a meaningful context that deals with other planets and other planetary characteristics (cf. Frase, 1969). Even the topic sentence of a paragraph, which suggests a larger context for the individual facts within it, may have this effect on learning. The method used by Ausubel (1968) to provide a context of meaning involved the use of an *advance organizer*. Before learning an organized set of new factual information, the learners are provided with a brief textual passage which orients them to the subject matter and relates the latter to the pre-existing knowledge they already have.

As a practical method, questions or statements of objectives may be introduced before or after the presentation of facts. One effect these may have is to direct the learner's attention to the categories of information to be learned. An even more direct effect, however, is to influence the kind of encoding that the learner undertakes with the material, and thus to enhance its retrieval (Frase, 1970; Rothkopf and Kaplan, 1972).

As for the learning of larger bodies of information, this too is presumably influenced by the degree of meaning the passages convey to the learner, or by the amount of "deep processing" she does with them. For example, the work of Ausubel and Blake (1958) showed that learners with greater knowledge of the principles of Christianity learned and retained more information about Buddhism. Presumably, external conditions must accomplish the activation of internal processing strategies that favor the *constructive* aspects of memory described by Bartlett (1932). By this means, memory is enhanced not only for the main themes of the information passage, but for the details as well.

INCREASING DISTINCTIVENESS OF CUES.　While the retention of verbal information is sometimes enhanced by the subsequent learning of other, new, information (as when new facts are added to an existing body of knowledge), it is also true that *interference* can occur. Thus, R. C. Anderson and Myrow (1971) demonstrated that high school students remembered fewer facts about a fictitious primitive tribe when they subsequently were asked to learn "similar but confusing" facts about another primitive tribe. External conditions or learning can be designed to reduce the probability of interference among potentially confusable information. The external cues for the recall of one set of facts can be made as distinctive as possible. In part, this may be done by tabular organization of facts to be learned, or by the images suggested by location maps or diagrams. Also, physical cues of different colors, shapes, type styles, and so on may be used in the presentation of text. The purpose of enhancing the distinctiveness of different and potentially confusable facts is simply to increase their "dissociability" (Ausubel, 1968), and thus facilitate their retrieval.

THE EFFECTS OF REPETITION.　Sheer repetition of labels or facts, in a kind of "overt rehearsal," does not necessarily lead to better encoding or retention (Meunier, Ritz, and Meunier, 1972; Tulving, 1966). However, when *retrieval* is practiced, substantial improvement occurs in the later recall of learned information. An early study by Gates (1917) demonstrated that "recitation" was clearly more effective than "reading" for the memorization of passages of text. Similar findings have come from studies which dealt with the learning of the substance of factual passages (Ausubel and Youssef, 1965; T. H. Gilbert, 1957). The text-inserted questions used in the studies of Rothkopf (1970) and Frase (1970) may also be considered to have the effect of introducing practice of the items of information whose retention was later assessed.

　　The practice of verbal information items, when it involves retrieval on the part of the learners, constitutes a *review* of the information being learned and stored. Such review can provide the occasion for additional and more elaborate encoding. It can also increase the variety of retrieval cues the learners have at their disposal. Thus, while repetition in the form of mere rehearsal does not appear to be an effective condition for the learning and retention of information, repetition which takes the form of review is highly effective.

EDUCATIONAL IMPLICATIONS

Students in schools learn a great deal of verbal information—names for objects; technical terms; facts of history, science, and social living; main themes of fiction and philosophical and political thought. In applying knowledge about learning to school instruction aimed at imparting this kind of knowledge, we need to consider two questions: (1) of what use to the individual is factual verbal knowledge; and (2) what conditions of learning, internal and external to the student, can be reflected in the design of instruction?

Usefulness of Verbal Information

It is not uncommon to hear disparaging statements about "facts" and "mere verbal knowledge" among teachers and other educators. The major reason for the expression of this point of view may be a desire to emphasize high-priority goals that are more difficult to attain, such as "teaching students to think creatively." Verbal information, after all, is learned quite readily; and much of it will be acquired incidentally in study that has other primary objectives. However, the priority assigned to information (knowledge) should be tempered by considerations of the positive usefulness of this type of human capability.

Verbal information of some kinds has a usefulness that extends throughout the individual's lifetime. We all need to know the names of common objects, the names of numerals, the days of the week, the months of the year, and many other facts simply essential for daily living and communication within a society. Of course, many labels and facts of this sort are normally learned in the early grades of school. In later grades, depending upon the occupational specialty chosen by the individual, a great many additional items of information must be learned. A person who becomes a carpenter must learn many names and facts about lumber and the tools used for building; one who becomes a botanist must learn many names and much other information about plants.

Another use for verbal information is as a component in the learning of other kinds of capabilities. Such information forms the "content" of the specific instances to which intellectual skills (concepts, rules) are applied, and in connection with which they are learned. The student who is learning a principle of government such as "the separation of church and state" must use many different items of verbal information about particular instances of the principle. Similarly, other kinds of capabilities, such as cognitive strategies and attitudes, require specific informational content in order that they can be exhibited by the learner. In general, except at the most elementary level, learning takes place against a background and within a context of verbal information. It is true, of course, that the necessary information can always be looked up; but a complete dependence on this method would be very inefficient. Much information, carried "in the head," is prerequisite to other learning.

A third and very important use for verbal information is as a vehicle for thought. One should not lose sight of the fact that the great thinkers we admire are likely to be men and women who have vast stores of knowledge. How is deliberative and reflective thought carried out? In part, no doubt, by means of images. But the relational, connective, functions of thought seem to require the propositional form presumably taken by information in the organized mode it assumes in human memory.

Instruction for Verbal Information Learning

The external conditions for effective learning of verbal information can be reflected in instructional materials and procedures, as summarized in Table 8.1. These examples are of necessity abbreviated, and the reader will probably be able to provide additional ones.

The role of previously acquired information, an internal condition for learning, needs to be taken into account in the design of instruction. Acquiring a new fact, or a new set of facts, will be easier for the learner who has a larger pre-existing structure of knowledge in memory than for a learner with a small amount of prior knowledge. Thus, if one asks a young child to learn about howdahs, careful attention must be given to the kinds and amount of knowledge the child already has. For an older learner, a greater amount of pre-existing knowledge about animals and animal seats may usually be assumed. The appropriate "advance organizer" would surely vary with age-correlated differences in learners.

The dependence of new learning of information on the existence of previously learned knowledge implies that the more people know, the easier it is for them to acquire new knowledge. This

TABLE 8.1   Instructional Procedures for Verbal Information Learning Using the Example "Howdah"

Learning Outcome	Procedure	Example
Name/Label	1. Providing a sentence context.	1. Bow to the sultan in his HOWDAH!
	2. Suggesting an image.	2. Imagine the sultan saying "how-de-do" from his HOWDAH.
	3. Furnishing distinctive cues.	3. Picture of a howdah on an elephant; label HOWDAH in capitals.
Facts; Connected Discourse	1. Using an advance organizer.	1. Orienting text on seats for riding animals.
	2. Providing a larger meaningful context.	2. Information about seats on various animals, including the fact that the howdah may have a canopy. For connected discourse, organized facts about howdahs.
	3. Review	3. Inserted questions, e.g., "How wide must a howdah be?"
	4. Furnishing distinctive cues.	4. Picture of a howdah on an elephant; label HOWDAH in capitals.

cumulative effect of learning seems to be a well-known fact which is readily observed in educational settings.

GENERAL REFERENCES

LEARNING NAMES AS VERBAL ASSOCIATES

Cofer, C. N., and Musgrave, B. S. (Eds.) *Verbal behavior and learning: Problems and processes.* New York: McGraw-Hill, 1963.

Dixon, T. R., and Horton, D. L. (Eds.) *Verbal behavior and general behavior theory.* Englewood Cliffs, N.J.: Prentice-Hall, 1968.

Goss, A. E., and Nodine, C. F. *Paired-associates learning.* New York: Academic Press, 1965.

MEANINGFUL INFORMATION LEARNING

Ausubel, D. P. *Educational psychology: A cognitive view.* New York: Holt, Rinehart and Winston, 1968.

Bartlett, F. C. *Remembering.* Cambridge: Cambridge University Press, 1932.

INFORMATION PROCESSING IN LEARNING AND MEMORY.
Anderson, J. R., and Bower, G. H. *Human associative memory.* Washington, D.C.: V. H. Winston, 1973.
Lindsay, P. H., and Norman, D. A. *Human information processing: An introduction to psychology.* New York: Academic Press, 1972. Chaps. 10, 11, 12.
Klatzky, R. L. *Human memory: Structures and processes.* San Francisco: Freeman, 1975.
Melton, A. W., and Martin, E. (Eds.) *Coding processes in human memory.* Washington, D.C.: V. H. Winston, 1972.
Tulving, E., and Donaldson, W. (Eds.) *Organization of memory.* New York: Academic Press, 1972.

9

MOTOR SKILLS

Many important human activities require the coordination of muscular movements. Some acts of this nature—such as reaching, grasping, and following moving objects with the eyes—are acquired very early and appear to be determined largely by response patterns that are innate. Others, often incorporating these basic patterns of movement, must clearly be learned at early ages; examples are projectile throwing, the using of food utensils, shoelace tying, the pronunciation of language sounds. Many motor performances of this sort are necessary to the individual's self-maintenance and survival. We learn a great many motor skills in early life, such as those involved in dressing and eating, and seldom think much about them thereafter. Yet they stay with us and are put to constant use throughout our lives.

By the time of kindergarten age, motor performances that children learn begin to have a definitely forward-looking purpose. The children need to learn to execute the motor acts that will serve them again and again in many future situations. Arrangements are made, therefore, for children to learn motor skills pertaining to clothing themselves: getting limbs into sleeves and legs, buttoning, zipping, typing, and so on. Children continue to learn the motor patterns of communicable speech. They learn the basic bodily control activities of balancing, running, jumping, throwing. And they begin to acquire some "fine" motor skills, which involve manipulation of the tools of written communication such as pencils and crayons.

Once the skills for these motor performances have been learned, the emphasis in school learning shifts progressively to tasks of a more intellectual cast. The student now uses these fundamental motor skills in the performance of other activities—singing songs, playing games, writing words and sentences and stories. The new motor skills to be learned are increasingly complex, and require the integration of simpler motor acts. The child learns to print letters and numerals, to make simple written figures like circles and squares, and to write cursive letters and words. On the playground, children learn skills of great precision, such as yo-yo spinning, rope jumping, and ball pitching. Further, these and other precision skills are incorporated into the larger and more complex activities of games, which require the carrying out of comprehensive procedures according to rules of play. Meanwhile, in the schoolroom, the introduction of new kinds of motor performances becomes less and less frequent, as the students devote attention to the learning of intellectual skills and information. Children continue to use the motor skills learned previously—they print letters, draw lines and figures, voice the sounds of language, move and carry objects—all as part of more comprehensive activities that are involved in their intellectual development.

Other kinds of new motor skills, however, must be learned as the individual's education proceeds. Of course, games and athletic activities become progressively more demanding in their rule complexity and in their precision of bodily movement. Aside from the objectives of physical education, motor skills are involved in a variety of school learning. The student learns to use new kinds of tools—compasses, protractors, and other drawing instruments; typewriters; clamps, ringstands, and microscopes. The child studying a new language may need to acquire new skills involving mouth and tongue in the pronunciation of sounds that are foreign. And then, as activities which are vocationally useful begin to be learned, the child may undertake to learn motor skills of the great variety found in sewing, cooking, welding, materials construction, equipment repair, and so on.

Motor skills, then, have a certain importance for the individual. Basic varieties of motor skills, useful throughout one's lifetime, are learned in early life and become a seldom-thought-of part of the individual's repertoire. These skills are nonetheless essential to daily living and survival. Many motor skills involved in the pursuit of play, sport, and organized athletic activity are essential to the maintenance of physical and mental health. Here and there specialized motor skills, such as the use of scientific instruments, are intimately involved with the pursuit of learning in the intellectual sphere. And of great significance are the motor skills that underlie the performances of vocationally useful activities.

THE STRUCTURE OF MOTOR SKILLS

The extent and variety of motor acts may be contemplated by thinking of (1) executing a dive, (2) using a typewriter, and (3) adjusting an internal part of a watch. Motor performances have in common dependence on the precision and timing of muscular movement. The acquisition of these qualities of action, precision, and timing is the primary meaning of *motor skill learning*, since these characteristics are common to all varieties of such learning. It is of some usefulness, nevertheless, to consider some major dimensions that determine differences in motor performance.

Dimensions of Motor Performance

Investigators of motor skills have distinguished three important dimensions of the motor performances that result from motor skill learning: (1) fine versus gross; (2) continuous versus discrete; and (3) open loop versus closed loop.

FINE VERSUS GROSS PERFORMANCE. The distinction between fine and gross refers to the amount of body musculature that is involved in the performance. A "gross" motor act is one that uses the large muscles and often involves the whole body. Examples are skills of swimming, jumping, playing tennis, lifting weights. Note that such activities may also require the development of muscular strength, but this is not what is meant by the learned motor skill. The latter is confined to the precision and timing of the performances. In contrast, at the other end of the continuum, are motor skills that are exhibited in movements of wrists and fingers; these are considered "fine" because they appear to require extremes of precision. Examples are threading a needle, printing letters, operating a typewriter. Manual skills obviously constitute a large portion of the category of "fine" motor skills, although the term is not necessarily intended to exclude other muscle groups. Using the vocal chords in speech or singing must surely be classified in the fine motor skill category, as would be wiggling the ears.

Individual differences apparently exist with respect to the ease with which different people acquire fine and gross motor skills (Hempel and Fleishman, 1955). Studies have shown low correlations between the two kinds of performances; and this small relationship constitutes one of the main reasons for believing that the gross-fine distinction is more than a superficial one. At the same time, the conditions for learning the two types of skills have much in common, as we shall see later in this chapter.

CONTINUOUS VERSUS DISCRETE.   A discrete motor task is typically one in which a particular movement is made in response to a particular *external* stimulus. Of course, a total task may be composed of different movements, each of which is "set off" by a different external stimulus. Reduced to its simplest form, a "discrete" task is the movement of the hand and arm in a single direction, as in the measurement of reaction time. The Discrimination Reaction Time Test, used in classifying aircrew trainees during World War II, is a good example of a discrete motor task, and is shown in Figure 9.1. In performing, the individual was required to make four different discrete movements, one to each of four switches. Each movement was made to a different stimulus, a pattern of lights which appeared on the upright panel.

In contrast, a "continuous" task is one that requires the individual to make continuous adjustments and corrections to a combination of stimuli, some of which are internal (stimulus feedback from the muscles). The movement which results may be a continuous one, although this continuity may result from frequent adjustments in the correction of slight over- and underreactions (Poulton, 1957). An example of a continuous motor task is provided by another aircrew classification test called the Rotary Pursuit Test. This task has

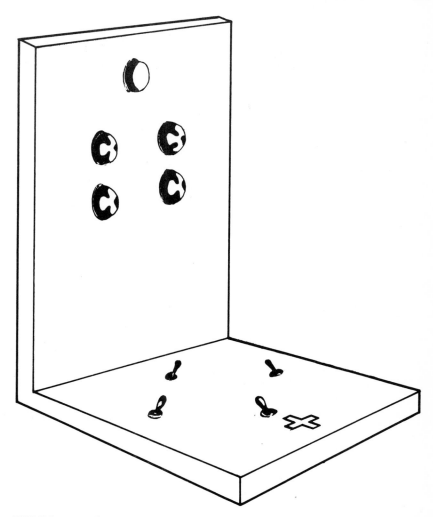

FIGURE 9.1   The Discrimination Reaction Time Test, an example of a task
requiring discrete motor performances. (Adapted from Fleishman, E. A. *A factorial study of psychomotor abilities.* Research Bulletin TR-54-15. Lackland Air Force Base, Tex.: Air
Force Personnel and Training Research Center, 1954).

been studied extensively in psychological laboratories for many
years. It is shown in Figure 9.2.

The plastic disc with an inserted flush metal "target" rotates
at 60 RPM. The performer follows the movement of the target with

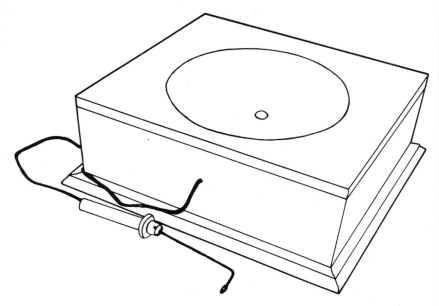

FIGURE 9.2   The Rotary Pursuit Test, an example of a task requiring continuous motor performance. (Adapted from Fleishman, E. A.
A factorial study of psychomotor abilities. Research Bulletin
TR-54-15. Lackland Air Force Base, Tex.: Air Force Personnel
and Training Research Center, 1954).

a stylus, attempting to maintain electrical contact between the metal
tip of the stylus and the target. The resulting skill is a continuous,
smooth movement of the arm and wrist, timed so as to correspond
to the speed of the target in its revolution.

CLOSED-LOOPED VERSUS OPEN-LOOPED TASKS. A "closed-
loop" skill is one that depends entirely upon internal feedback
from the muscles as guiding stimuli. Such a task can be performed
with the eyes closed. Making a smooth, continuous movement in a
particular direction with the arm would be an example; performing
the rotary movement of the Rotary Pursuit Test "in the air" while
blindfolded would constitute a closed-loop skill. The rapid freehand
drawing of a large circle on the blackboard comes close to being
a closed-loop skill, since the movement is not adjusted in response
to the external appearance of the line as it is being drawn.
        Most practically useful motor tasks have some open-loop
characteristics, that is, their responses are influenced to a greater or
lesser degree by external stimuli. The printing of letters is obviously

largely influenced by the stimuli provided by the lines as they appear on the paper. Catching a ball, jumping a hurdle, making a dive, are athletic skills that are obviously dependent upon the presence of external stimulation for their proper and precise performance.

Some kinds of open-looped skills are controlled in part by stimulation which must have the form of an intellectual plan, distinct from muscular feedback. Such is the case with the skills of piano playing and typewriting. In these instances, the individual discrete movements occur with rapidity that is too great to allow for correction based upon feedback from the muscles. The attainment of skill in such activities can apparently not be accounted for on the basis of a simple "linking" of specific motor movements. Instead, it seems reasonable to suppose that the individual must acquire "executive routines" (Welford, 1968) or "motor programs" (Keele, 1968). A comparative review of theories of motor learning, containing a discussion of these issues, is provided by Singer (1975).

LEARNING MOTOR SKILLS

Human performances are of many kinds. They not only involve different portions of the body musculature; they also bring into play a variety of internal processes. Since any performance is assessed (at least ultimately) in terms of *overt action*, some aspects of the performance are bound to be "motor." Yet we do not customarily consider that any action which eventuates in muscular movement (such as recording the answer to a problem in addition) has involved the learning of a motor skill. It is necessary, therefore, to address the question of when and under what circumstances motor performances are to be considered as instances of *motor skill learning*.

Another related matter is that skilled motor performances often occur as parts of larger units of human action, which may be given the general name of *procedures*. Putting an automobile into motion from a state of rest is a procedure. If we examine this procedure, or any procedure, as a sequence of actions, we find that some of the component actions may indeed require skilled motor performances, and that one or more of these performances may require the learning of motor skills.

Focusing on the single motor skill, most investigators have become aware that learning typically progresses through certain *stages*. The performances exhibited by a novice and an expert differ most apparently in the observable degrees of precision, smoothness, and timing. Besides this apparent change in the motor performance, however, are other evidences of changes in the quality of the skill as it is progressively mastered. These changes imply shifts in the kind of internal processes that control the motor performance. And these changes have definite implicatons for the learning of motor skills, which are reflected in the conditions of learning to be discussed later in this chapter.

Human Performance

Overt performances of human beings, often used as evidences of learning, take many forms. They may involve the entire body, as in running, jumping, swimming, or skating. They may require the movement of primarily one limb, as in turning a crank with one's arm. Very often, performances are executed with the primary involvement of a single hand and its fingers, as in writing, printing, or operating a small calculator. Other parts of the body may participate in a performance, as when the vocal chords and throat are used in forming language sounds.

It is evident that except for special purposes, we do not depend upon the overt motor action for an identification of the type of human performance we wish to observe or examine. A student may be asked to "make a sentence using the word 'exemplary'." His performance (if oral) obviously involves the use of mouth, tongue, and vocal chords in forming and uttering the speech sounds that make up a sentence. Yet we do not consider that his performance is "motor," or that it has involved the learning of a motor skill. Similarly, a student may use her hands and fingers to manipulate a pencil in recording the answer to the multiplication problem: $12 \times 7 = \square$. We look upon this behavior as the exhibition of an intellectual skill, but not as a motor skill.

Motor skill learning, then, cannot be identified simply by observing the overt motor performance of the learning. This means that it is of critical importance to observe what the learner is able to do before learning, as well as afterwards. In order to infer that a motor skill has been learned, we must first see what the learner's "entering behavior" is. The student who is learning to use the word "enabling" in a sentence is *already* able to form the necessary words in speaking the sentence. The student who is performing multiplication already knows how to print the necessary numerals on a piece of paper. Although these performances are motor, the learning of a motor skill has not occurred. Of course, we know that at some time in their lives, perhaps much earlier, these students actually had to learn the motor skills that make possible the motor performances of speaking words and writing numerals. But the identification of newly learned motor skills must be done by considering the aspects of *motor* performance that are new and that were not present *before* learning began.

Even when tasks are deliberately designed to require motor action, the motor skills that must be learned may be minimal. This is the case, for example, with a task like the Discrimination Reaction Time Test (Figure 9.1). This test requires the learner to make rapid movements to any one of four switches. But to a considerable degree, the motor skills of pressing switches (forward, backward, to the left, or to the right) have already been learned and are well established. What, then, is being learned as the learner is given practice in responding to this device? The name of the task provides the answer—the learner is acquiring *discriminations* (or a *multiple discrimination*, since four stimuli and four responses are involved). Some degree of motor skill learning may take place, in which the learner acquires greater precision and speed in pressing the switches of the device. But the amount of performance improvement attributable to this "motor learning" is minimal. The primary task is learning stimulus pattern 1 → response to switch 1, stimulus pattern 2 → response to switch 2, and so on.

Evidence that discrimination learning, rather than motor learning, is the primary component in such a task may be found in the results of an experiment by Gagné and Foster (1949). They used a four-switch task with switches and light patterns arranged somewhat differently from those of the Discrimination Reaction Time Test, but which was otherwise similar. Learners were given practice on the discrimination learning task, before they attempted to learn the task with the actual device. Practice was provided on a "pictured representation" of the lights and switches, in a paper-and-pencil form. The motor responses for this discrimination-learning task consisted simply of marking positions with a pencil on paper—very different from the responses required in pressing switches. Following practice in discrimination learning, the learning of the light-switch task was undertaken. The transfer of learning was very great, amounting to 80 percent. Only a few trials of practice were needed for these learners to achieve a degree of mastery on the final task comparable to that of skilled performers who had not learned the "pictured" task first. It is quite clear, therefore, that the major component learned on this device is not a motor skill, but the simple intellectual skill called a multiple discrimination.

Similar conclusions can often be reached by analyzing more complex human performances. Running the bases of a baseball diamond is obviously a motor performance. Yet to a large extent, the motor skills involved are already present in the novice baseball player. They consist of running rapidly in an approximately straight path from one position to another, which the rookie already knows how to do. If additional motor skills are acquired, they must consist of touching bases with the foot, "rounding" a base, coming to a stop with foot on base, and other skills of this nature. Undoubtedly, these motor skills are learned as the player progresses from novice to expert status. The important point to be made, however, is that in identifying motor skills to be learned, one must first have a clear idea of what the "entering behavior" is—of what has already been learned. It would be best not to think of base running as a "motor skill," but as a total performance which involves the learning of several component motor skills.

Procedures

The running of bases is an example of many kinds of human performances which may be called *procedures*. While procedures that result in overt action are motor performances, they do not always require the learning of (new) motor skills. An order clerk, for example, may need to learn how to fill out a newly introduced order form, with coded symbols for the consignee, method of payment, stock numbers, and so on. The completion of this form may require that entries be made in a certain sequence, and that various intellectual operations (subtraction, matching, etc.) be carried out along the way. The overt actions required may be printing, making checkmarks, filling blanks, stamping with a rubber stamp. Obviously, though, motor skills do not have to be learned by the clerk, since the skills which make possible these performances have been learned long ago, and practiced for many years.

What is learned when the capability of performing a procedure is acquired? A procedure is in fact an *intellectual skill*, often a *rule* determining sequence (a *sequential rule*), with which certain subordinate rules are also associated. In filling out a form, the sequential rule controls the order in which actions are taken—the date is entered first, the name of the consignee next, the code for the type of goods next, and so on. The total procedure may also require the use of subordinate rules, as for example, when a step requires that a subtraction rule be applied to "current balance" to find "amount due." Sequential rules are not new or strange entities; for example, the intellectual skill of long division obviously involves a sequence-governing rule, along with other subordinate rules for factoring, subtraction, and so on (see Chapter 6).

What is new at this point is our consideration of procedures made up of steps involving different motor performances, which in turn may or may not require the learning of new motor skills. An example is provided by the procedure of parking an automobile parallel to a curb. An analysis of this procedure is presented in Figure 9.3.

The procedure itself is seen to consist of a *sequence of rules*: first, the car must take a position about a foot away from, and even with, the vehicle in the next forward parking space. As a next step in the sequence, the car must be backed at an angle of 35 to 40 degrees, at low speed. Then the front wheel must be turned sharply so that the car will approach a position near the curb. And as a final step, the front wheels must be straightened so that they are parallel to the curb, while the backing of minimal speed continues. The rules that constitute the procedural sequence can be seen to require

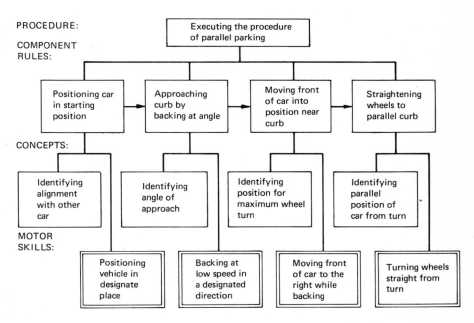

FIGURE 9.3   The procedure of parallel parking, analyzed to show the major component rules, concepts, and the motor skills on which it depends.

certain subordinate concrete concepts to be identified (position of the car, etc.). Most importantly, though, the execution of the procedure requires the possession of certain *motor skills*, indicated in the bottom row of Figure 9.3.

Evidently, then, this procedure of parallel parking is one that includes a number of component skills, some of which are intellectual skills (such as identifying the "lined-up" position of the front of the car), whereas others are motor skills (such as backing the vehicle at minimal speed). Shall we call the whole procedure a "motor skill"? That would be only approximately correct, although it is often done. Preferably, it should be identified as a procedure. It is sometimes called a motor skill because, in contrast with certain other procedures, the major new components to be learned are motor skills. In this case, the procedural components that are intellectual skills (lining up the car, estimating a backing angle, etc.) are likely to already have been fairly well learned. The skills to be learned and brought to a stage of reasonable mastery are the motor skills—turning the car to a proper angle, backing at minimal speed, and so on.

Most sports activities are also composed of procedures, which in turn consist of separately identifiable motor skills. For example, making a tennis serve requires that the player stand in a specific part of the court, and aim the serve so that the ball will land within certain bounds in the opposite court. In short, the player follows a particular procedure in serving. The serve itself, however, insofar as the direction, speed, and rotation of the ball is concerned, is a performance that depends upon an organized motor skill.

The frequent occurrence of motor skills within larger frameworks of activity called *procedures* leads to a question regarding the learning of the latter. Can one learn the procedure separately from its component motor skill or skills? Of course this can be done, although the result would not be judged as highly "skillful." When the component skills of a procedure are already well learned (as in the case of printing or switch pushing), the sequence of steps in the procedure may be practiced separately, with favorable results for a later learning stage when "everything fits together." As indicated by a previous example, the transfer of learning from practice in a "representation" of the task may be quite substantial. In contrast, when the component motor skills of a procedure have not been fully learned, practice of the procedure *without* simultaneous practice of the motor skill components cannot be expected to contribute very much to the learning of the total activity.

These various examples lead to a number of conclusions

about the learning that underlies human activities of a motor sort. Many practical motor performances involve separately identifiable *action steps*. Sometimes, these action steps are arranged sequentially (as in parking a car); sometimes, the individual steps are chosen as alternatives (as in the choice of which switch to press). Each action step may be a motor performance previously well learned, or it may be a performance for which a motor skill must be newly learned. The total performance is often spoken of as a *total skill*. It is noteworthy that a total skill has the characteristics of a *procedure*, and that its components may be called *part-skills*. The learning of the procedural aspect of a performance results in the acquisition of what is sometimes called a *movement plan* (Singer, 1975) or an *executive subroutine* (Fitts and Posner, 1967). Part-skills may be learned and practiced separately as motor skills, but integrating them into practice for the total skill is essential.

The Acquisition of Skill

The course of learning for a motor skill depends, among other things, upon the task to be learned: the nature and length of the procedure, the type and number of part-skills that compose the total skill. If the component motor acts of a total skill have been previously well learned, a minimal amount of time may have to be spent in "putting them together" in a procedural sequence. Conversely, if the component motor skills have not been learned to the point at which they exhibit adequate precision and timing characteristics, further practice on the procedure by itself will not yield added proficiency. In the latter case, additional periods of learning devoted to part-skills, to the total skill, or to both will be required.

PRACTICE.   Surely, the most obvious feature of motor skills is that they improve with practice. That is, the movements that make up the desired performance attain greater precision and more appropriate timing characteristics as the performance is practiced. By "practice" is meant the repetition of the procedure (1) with intent on the part of the learner to achieve an improved performance, and (2) with "feedback," which provides information to the learner. Repetition of the motor act without these two conditions is not normally meant by the word "practice"; learning under such negative conditions is essentially nil.

The effects of systematic practice on the acquisition of motor skill are shown in performance on the Rotary Pursuit task (previously described), in Figure 9.4. In fifteen practice trials, learning shows steady improvement, with a gradual decrease in amount of improvement from trial to trial. It is notable, however, that small variations in this general trend occur, even when the curve is based upon the average performance of 403 learners, which is the case with Figure 9.4. After fifteen 20-second practice periods, learning is still going on, and it appears that performance improvement would not slow appreciably for many practice trials.

Typically, the *learning curve* for a motor skill exhibits a rapid rise in proficiency during its early portion, with a gradual tapering off of improvement as practice proceeds. The curve is a negatively accelerated one, which appears to approach an asymptotic limit.

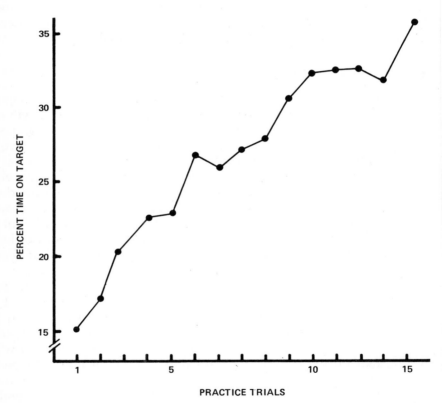

FIGURE 9.4   A learning curve for the Rotary Pursuit task, showing the change in average performance of 403 learners during fifteen practice trials each of 20-seconds duration, with 10 seconds rest between trials. (Data from Melton, A. W. (Ed.), *Apparatus Tests*. Army Air Forces Aviation Psychology Program Research Report No. 4. Washington, D.C.: 1947).

Sometimes, the learning curve for a motor skill has an initial portion of gradual improvement before the period of rapid accleration. This initial portion can usually be attributed to the necessity for learning the procedure, before the effect of practice in increased motor precision can show itself.

Why is practice necessary for the learning of a motor skill? We have seen that practice is not a factor which affects the learning of rules and concepts or of factual information. Yet we do not expect that shooting baskets or printing letters or turning stock in a lathe can be adequately achieved without practice. The reason appears to lie in the nature of *stimulus control* for motor skills. The desired movements must be cued by stimuli that are only partly outside the learner. Some very important stimuli (cues) are internal to the learner and arise as feedback from the muscles. As we have seen, this is true when the motor skill to be learned is of the open-loop sort, as well as when a closed-loop skill is to be learned. By repeating the essential movements in successive trials of practice, the learner is discovering the kinesthetic cues which signal the difference between error and error-free performance. In addition to the external cues, these internal cues come to control and regulate the performance, and thus lead to increasing degrees of precision and timing accuracy. Practice is necessary, then, because only by repeating the essential movements can the learner be provided with the cues that regulate the motor performance. As practice proceeds (with suitable feedback), internal cues leading to error are progressively rejected, and internal cues associated with performance smoothness and precision become established and retained as regulators of skilled performance.

Improvement of motor skills with practice is often gradual; and the more difficult it is for the learner to detect the "correct" internal kinesthetic cues, the slower learning occurs. A *New Yorker* cartoon once depicted a golfer who had just completed a drive that placed the ball inches from the cup. Her remark was, "I wish I knew what I did right!" Thus a golfer may be aware of her difficulty in detecting the exact set of cues to posture and swing which have resulted in an excellent performance. The likelihood is that many more trials of practice, some good and some bad, will be needed before the internal stimuli which control the good performance are established as regulating cues.

There is much evidence to indicate that improvement of motor skill can proceed with continued practice for very long periods of time (Fitts and Posner, 1967). For example, Crossman (1959) made a study of the speed with which cigar-makers completed the manufacture of a cigar on a hand-operated machine. The workers had varying amounts of experience, up to seven years. Gradual increases in skill occurred for at least four years, or during the time workers were producing an estimated two million cigars. Similar findings concerning continued gradual improvement in motor skills over long periods of practice have been obtained with a variety of practical and laboratory tasks (Stevens and Savin, 1962).

The difficulty of selecting internal cues for correct performance can sometimes be overcome by providing additional *external* cues, in a method usually referred to as *augmented feedback*. An interesting practical example is provided by a device known as a Golf-Lite, described by Mathews and McDaniel (1962). A small light attached to the shaft of a golf club is powered by a battery in the player's pocket. The light projects a bright spot on the ground, and permits the golfer to receive visual feedback on the direction and accuracy of his swing, with reported improvement in the acquisition of skill. Smode (1958) studied the performance of learners on a tracking task which required keeping a moving needle centered on a scale by rotating a dial. One group of learners was provided after each practice trial with information about their time on target. The other group was given augmented feedback by viewing a counter which accumulated the time on target as it occurred during each trial. This second group attained considerably higher proficiency scores than did the first group. The time-on-target scores were 63 percent versus 51 percent after eleven practice trials. Furthermore, the advantage for the augmented-feedback group was retained as greater skill: the group's performance remained better on a second day, when it was tested without the presence of the counter.

School learning tasks may also take advantage of augmented feedback to speed the learning of motor skills. An example is the use of specially prepared guides to the printing of letters. When the child's hand movement departs from the form of the desired letter, a carbon impression shows the nature and extent of the "error." Thus immediate feedback is given during the practice trial, as opposed to after the total letter is completed. Such a device appears particularly useful during the early stages of acquiring the skill.

Combining Part-Skills into Skilled Procedures

We have seen that individual motor skills often occur within larger units of activity called procedures. Learning motor skills, in a general sense, often means combining part-skills into these larger units. Procedures which are to be executed in a particular order are often considered to require the learning of *behavioral chains*.

When one says to a novice driver, "Now start the engine," one is asking for the execution of a learned behavior chain containing several component skills. If the training of the driver has been successful, what will take place is the reinstatement of a sequence something like this: S ("Start the engine") → R (looking forward and to the rear) . . . S (sight of clear road) → R (testing for gear in neutral) . . . S (gear in neutral) → R (turning key to activate starter) . . . S (sound of motor catching) → R (release of key) . . . S (key released) → R (depressing accelerator). Each of the individual acts in the chain is something that the learner knows how to do. What must be learned is to get them done in the proper order.

There are many varieties of sequential procedures. Sometimes the linked components are intellectual skills, as in the operations of long division; sometimes the components are entirely motor skills; but most often, both are involved. T. F. Gilbert (1962) describes the analysis of several varieties of procedural chains. He indicates how such an analysis can simplify the requirements for learning a procedure such as multiplication with the slide rule. Gilbert's derivation of learning principles from these analyses emphasizes several points. One is the desirability of learning a chain by beginning with the final "link" and working backwards, in order to insure that each newly learned act is optimally reinforced. Another is the importance of making each link as distinctive as possible, in order to reduce the tendency for "competition" (or interference) to occur among them. When tendencies to interference exist, preference in learning practice should be given to links most prone to competition. Verbal mediators (that is, extra verbal cues) also have the effect of reducing competition by increasing the distinctiveness of the component links of a chain.

CONDITIONS FOR LEARNING MOTOR SKILLS

Motor skills that are practically useful are frequently complex. They may be composed of a number of unitary part-skills, which themselves are made up of different body and limb movements. Single motor skills often occur as components of procedures such as parking a car, making a tennis serve, drawing a square.

As a consequence of this complex structure, the learning of

motor skills during periods of practice appears to emphasize the establishment of different aspects of skilled capability in several *phases.* Fitts and Posner (1967) distinguish three main phases of learning:

1. *Early, or Cognitive, Phase.* The beginning learner attempts to "understand" the task and what it demands. The instructor provides verbal guidance directing the learner's attention to the proper sequence of actions, and also to the external cues which signal the start of each subordinate movement. During this stage, previously acquired part-skills (subroutines) are selected by the learner and put together into the required procedure. The primary consequence of this phase is the learning of an *executive routine;* in other words, the *procedure.* Fitts and Posner (1967) identify this learning of a procedure as "cognitive." The intellectual skill guides the entire complex of subordinate movements.

2. *Intermediate, or Associative, Phase.* During the intermediate phase of learning practice, two kinds of change typically take place. First, part-skills not previously brought to high degrees of smoothness and timing are achieving these qualities. Second, unitary subskills are being integrated into the total skill, in the sense that competing responses (interference) are being eliminated. Actually, separate practice is sometimes given to achieve these two learning effects. Part-skills may be practiced separately, before or alternately with the total skill. An example is the crawl swimmer's separate practice of the kick and the head movements associated with breathing, alternating with practice of the total skill. For some skills, part-skill practice may be advantageous in terms of total-skill learning. This seems particularly true when the components of the skill are independent (Fitts and Posner, 1967). When part-skills must be coordinated to achieve the total performance, however, practice in the total skill is usually a more efficient learning procedure.

3. *Final, or Autonomous, Phase.* During the final phase of learning, the motor skill becomes less subject to interference from other ongoing activities. The procedural steps no longer need to be initiated by cues supplied by the learner; that is, the learner no longer needs to "think of what to do next." The skill becomes *autonomous,* which means that it can be executed while the individual is engaged in other activities (such as conversing, or solving intellectual puzzles). Improvements in smoothness and precision of the skill continue to take place as practice continues, although at a continually decreasing rate.

This account of motor skill learning, derived from observations of learners during practice, and also from interviews with skill instructors (Fitts, 1964), implies that the conditions for learning motor skills must take cognizance of the *different* primary outcomes of these three phases of learning.

Following our general plan, we proceed here to describe the internal and external conditions that lead optimally to the learning of motor skills.

Internal Conditions

RECALL OF PART-SKILLS. A new motor skill is typically assembled from part-skills, some of which have been previously learned. Even the execution of a "simple" skill such as the drawing of a square by a child requires the part-skills of holding the pencil and making directional marks on paper be employed. For an adult learner, a skilled procedure such as removing the wheel from an automobile involves the part-skills of fitting a wrench to a nut, loosening a nut by turning, and so on. Often, part-skills have been learned and practiced over many years. In order that a total skill be learned, these component skills must be recalled. That is to say, the internal cues which set each part-skill into motion must be retrieved and made accessible in the working (short-term) memory. Of course, some of the part-skills of a total motor skill may have to be newly learned. As we have said, this new learning may be done by separate practice of novel part-skill, or as a part of the practice provided for the total skill.

It is important to note that previously learned part-skills, depending on their nature, may actually interfere with the learning of new skills. Thus a previously well-learned relationship such as that between a light located on the *left* of a panel and a response to the *left* may have a low degree of "compatibility" with a new skill which requires a response to the *right* to the same left-located light. Considerable variations in the difficulty of learning new skills of varying degrees of compatibility with old part-skills were demonstrated by Fitts and Seeger (1953). Previously learned part-skills are completely incompatible with new skills when all of the relationships between stimuli and response movements are reversed; and this condition results in *negative transfer* (Lewis, Shephard, and Adams, 1949).

RECALL OF EXECUTIVE ROUTINE. The execution of a motor skill involves a pattern of movements, often a sequence of movements. This *procedure* must be recalled as a movement plan during the second phase of motor skill learning, when increasing smoothness and precision are being acquired. For example, a bowler who is practicing his skill follows a procedure of positioning the ball, approaching the release line, selecting an aiming point, imparting a twist to the ball, and so on. This executive routine must be learned by a novice during an early phase of motor skill learning, as Fitts and Posner (1967) suggest. It is actively retrieved and employed in the working memory during the intermediate phase of learning. The learner must continue to "think of what he is doing."

External Conditions

VERBAL INSTRUCTIONS.   Verbal instructions have an important, but limited, role in the learning of motor skills. In the early phase of learning, when the executive routine (movement plan) must be acquired, verbal instructions can provide the cues for procedural steps. The instructor tells the novice driver to "line the front of your car with the front of the forward car," "turn your wheels so that the car will back at a 40-degree angle," and so on. As learning proceeds, the learner may rehearse these verbal instructions in her short-term memory, and thus supply them "to herself." They are stimuli, initially external, which guide the learner as to "what to do next."

Verbal instructions have a second function, which is sometimes of considerable importance: they can operate to increase the distinctiveness of external cues (Ellis, 1965). Thus, in responding to the light patterns of the Discrimination Reaction Time Test (Figure 9.1) or similar tasks, the learner is aided by verbalizing the relationships between patterns of lights and response directions (as in saying to oneself "red-left, green-right," or similar appropriate word phrases). This effect may be conceived as a *mediational* function of verbal self-instructions (T. F. Gilbert, 1962). Of course, these instuctions may originally have been provided by the instructor as part of the external conditions of learning.

PICTURES.   Pictures of the movement involved in a motor performance, whether still or moving, may serve functions similar to those of verbal instructions. Often pictures can accomplish these purposes more effectively than words can. Diagrams which depict for children the separate steps in the procedure of printing an *E* may be more effective than a verbal instructional sequence, which they may have some difficulty retaining in their short-term memories. In motor tasks undertaken by adults, pictures may provide an effective medium for the presentation of procedural sequences to be learned and remembered, as in knot tying (Roshal, 1961) and operating a cutting press (Lindahl, 1945).

Pictures can also aid the learning of motor skills by directing the learner's attention to the external cues for the control of motor responses. This function is served, for example, by training in the identification of the "correct sighting picture" in rifle firing at a target (Gagné and Fleishman, 1959, p. 249). During the intermediate stage of motor skill learning, the selection of appropriate external cues is an event of considerable significance to the attainment of increased performance precision (Singer, 1975).

DEMONSTRATIONS.   Actual demonstrations of the execution of a motor performance, when observed by learners, can serve functions similar to those of pictures. The "motor plan" (Singer, 1975) or the steps in the sequence of movements comprising the executive routine (Fitts and Posner, 1967) can be acquired by learners as they observe the act of a skilled performer.

Interestingly enough, learners may accomplish a substantial amount of motor skill learning by engaging in *mental practice* after watching a demonstration of the motor performance. Usually, such practice in actively imagining the movements involved is most effective when the learners have had some initial experience with the motor act, followed by mental rehearsal. For example, Clark (1960) found that mental practice of basketball foul shots was nearly as effective as physical practice in producing a moderate amount of skill. Mental practice has been found to have some effectiveness when employed in connection with the learning of many different types of motor skills (Richardson, 1967).

PRACTICE.   An essential part of externally arranged conditions for the learning of a motor skill is provision for repeated *practice* of the motor performance. As we have seen in previous sections, a motor skill is typically acquired in a gradual fashion; and increasing degrees of smoothness, timing, and precision of movement are acquired in successive practice periods. The effects of practice are presumably due to the progressively greater precision with which stimuli, both external and internal, come to exert control over the responses of the learner.

Periods of practice naturally alternate with periods of no practice, or "rest." Thus practice may be *distributed* or *massed*. *Continuous*, or *massed*, practice typically has the effect of depressing the level of performance, which then recovers during any subsequent rest period. The effect of massing seems to be confined to this phenomenon of "performance inhibition." So far as learning is concerned, massed practice has not been shown to be inferior to distributed practice. A number of studies (e.g., Whitely, 1970) have shown that the performance of learners under massed-practice conditions recovers, following a rest, to the level of performance of learners given distributed practice. It appears, then, that amount of practice, rather than its "distribution," is the important variable in determining the level of learning achieved. Of course, practical considerations such as avoiding learner fatigue and lowered motivation need to be considered in planning practice sessions. Reasons such as these may favor the "distribution" of occasions for practice, or at least the avoidance of extreme "massing."

FEEDBACK.   Practice in the sense of repeated movement contributes to learning only when learners receive feedback from their performance or its results. Thus, one of the most important external conditions for the learning of a motor skill is the provision of *informative feedback*, providing reinforcement for the motor performance. It is evident that some feedback is *intrinsic* to the motor act. A single performance of a swimming stroke or the swing of a hammer may not "feel" right to the performer, and this kind of feedback from the muscle is an inherent property of the motor act. Feedback may also be intrinsic in the sense that the external results of the performance are immediately obvious, as when the archer sees the arrow hit the target or when the basketball player perceives the ball going into or out of the net.

Informative feedback may also be furnished externally as *knowledge of results* (Bilodeau, 1966). Besides the kind automatically provided by target information, *supplementary*, or *augmented*, feedback may be supplied by a device or by an external observer. Such feedback may be used to provide more precise or more immediate information about performance than can ordinarily be obtained. For example, children may view the squares they have just drawn as perfectly good. Augmented feedback can be provided by comparison of their squares with a printed square on a plastic overlay. The degree of precision of the drawing thus becomes immediately apparent; the feedback is more direct than that provided by comparison with a model located at some distance away. Of course, knowledge of results can also be given verbally or in some other form by a teacher. Generally, it has been found that augmented feedback which adds to the precision, or improves the immediacy, of knowledge of results is beneficial to motor skill learning (cf. Singer, 1975, pp. 429–433).

EDUCATIONAL IMPLICATIONS

Although not the most highly visible part of the curriculum of schools, the learning of various kinds of motor skills nevertheless has a definite part to play in education. In the primary grades, motor skills are involved in many personal and social activities, as the child learns to manipulate clothing, articles of furniture and equipment, and other physical objects. In addition, basic tool skills such as printing, cursive writing, drawing, and the pronunciation of language are essential motor skills which have long-term uses and implications for further school learning. In grades beyond the elementary, motor skills occupy a less important place in the curriculum, but they are present in the manipulation of the implements of science, in musical instrument playing, and in many activities of a vocational nature such as mechanical drawing, wood and metal working. And, of course, motor skills are prominent in all physical education and sports activities.

In designing instruction for motor skills, it is of considerable importance to recognize that they are more than merely "muscular" in nature. Very often, even usually, motor skills occur as components of *procedures*, involving either choices of alternative movements or sequences of movements. In its totality, a procedure is an intellectual skill, since it it is a complex combination of rules. Executing the procedure may be a matter of using these rules in a certain order; and in doing so, the individual must employ the motor skills that comprise the desired activities. For this reason, the learning of a complex procedure requires that a *motor plan*, or *executive routine*, be acquired at an early stage. Children do not learn to print an *E* simply by seeing the model of an *E* or by practicing random movements with a pencil. Somehow, they must acquire the executive routine that organizes the individual vertical and horizontal pencil-strokes that make a printed *E*.

Various kinds of external stimulation may be employed to guide the learning of a motor skill. Verbal instructions may be given; pictures or actual demonstrations may be used. By means of such "guidance," two functions are accomplished. First, the executive routine may be learned and "internalized" either as an image or as a verbal sequence. Second, pictures or demonstrations serve to highlight the external cues which partially control the desired motor responses. The model of an *E*, for example, shows the middle bar to be shorter than the top and bottom bars, and thus provides an external stimulus which guides the learner's performance. The model of the correctly spoken French word *rue* provides guidance for the performance of the motor skill of pronouncing words containing the "u" sound.

External stimuli play an important role in the learning of motor skills, but it is also a limited role. Crucial stimulation is provided by internal feedback from the muscular movement itself. This internal stimulation makes possible the attainment of precision, smoothness, and timing which characterize high levels of skill in motor performances. To obtain and utilize the control of this internal stimulation, the learner must engage in *practice*. By this word is meant repeated attempts to execute the correct movements, followed in each case by *informative feedback*. Periods of practice, interspersed with periods of "rest," bring about continued improvement in the motor performance; and the improvement may go on for long periods of time as the practice continues.

The essentiality of practice to motor skill learning should not be generalized to other activities. "Practice makes perfect" is not a bad principle so far as motor skills are concerned. But the same requirements for practice do not apply to the learning of other capabilities such as intellectual skills, information, and attitudes. For these types of performances, practice does not have the meaning of "repetition of a set (or sequence) of overt responses." Nor is their learning characterized by the gradual improvement that is so typical of motor skills. The teacher, therefore, must think of arranging suitable periods of practice when motor skills are to be learned; but quite a different set of conditions are implied by "practice" in the learning of other capabilities.

GENERAL REFERENCES

MOTOR SKILL LEARNING
Cratty, B. J. *Movement behavior and motor learning.* Englewood Cliffs, N.J.: Prentice-Hall, 1973.
Fitts, P. M., and Posner, M. I. *Human performance.* Monterey, Calif.: Brooks/ Cole, 1967.
Gagné, R. M., and Fleishman, E. A. *Psychology and human performance.* New York: Holt, Rinehart and Winston, 1959. Chap. 8.
Robb, M. D. *The dynamics of motor-skill acquisition.* Englewood Cliffs, N.J.: Prentice-Hall, 1972.

Singer, R. N. (Ed.) *Readings in motor learning.* Philadelphia: Lea & Febiger, 1972.

Singer, R. N. *Motor learning and human performance*, 2nd ed. New York: Macmillan, 1975.

Welford, A. T. *Fundamentals of skill.* London: Methuen, 1968.

MOTOR LEARNING AND PHYSICAL EDUCATION

Cratty, B. J. *Teaching motor skills.* Englewood Cliffs, N.J.: Prentice-Hall, 1973.

Knapp, B. *Skill in sport: The attainment of proficiency.* London: Routledge, 1964.

Singer, R. N., and Dick, W. *Teaching physical education.* Boston: Houghton Mifflin, 1974.

10

ATTITUDES

Besides capabilities for action, learning also results in the establishment of internal states that influence the individual's *choices of action*. These outcomes of learning are called *attitudes*. Their relation to the behavior of the individual is somewhat less direct than is the case with capabilities like intellectual or motor skills. Attitudes do not determine particular actions; rather, they make certain classes of individual action more or less probable. For this reason, attitudes have often been described as "response tendencies," or as states characterized by "readiness to respond." A valuable definition which has withstood the test of time is Allport's (1935, p. 810): "An attitude is a mental and neural state of readiness, organized through experience, exerting a directive or dynamic influence upon the individual's response to all objects and situations with which it is related."

The indirect (or complex) relation that attitudes have with human action means that their attainment and their modification pose difficulties for assessment. It is not easy, in other words, to be sure that one is measuring a change in attitude as a result of learning, rather than of something else. In addition, it appears that the conditions for learning attitudes are more complex than the conditions pertaining to other kinds of learned internal states. Nevertheless, there can be little doubt, as Allport's definition suggests, that attitudes are established and "organized" by learning.

Historically, attitudes have been considered to constitute the basic core of the discipline of social psychology. Consequently, they are often exemplified with a "social" orientation—as in "attitude toward religion," "attitude toward marriage," or "attitude toward Jews." In the very extensive research literature on attitudes, social themes are prominent; that is, the "situation" in which the attitude is detected and the "object" at which it is directed are often defined in social terms. Regardless of this focus, however, it is generally recognized that the meaning of attitudes is quite broad, and need not be restricted to the social realm. A lathe operator, for example, may display an "attitude of precision" towards his task, in which the object of the attitude is a steel rod. An "attitude of carefulness" toward situations not directly involving other human beings may be possessed by a farmer, a hunter, or a housepainter. Attitudes need not be social in their orientation, although many of them are.

Most of our attitudes are learned incidentally, rather than as a result of preplanned instruction. Conditions that form and modify attitudes surround the individual constantly, from birth onward. As a young child, a person acquires attitudes toward parents, brothers and sisters, other children, and adults. The child's experiences lead to attitudes towards animals, such as cats, dogs, snakes, spiders, and insects. Some of the attitudes acquired early in life are remarkably persistent and resistant to change. Usually as a result of family living, the young child also acquires attitudes related to sharing possessions, keeping promises, helping people, and making truthful statements. From association with playmates, the child may also acquire attitudes of cooperation, competition, compromise, and "fair play," as well as combativeness and vengeance.

Social institutions conduct various kinds of activities primarily aimed at the establishment of attitudes. Families may be very deliberate about the instruction of children in the "virtues" of trustworthiness, promptness, cleanliness, politeness, helpfulness. In carrying out family chores or the work tasks, the individual may encounter intentional feedback supporting attitudes of "good workmanship" and "perseverance." Religious organizations, of course, spend a great deal of time and effort on planned educational programs designed to establish desirable social attitudes such as those embodied in the Ten Commandments and the Golden Rule. And the attitudes that various manufacturers wish us to learn are very apparent from the product advertisements we see and hear.

Although many different attitudes are acquired in the home, in the church, and in the neighborhood, there is a definite expectation that some attitudes will be learned or strengthened in the school, as a result of deliberate planning (Gagné, 1972). Actually, it has always been considered appropriate for the school to undertake the establishment of attitudes. If there has been a change in recent times, it consists in the *kinds* of attitudes that are thought to be appropriate or inappropriate as objectives of the curriculum. In an earlier age, "reverence toward God" was considered an appropriate attitudinal goal of the school as well as the home and the church; whereas this objective is no longer deemed appropriate for the public school curriculum. In an earlier age, education in "manners" (attitudes of courtesy) was thought to be primarily a responsibility of the family; nowadays a great deal more dependence is placed upon school education for the establishment of such attitudes.

Planned objectives of attitude learning, whatever their specific nature, are definite components of educational programs for children and adults. The curriculum is said to include an *affective domain* (Krathwohl, Bloom, and Masia, 1964); this term emphasizes the "feeling tone" of these learned internal states. The kinds of attitudes to be established sometimes become the subject of controversy between school and community, or even within the community itself. At the same time, many attitudes appropriate for school learning would hardly be controversial. Here, for example, is a list of such attitudes, many of which are suggested by Klausmeier (1975, p. 375):

Respect for the individuality of others
Acceptance of responsibility for one's own actions
Positive liking for a given subject matter
Positive attitude toward classmates
Positive attitude toward the teacher

Enthusiasm for work
Promptness in beginning schoolwork
Taking care of own and other's property
Cooperation in working with others
Courtesy to others
Carefulness in observing safety rules

Despite differences in opinions about which attitudes are legitimate and which are of high priority to adopt as curriculum objectives, educators seem in substantial agreement about the importance of attitudes in educational programs of all sorts. It is generally recognized that attitudes of a social nature, such as those pertaining to personal violence or the use of harmful drugs, play a critical role in the operation of our modern society, and affect the quality of life for all individuals in that society. If desirable attitudes could be identified, agreed upon by the community, and taught as part of educational programs, a better quality of life would presumably be insured. The major hitch in such a plan devolves to "community agreement."

THE NATURE OF ATTITUDES

There is much disagreement about the nature of attitudes. We shall be unable here to resolve these differences in points of view, and can only describe them in general terms. It will be apparent from this discussion that we are not so concerned with what attitudes *are*, as with what they *do* in the lives of the individuals who possess them. In addition, our discussion naturally emphasizes how attitudes are acquired and changed by the processes of learning.

Three Aspects of Attitudes

Attitudes are generally agreed to exhibit three different aspects, which may be investigated separately or together (Triandis, 1971). These features are (1) *cognitive*, pertaining to the ideas or propositions that express the relation between situations and attitudinal objects (as in "automobiles use too much gasoline"); (2) *affective*, pertaining to the emotion or feeling that accompanies the idea; and (3) *behavioral*, pertaining to the predisposition or readiness for action (such as the action of purchasing an automobile having a high miles-per-gallon rating).

Generally speaking, these aspects are considered to characterize the internal states that are the learned attitudes. In other words, each such state has an affective, or emotional, component; a cognitive component; and an "action-tendency," or behavioral component (Rosenberg and Hovland, 1960). Differences among theories of attitudes pertain to questions about which of these components is primary, or which is a cause of the others. Many theorists hold that discrepancies in "beliefs" (cognitive component) result in attitude change (e.g., Festinger, 1957). Others emphasize the learning of emotional (affective) responses to stimulus objects by conditioning (Staats and Staats, 1958). A third and different view maintains that attitudes follow from the individual's perception of his own behavior (Bem, 1970). Actually, there is evidence to support each of these viewpoints, and it is difficult to choose among them. For purposes of considering how attitudes function, such a choice may not even be necessary.

THE COGNITIVE COMPONENT.   Most theoretical accounts of the origins of the cognitive component of attitudes adopt the basic premise of the "need for consistency." It is postulated that human individuals strive for consistency in their own thoughts, beliefs, attitudes, and behavior. Various forms of this theory, including those emphasizing "balance" (Heider, 1958), "symmetry" (Newcomb, 1961), and "dissonance" (Festinger, 1957), have been given critical reviews by Kiesler, Collins, and Miller (1969). The basic idea is that when an inconsistency or dissonance among beliefs is encountered, the individual strives to achieve consistency, and in this process his attitude may undergo change.

In a well-known study (Kelman, 1953) whose results can be interpreted in accordance with this principle, children were offered prizes for writing essays favoring a particular type of comic book, which they actually did not prefer. When the essays had been written and the prizes received, it was found that the comic books they had praised in the essays were rated higher in attractiveness by the children. One way of viewing these results is to say that the children experienced dissonance (inconsistency) when they undertook to praise comic books they did not originally favor. Several ways of achieving consistency can be imagined—for example, the provision of some large external reward, or approval from the teacher. These justifications for writing favorable essays were not available to the children in this study. Consequently, consistency was achieved by a change in attitude in favor of the comic books they praised in their essays.

THE AFFECTIVE COMPONENT.   Evidence that attitudes are accompanied by positive and negative "feelings" derives largely from introspective accounts. A few studies, however, have shown changes in emotional states to accompany changes in attitudes, as revealed by physiological measures. For example, Rankin and Campbell (1955) measured changes in the galvanic skin response of experimental subjects when an experimenter entered the room to adjust the apparatus. The experimenter was either black or white. Changes in skin resistance (a typical emotional measure) were shown to be related to measures of racial attitudes obtained from a questionnaire. Other studies which have found relationships between physiological measures and reported attitudes include those of Westie and de Fleur (1959), Staats, Staats, and Crawford (1962), and Porier and Lott (1967).

Attitudes vary from "positive" to "negative." According to Triandis (1971), these positive and negative tendencies represent *two* dimensions, rather than only one. The most obvious quality is the behavioral tendency of *seeking* versus *avoiding* contact (with the person or other object of the attitude). The second dimension pertains to "affect," to *liking* and *disliking*. Thus an attitude may reflect seeking contact, when the individual is willing to pay money to attain the contact; such an attitude is "positive" in both the seeking and the affective dimensions. Suppose, though, that the attitude is positive in seeking contact, but seeks this in a wish to *destroy* the object. The latter represents a negative value of the affective component of the attitude.

THE BEHAVIORAL COMPONENT.   An attitude is defined as a disposition or readiness for some kind of action. What is the relation between the attitude and the actual behavior of the individual possessing that attitude?

The classic study of this question was done by La Piere (1934). He traveled through the United States with a Chinese couple, stopping at 66 different hotels and motels, and dining at 184 restaurants. Service was refused only once during this entire trip. Six months later, letters were sent to the hotels and restaurants visited, and the same letters to a similar "control" group, which had not been visited. Of the replies received, 92 percent indicated that they would not furnish service to Chinese guests. Thus the result showed a marked discrepancy between attitudes expressed in the letter replies and the actual behavior exhibited.

Many other studies have been performed which illustrate

the same basic trend: an absence of any high degree of relationship between attitudes as reported by responses to questions and actual behavior (Triandis, 1971). There are several possible reasons for this finding. The first is that attitudes, as customarily measured, are simply not the same as behavior; and such a relationship should not be expected. The situation of responding to a letter about Chinese guests contains many elements that differ from the situation of being confronted with an actual Chinese couple seeking accommodations. The two situations involve very different response thresholds, as Campbell (1963) has pointed out. Another way to say this is to state that social behavior is largely *situationally determined,* and attitudes play only a limited role in regulating behavioral outcomes.

A second reason for a small degree of relationship between measured attitudes and behavior derives from the methods used to assess attitudes, and pertains to the *validity* of such measures. Very often, attitudes are assessed by asking people to respond to verbal statements on scales which indicate dimensions of like-dislike or favorable-unfavorable. The statements themselves, however, may refer to *other people's* behavior, rather than to the behavior of the individual whose attitude is being tested. For example, it is not uncommon to find statements such as the following on a questionnaire assessing attitude toward religion:

A person who goes to church is likely to have a good moral character.
Agree __ __ __ __ __ Disagree

Conflicting doctrines of the church make religion confusing to the average person.
Agree __ __ __ __ __ Disagree

Statements such as these, and others like them, are commonly used to assess attitudes—the attitude "score" is obtained by accumulating values of responses indicating degree of agreement with each statement. Obviously, such measures are indeed indirect, so far as the individual's *own choices* of action are concerned. Scores based on such instruments can tell us the individual's opinions about other people's behavior, but not about her own. Part of the reason, then, for the lack of correspondence found between attitude measures and behavior may well be the lack of validity of the attitude measures.

As a first step to achieving validity in attitude measures, efforts may be made to insure that the printed statements used for assessment describe *choices of personal action.* Items of this sort were used originally by Bogardus (1925) to assess attitudes toward people of different nationalities, yielding a measure of what he called "social distance." The questions used asked people to indicate, with reference to different nationalities, whether they would (1) marry a member of the group, (2) have members of the group as close friends, (3) work in the same office as a member of the group, (4) have members of the group as speaking acquaintances, (5) exclude members of the group from the nation. The development of scales of social distance was pursued further by Triandis and Triandis (1960), and led to the development of the Behavioral Differential (Triandis, 1964), which measures the "behavioral intentions" of people toward any person or category of persons. This method employs items that first give a description of the person to be judged (the attitudinal object). A series of scales describing choices of personal action follows, each of which is to be checked as to likelihood of choice. For example:

A 50-year-old black minister
would __ __ __ __ __ __ __ __ __ would not
                    obey this person
would not __ __ __ __ __ __ __ __ __ would
                  ask this person for advice
would __ __ __ __ __ __ __ __ __ would not
                invite this person to dinner

Informative studies concerning attitudes toward persons of various nationalities have been carried out by Triandis and his associates using this method (see Triandis, 1967). Factor analyses of these results have indicated the existence of certain *dimensions* of attitude, which have been named as Respect, Marital, Friendship, Social Distance, and Superordination. Perhaps the most important point of this research, however, is the possibility of making a more or less direct assessment of behavioral intentions. In other words, the method provides *content validity* for the assessment of *choices of personal action*. The same kind of assessment could readily be applied to other "objects" than people of various nationalities. For example, attitude toward chemistry as a college subject might be assessed by a number of items including:

would __ __ __ __ __ __ __ __ __ would not
                elect this subject as a major
would not __ __ __ __ __ __ __ __ __ would
            drop the course if I could without penalty

The Scope of Attitudes

The objects of attitudes, as we have seen, may be classes of persons (such as Asians), or events (such as parades), or physical objects (such as auto trailers). Such object classes may be large and inclusive or small enough to contain only a single member. Does this variability in the scope of attitudes give us any clue as to how to delimit them? And if not, is there a way of conceptualizing how large or small an entity an attitude is?

PERSONAL ACTION.   A clue to the problem of attitude scope may be provided by the results of the factor-analysis study of Triandis (1964), based upon assessments of choices of statements describing *personal action* toward certain nationalities. It is notable that the items of this attitude measure which tended to be highly intercorrelated were those which pertained to certain classes of personal action, which were given names such as Respect, Friendship, and Superordination. Friendship, for example, was indicated by items which asked about (1) being partners in an athletic game, (2) eating with the person, (3) gossiping with the person, (4) accepting the person as an intimate friend. Superordination, as a distinct class, pertained to (1) treating the person as a subordinate, (2) commanding the person, (3) obeying the person, and (4) criticizing the work of the person.

Thus it appears that, regardless of the size of the class of objects to which the attitude refers, the kind of personal action delimits the scope of an attitude in the sense of defining a *consistent unit*. A unitary attitude is one which is defined by a *class of personal action* toward some category of objects, persons, or events.

The implication is that one cannot legitimately conceive of single attitudes such as "attitude toward Mexicans" or "attitude toward school" or even "attitude toward Calvin Coolidge." The size of the object class does not determine the unity of the attitude; instead, the singleness of an attitude is determined by the class of personal action which it influences. An instrument that purports to measure "attitude toward school" can be analyzed to reveal several different unitary attitudes: personal actions of *traveling* to school, of *associating with* schoolmates, of *interacting with* the teacher, of *doing* school assignments. Thus, an assessment instrument which includes all of these types of personal action actually measures a *collection of attitudes*.

Of course, it may be the case that what is wanted in assessing the outcomes of an instructional program aimed at changing attitudes is a measure of change in a collection of attitudes, rather than in a single attitude. An attitude questionnaire that measures such a collection would then be perfectly appropriate. If one is concerned, however, with the question of *validity* (that is, with what has actually been learned), the recognition that single attitudes are definable in terms of classes of personal action is an important one.

Attitudes and Values

Values are often spoken about in the same breath with attitudes. Some investigators make no distinction between these two words, and this is perhaps the simplest point of view to adopt at the present moment. Others consider that *value* is a name given to a social attitude that enjoys widespread societal acceptance. Examples of such attitudes would be *"respect for the law,"* "reverence toward God," and the Golden Rule. Different societies, of course, exhibit and reward different choices of personal action reflected in such values (Ringness, 1975).

INTERNALIZATION OF VALUES.   A widely held view of the relationship of attitudes and values is that the former may be arranged on a continuum that represents increasing degrees of *internalization* ranging from those that are lightly held to those that are strongly valued (and therefore highly resistant to change). This is the view described by Krathwohl, Bloom, and Masia in the *Taxonomy of Educational Objectives, Handbook II: Affective Domain* (1964).

The most lightly held attitudes, according to this conception, fall into the general category of personal action called Receiving. An example of *willingness to receive* is "accepting differences of race and culture, among people known." Increasingly greater degrees of internalization of attitudes are indicated by the categories of Responding and Valuing. *Preference for a value*, for example, is indicated by the kinds of action reflected in the descriptions "assumes an active role in current literary activities" and "writes letters to the press on issues he feels strongly about."

Still greater degrees of internalization of attitudes are indicated by the categories of Organization and Characterization by a Value Complex. Since more than one value may be relevant to a situation, values become organized, first, by being conceptualized and later by being formed into a value system in which some are more dominant than others. At the peak of the internalization process there is attained a generalized set and a characterization of values which is reflected in the development of conscience, codes of behavior, and a philosophy of life.

During the course of individual development, different kinds of values, perhaps exhibiting differing degrees of "internalization," may become evident from the individual's choices of personal action. Kohlberg (1973) has described six stages of moral development in the human individual. These range from the *preconventional level*, in which "right" action is determined by its hedonistic consequences; through the *conventional level*, characterized by conformity and maintenance of approved rules; to the *autonomous*, or *principled*, level, in which right conduct is chosen in accordance with self-conceptualized ethical principles.

Beliefs, Emotions, or Behavior?

The functionally important conceptions that may be derived from the voluminous literature on attitudes appear to be those of a *learned internal state* which influences *choices of personal action* toward some class of objects, events, or persons. Such a state possesses "affective," or emotional, components which have not figured largely in the characterization of the attitude, except in the generally recognized accompaniments of "good or bad feeling." An attitude also has a cognitive component, reflected in the conceptualization of principles which guide or influence action choices.

Some investigators conceive of attitudes almost entirely in cognitive terms, as "systems of beliefs" (Rokeach, 1969) or categories of concepts and their attributes (Kelly, 1955) or ideas arising from dissonances in other ideas (Festinger, 1964; Zajonc, 1960). Different communications of ideas which convey partially conflicting information are evidently integrated by an "averaging" process, as shown in a study by N. H. Anderson (1973). Surely the cognitive organization of attitudes is an important problem. It is a problem most readily approached by using systematic variations in the kinds of *verbal statements* people are asked to select or respond to when attempts are made to assess their attitudes. But the widespread use of the questionnaire with its propositional statements should not mislead us to conclude that these propositions are themselves attitudes.

Beliefs and ideas and the conflicts among them may be convenient descriptions of the cognitive components of the internal states called attitudes. They do not seem to be adequate, however, to account for the dynamic effects that attitudes have in their influence on the choices of action made by the individual. This latter characteristic of attitudes (sometimes called "behavioral") is their most illuminating feature.

AN OPERATIONAL DEFINITION.   In terms of the operations of an external observer, an attitude is a state that influences or modifies the individual's choices of personal action. Such influence can sometimes be observed in actual choices exhibited in overt behavior. Acts of kindness to other children may be taken to indicate an "attitude of kindliness"; the borrowing of books from the library can be used as an indicator of "preference for reading." However, the effects of attitudes on overt behavior cannot always be observed, given a limited period of time and limited access to individuals and all their situations. As is well known, attitudes are most commonly assessed by means of responses to verbal statements contained in questionnaires, rating scales, and other instruments of this general sort (M. E. Shaw and Wright, 1967).

How should an attitude be defined in operational terms when responses to verbal statements are used as measures? Obviously, with the use of such instruments, one wishes to make the inference of an *internal state*—just as one would if overt behavior choices were being made. Assume that the individual responds to statements by indicating the "degree of agreement" or the "degree of likelihood of choice" for each one. Then a cumulative score for each attitude measured could be described as *the degree of commitment expressed to statements describing choices of personal action (of a designated type)* toward some class of objects, persons, or events. Is the inference of the internal state, using such verbal instruments, as valid as the inference made from other behavior? This would seem to depend primarily on the learners' comprehension of the verbal statements, and their meaningfulness to the individuals whose attitudes are being assessed. For most adults, the inference appears a justifiable one; for young children, it does not.

ATTITUDE CHANGE

Many of our attitudes are learned as a result of a series of interactions with other people—with parents, friends, and associates. Attitudes may be acquired or changed rather suddenly as the result of a single experience. Or they may undergo gradual change over a period of years, presumably as the result of a cumulative series of experiences.

Three major kinds of learning situations have been extensively studied as producing attitude learning. We shall describe these here as (1) classical conditioning, (2) perception of success in behavior, and (3) human modeling.

Classical Conditioning

It has long been known that conditioning of the classical (Pavlovian) sort can produce learned emotional reactions to stimuli. The study of Watson and Rayner (1920) showed that an unconditioned stimulus for "fear" (sound of striking a metal bar), when paired with a conditioned stimulus (a white rat), quickly produced a newly conditioned response (withdrawing from the rat) in a child. This fear response, with its apparent "affect," might reasonably be taken as evidence of the establishment of an attitude toward the animal. It is generally believed that certain irrational fears of childhood, such as those toward snakes, spiders, or other animals, probably arise through the accidental pairing of stimuli as in classical conditioning. Sometimes these attitudes persist for many years, and are changed only with difficulty.

The establishment of attitudes by means of classical conditioning methods has been studied in experimental settings. For example, Razran (1940) showed that the presentation of a set of political slogans along with a free lunch resulted in a change to positive acceptance of these slogans, whereas presenting another set of slogans accompanied by unpleasant odors brought about a change in the opposite direction. The participants could not recall, when they were asked, which slogans went with which condition. (This control is used to demonstrate that conditioning, and not deliberate choice, was the causal factor).

Staats (1967) considers that attitudes are acquired by classical conditioning, in the sense that an object takes on an emotional meaning by this means. A laboratory study by Staats, Staats, and Crawford (1962) demonstrated that words paired with shocks or with loud sounds (unconditioned stimuli) came to evoke the galvanic skin response (an emotional indicator) and also to exhibit changes in their ratings. In another study, (Staats and Staats, 1958) "favorable" words like "beauty," "sweet," and "gift," were presented together with one set of male first names ("Tom," "Bill," "Jack," etc.); whereas "unfavorable" words such as "bitter," "ugly," and "sad," were presented together with another set of male first names. The first condition resulted in an increased positive rating of the names; the second in a decrease in positive attitude.

Reinforcement

Operant conditioning, involving the manipulation of contingencies of reinforcement, has also been used as a method for the learning of attitudes. For example, Insko (1965) reinforced students over the telephone, using the word "good" when they agreed or disagreed with particular statements of opinion. A week later the same students were asked to respond to these opinion statements presented in questionnaire form. The reinforcement was found to influence their attitudes in the predicted direction. In a study by Scott (1957) attitudes of students engaged in a debate were shown to change in the direction in which they had argued when they won the debate, and in the opposite direction when they lost. The reinforcement provided by letter grades (A versus D) has been shown by Bostrom, Vlandis, and Rosenbaum (1961) to alter the attitudes of students who were required to write essays advocating a position inconsistent with their original attitudes; in this case, A was a more effective reinforcer than D.

Studies such as these appear to show that favorable attitudes may be established by suitable arrangement of reinforcement contingencies. They also appear to be interpretable in a somewhat different way, which is that favorable attitudes arise from the *experience of success* (which is itself dependent upon reinforcement). Many incidents of everyday life attest to the importance of success in an activity in attaining a positive attitude. The child who has not yet become successful at skating tends not to "like to skate"; her attitude changes rapidly to the positive once she achieves success in this performance. Schoolwork, of course, exhibits the same phenomenon. Positive attitudes toward mathematics or English composition or public speaking follow one or more experiences of success in these activities. Conversely, attitudes of dislike result from repeated instances of failure. Practical methods of establishing attitudes, based on reinforcement principles, are the subject of a book by Mager (1968).

Bem (1970) marshals evidence that "attitudes follow behavior." This is the case, he says, because individuals infer their own inner states on the basis of clues which come from their own behavior; they engage in *self-perception*. It is not unreasonable to suppose that individuals' perception of successful behavior provides them with one of the strongest clues to their own "feelings" toward some external object. It may be, then, that reinforcement contingencies affect attitudes not simply because the reinforcement occurs, but more importantly because such occasions produce suc-

cess. The perception of success (in some activity) leads to the establishment of a positive attitude. The perception of lack of success
may accordingly be expected to change the attitude (toward some
particular activity) in the negative direction.

Human Modeling

One of the most dependable sets of events that has been found to
produce changes in attitudes is the phenomenon of *human modeling*. In these circumstances, learning results in imitation of the
model's behavior, or more precisely, in imitation of action choices.
When suitably designed learning conditions are present, the learner
acquires an attitude which reflects that expressed or demonstrated
by the human model. The process of human modeling has been
extensively studied by Bandura and his associates (Bandura,
1969).

The basic design for human modeling is as follows. A person
who is admired, respected, or perceived as having "credibility" is
observed (by one or more learners) to exhibit certain behaviors, or
to make certain choices of personal action. For purposes of study,
the model may exhibit choices of undesirable behavior (such as
aggressiveness) or desirable choices (such as making objective
moral judgments). The demonstration may take the form of acting
out the behavior concerned and may or may not be accompanied
by appropriate verbal remarks. Or the model may use only verbal
descriptions of the behavior choices being modeled. As part of the
demonstration, the impression is usually conveyed that the action
choices exhibited are either "good" (when socially desirable) or
"bad" (when undesirable). This may be done when the learners
observe the model being rewarded or being punished, whichever
is appropriate.

In one study (Bandura, 1965), nursery school children observed a model (an adult male) exhibiting several sorts of aggressive
behavior toward an adult-sized Bobo doll. Following this demonstration, another adult praised the performance and rewarded the
model with soft drinks and candy. For another group of children,
this second adult scolded and punished the model for his aggressive
behavior. A third group of children saw the demonstration with no
following consequences. Then the children were led (individually)
to a room containing toys including a Bobo doll, and their behavior
was observed and recorded during a 10-minute period. The results
showed that the observation of reinforcement to the model had a
significant effect on the amount of aggressive behavior exhibited by

the children. That is to say, the children who observed positive rein-forcement of the model tended to increase their aggressive behav-ior; those who observed punishment of the model tended to show decreased amounts of aggression. This phenomenon is called *vicari-ous reinforcement* by Bandura.

A study by Chittenden (1942) undertook to test the effec-tiveness of dramatic presentations in changing choices of personal actions in a set of preschool children who were domineering and hyperaggressive when frustrated in their activities. These children observed and discussed a series of eleven 15-minute plays in which dolls (representing children) displayed aggressive solutions to inter-personal conflict, and alternative solutions which were cooperative. The children's behavior in their nursery school environment was observed before they saw and discussed the plays, immediately afterwards, and again a month later. Increases in cooperative be-havior and decreases in domination behavior were observed on both post-play occasions, as illustrated in Figure 10.1.

The many studies of behavior modeling and attitude change through human modeling suggest that human beings play an essen-tial role in the conditions for effective learning of attitudes. Pre-sumably, the learners acquire a "conception" or "image" of the human model. Since the model is in some sense an admired person, the affective component of this image is distinctly positive. The learners then "imitate" the model, in choosing identical or similar courses of personal action. As a consequence, they may themselves receive positive reinforcement (cf. Baer, Peterson, and Sherman, 1967). Often, though, the attitude is established following obser-vation of rewards to the model, that is, by means of vicarious rein-forcement (Bandura, 1965). The attitude acquired by this means is not limited to the specific behavior exhibited by the model, but generalizes broadly to other behavior and situations (Bandura and McDonald, 1963; Bandura and Mischel, 1965).

Human modeling may occur in many learning situations. The model may be presented to the learner in pictures, movies, or TV scenes, and need not appear in person. Presumably, modeling can occur in older children and adults when the model is merely de-scribed, as in a biography, a history text, or a novel. Thus, the ways of introducing conditions of learning for attitude change by model-ing are many.

Most probably, parents are the primary human models for the transmission of attitudes in the young child. As Thornburg (1975) points out, the family is the locus of the child's initial social learning. In the early years, the teacher, as well as the parent, can serve as a human model for the child's learning of desirable atti-

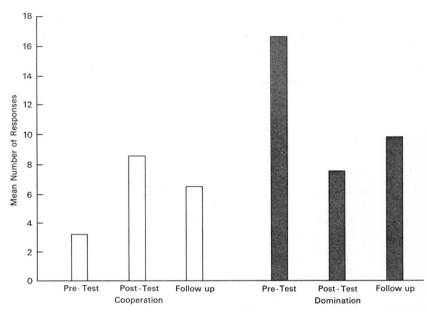

FIGURE 10.1 Amount of cooperative and domineering behavior exhibited by a group of hyperaggressive preschool children before and after seeing and discussing plays in which the desirable choices of behavior were modeled. Drawn from data of Chittenden (1942). (Reprinted from Figure 3-7, in A. Bandura, *Principles of Behavior Modification.* Copyright © 1969 by Holt, Rinehart and Winston. Reproduced by permission of Holt, Rinehart and Winston.)

tudes such as consideration for others, completion of tasks, and fairness. As adolescence is approached, the typical rejection of adult models may herald the period when peer models become predominant, conflicts occur between values and behavior, and many new attitudes are acquired from admired schoolmates. When adulthood is reached, the "selection" or acceptance of models becomes related to the adoption of the individual's own social role (Thornburg, 1975); and the model's credibility is a dominant factor in the changing of attitudes.

Message Content and Attitude Change

Research on the attitude-changing effects of various kinds of communication has been conducted for many years by investigators at Yale University. Studies of "communication and persuasion" were begun during World War II, when the effects of various communications in motion picture form were investigated (Hovland, Lumsdaine, and Sheffield, 1949). Subsequent results of the program have been reported in several volumes, beginning with that of Hovland, Janis, and Kelley (1953).

Perhaps the most important findings obtained in this program of research pertain to the effects of the *kind of communication*. What kind of message is most effective in changing attitudes? The most interesting generalization of the research findings is this: most variations in type of message make no appreciable difference in attitude change. No dependable effectiveness has been found for verbal communications which (1) present rational arguments, (2) give both sides of a question, (3) appeal to emotion, (4) contain fear-arousing stimuli, or (5) draw specific conclusions. While single adjurations such as "Drive safely!" have long been known to be ineffective in changing attitudes, these studies found that various elaborations on the basic message theme also are not effective.

THE SOURCE OF THE MESSAGE.   In contrast with the findings concerning the *content* of the communication, the Yale investigators early discovered that the "communicator," or "source," of the message made a considerable difference in determining its effectiveness for attitude change. A variety of studies have confirmed the importance of the source as an important determiner of attitudes. The relationship between the characteristics of the source and those of the learners is naturally a critical matter. Triandis (1971) has summarized findings about these characteristics as including (1) physical attractiveness; (2) clothes and speech as indicators of status; (3) demographic qualities such as age, race, nationality; (4) the source's attitudes; and (5) evidence that the source's past behavior relates in a rewarding (or punishing) way to the learners.

Attitude theorists generally emphasize the importance of the communicator to the process of attitude change. Kelman (1958), for example, has proposed that effective attitude change requires that the source deliver a "compliance communication," indicating that he possesses means of control (as would be the case with a police officer, a college dean, or the manager of a baseball team). A second kind of message is an "identification communication," which conveys to the listeners the attractiveness of the communicator (as would be the case with an admired sports figure, a student class president). Still a third kind of communication pertaining to the source is called the "internalization combination," which conveys the idea of the communicator's high degree of credibility (as would be the case with an expert in art criticism, race relations, or whatever).

It is evident, then, that whatever aspects of the communication may be found to be effective, a great mass of evidence indicates that these effects are overwhelmed by the influence of the *source*. Obviously, the source is simply another name for the *human model*. Thus it is most illuminating that two or more different lines of evidence, beginning with separate problem definitions and approaches, converge in their agreement that the *human agent* is one of the critically important conditions for attitude learning and change.

CONDITIONS OF LEARNING— ATTITUDES

Having discussed the major theoretical positions concerning the nature of attitudes, and some relevant evidence regarding attitude change, we should now be able to describe the conditions that are optimal for attitude learning. It will be recalled that we view an attitude as a learned internal state, whose function is to influence choices of personal action. We are ready now to examine the internal and external conditions that need to be present when the learning of an attitude takes place. Such learning, of course, may establish an attitude that was not previously present in the learner, or it may change an existing attitude in either the positive or negative direction.

Internal Conditions

As is the case with other kinds of learned capabilities, attitudes require that certain *prerequisite* capabilities be present in the learner. Primarily, these are intellectual skills of the *concept variety*, and a certain amount of relevant *information*.

CONCEPTS. First, it is evident that the learner must possess the concept of the class of object, event, or person to which the new (or newly changed) attitude will be directed. For example, if the attitude is directed at people of the nationality called Estonian, the meaning of Estonian people must be present in the learner's memory. Otherwise, instruction must establish this concept prior to the delivery of the "attitudinal message." Similarly, if attitude is directed at a harmful drug such as cocaine, this concept must be present internally.

Of major importance, as we have seen, is the concept of the "source," or human model. The characteristics which insure the learner's identification with the human model must have been previously acquired, or "internalized." For best effects, the model needs to be conceived as attractive, powerful (in the sense of being capable of control), and highly credible. When the concept of the model is already present (as might be the case with a student leader, or a popular sports figure), the designer of instruction may simply *select* the model who has appropriate characteristics. When the model is not already known, his appealing characteristics may need to be established as prerequisite to the communication of the attitude itself.

A third necessary internal condition is a set of concepts pertaining to the personal action to which the attitude relates. In the case of harmful drugs, for example, concepts are necessary of the *situations* in which such drugs are likely to be encountered, as well as of the *actions* likely to be involved in using them (smoking, sniffing, injecting, etc.). As another example, consider the concepts required as prerequisites in the establishment of a consumer attitude of price comparison of packaged foods. If comparison of cost per unit is to be established as an attitude, the learner must possess the concepts of pounds, ounces, dollars, and cents, as well as the rules which permit ratios to be made and compared (cf. Gagné and Briggs, 1974).

INFORMATION. Relevant information is also an important prerequisite to the learning of attitudes. In particular, such information is likely to pertain to the *situations* in which choices of action are likely to be made. Thus in the case of attitude toward harmful drugs, the learner may need to know the "street names" of the common drugs, as well as the social situations in which they are likely to be available. If the target attitude is one of refusing to drink alcoholic beverages before driving, information concerning the situations in which such drinking is likely to occur (or to be rejected) is necessary as a background for attitude learning.

It is not uncommon for teachers who wish to establish positive attitudes to place undue dependence upon concept learning and information learning. These kinds of learning outcomes constitute *essential prerequisites* for the acquiring of attitudes, and they may, of course, be learned within the same unit of instruction that contains the attitude communication. Their learning, however, does not in itself produce attitude learning or attitude change. The learner may acquire many new concepts about ethnic characteristics, for example, or obtain masses of information about ethnic customs; but it is perfectly possible for these to be learned without any attitudinal change. Concepts and information are merely pre-requisite internal conditions. They are not the crucial events that bring about attitude learning.

External Conditions

The conditions external to the learner that are favorable to the establishment of attitudes may take a number of different forms, depending upon what model of attitude change in favored. Thus, it is possible to employ classical conditioning techniques for some kinds of attitude change, but this method would hardly be appli-cable to the broad range of attitudes with which schools or other educational establishments might be concerned. Reinforcement contingencies may be suitably arranged to provide the perception of success on the part of the learner, for a great variety of attitudes. It would seem by all odds, however, that the method employing human modeling is the most generally applicable, and quite pos-sibly the most effective, approach to attitude learning.

OBSERVATION OF THE HUMAN MODEL'S CHOICES. The set of events that result in learning from human modeling occur in approxi-mately the following order:

1. *The model's appeal and credibility is established.* If the model (such as a teacher, parent, or prominent person) is already known to the learners, this step is assumed. If the model is un-known, information is provided to the learner with the purpose of bringing about "identification" and belief in the model's credibility.
2. *The learner's recall of the object of the attitude and the situa-tions to which it is applicable is stimulated.* The learner recalls relevant intellectual skills and information previously described as internal conditions for learning. For example, to impart the attitude of refraining from drinking before driving, situations are recalled in which drinks are offered, followed by situations in-volving automobile driving.
3. *The model demonstrates or communicates the desired choice of personal action.* For example, the human model indicates that he or she refuses offered alcoholic drinks in anticipation of driving.
4. *A demonstration or communication indicates a reinforcing state of affairs for the model.* For example, the model may be shown keeping a cool head in a difficult driving situation. Further (if

appropriate), the model may be seen receiving a "safe driving" award. Or a model who happens to be a professional automobile driver may be seen receiving an award for skillful driving on a difficult course.

The presentation of these steps may be more or less elaborate, depending upon the attitude to be imparted and the nature of the learners. One can see that the steps occur in fairly simple form when a teacher of first-grade children undertakes to teach an attitude of helpfulness. In this case, the teacher is the model. For step 2, she reminds the children what "helping" means and in what kinds of situations it occurs. She demonstrates the choice of personal action by actually helping a child with a task (such as lifting a piece of furniture). The task is seen to be accomplished readily with "helping." The child who is helped is pleased. The teacher shows satisfaction in the pleasure of another person (the child who is helped). The children also experience pleasure; that is, they are vicariously reinforced. By this means, the children's attitudes are changed in the positive direction toward "helping others."

VARIATIONS ON THE HUMAN MODELING THEME.   The effects of human modeling on attitudes are considered to occur widely in many kinds of situations. Obviously, the basic events of human modeling occur when dramatic presentations are employed, as in actual plays and in television programs. Another form that human modeling can take is *role playing*, in which the actor is influenced by the role of an imagined person, rather than by an actual person. Fictional characters encountered in reading can be human models, and often are. Presumably, human modeling represents the basic psychological process involved in the acquisition of values from the reading of history and literature.

Particular mention may be made of the way in which the factors in human modeling come into play in class discussion. The class may be presented with a problem, perhaps one involving moral values. The students' discussion leads to the presentation of various and sometimes conflicting attitudes. Each person who presents a point of view (towards the choice of personal action) is, for the moment, behaving as a model. The discussion typically leads to the rejection of extreme attitudes which are unacceptable to the group as a whole. More importantly, the communications of attitudes are progressively expressed with greater precision. The teacher or discussion leader (again, acting as a model) may help in the process of reasonable expression of attitudes. Some consensus emerges from the discussion, which is satisfying to most or all of the members; there is, then, reinforcement of both direct and vicarious sorts. Socially acceptable attitudes and changes in attitudes emerge from events of this nature. To be noted is the effectiveness of group discussion in changing attitudes, as contrasted, say, with the ineffectiveness of a verbal communication delivered to the learner without the presence of other human beings.

REINFORCEMENT OF ACTION CHOICE.   Whether or not the attitude has been initially conveyed to the learner by a human model, its establishment is aided by direct reinforcement of the choice of personal action concerned. If a child has learned an attitude of "helping others," the probability of choice of this class of personal action is increased when the child receives direct reinforcement. Having heard about helping, a young child may choose to help another in some task requiring cooperation. When such an act is followed by indications of pleasure or thanks or a returned favor, the conditions of reinforcement are present. In such circumstances, the helping attitude is strengthened; that is, the choice of "helping" actions is made more probable in the child's future behavior.

Reinforcement works equally well at all age levels. Adults who have acquired attitudes against cigarette smoking have their attitudes strengthened when they receive social approval for not smoking, and perhaps also when they see "No Smoking" signs in public buildings. People who have learned to be skillful at certain activities (typing, diving, mountain climbing) acquire strong positive attitudes of liking toward these activities. The experience of success, or in other words, the fulfillment of an expectation, is a powerful factor in the establishment of positive attitudes. Conversely, the absence of success often leads to negative attitudes of dislike for an activity.

EDUCATIONAL IMPLICATIONS

The learning and modification of attitudes, referred to by some as the affective domain of objectives, is surely of great importance to educational programs of almost every kind. It is customarily desired that students acquire positive attitudes toward any subject they are studying, and more broadly toward the activities of learning in general. Practical training programs usually incorporate objectives that represent attitudes toward work, toward performance standards, toward safety measures. School programs are expected to produce in their students attitudes useful for social living, such as consideration for others, cooperativeness, and tolerance of cultural and ethnic differences. In addition, many school programs are concerned with teaching attitudes favoring protection of the environment, avoidance of harmful drugs, and exercise of citizenship responsibilities.

Although many kinds of attitude education are deliberately instituted, human individuals acquire a host of attitudes as a result of their experiences in the larger social and physical environment. Family influences are particularly important in establishing attitudes affecting personal conduct and interpersonal behavior, as well as precision of language and thought. The church, the labor union, the social club, the peer group, and other social organizations and groups to which the individual holds allegiance likewise have strong effects in determining attitudes. Then, too, the various media from which the individual seeks information or entertainment are often powerful sources of attitude change.

Attitudes have both cognitive and affective components. That is to say, they are internally mediated, in part, by propositions which incorporate the category of "object" (events, persons, things) to which the attitude is directed. Usually, they appear also to be mediated, in part, by feelings which give them their "affective" nature. These characteristics, however important they may be in understanding the essential nature of attitudes, give few clues regarding the *function* of attitudes. It is this latter aspect of attitudes that is of central importance to educational programs. If attitudes are to be established or changed, they must be identified as *learning outcomes* and as instructional *objectives*. For such purposes, a useful definition of attitude is a *learned internal state which influences choices of personal action towards some category of persons, objects, or events.* The aim of instruction in this domain is to establish or to strengthen particular internal states which perform this function.

Although attitudes may be formed and changed in several ways, the principles of *reinforcement contingencies* can usually be readily recognized as playing an important part in attitude learning. However an attitude is originally introduced or communicated, its establishment (as is true of other kinds of behavior) depends upon the occurrence of reinforcement to complete the act of learning. It is also true that people like what they do well. The kinds of personal action that lead to *success* are most likely to be those toward which the individual displays a positive attitude. In many educational situations a desired positive attitude may most readily be assured by making it possible for the student to achieve success.

One of the most dependable methods of establishing attitudes is by means of a set of learning conditions that includes *human modeling*. In brief, this method involves the demonstration or communication of the desired choice of personal action (the attitude) by a respected or admired person. Such a person may be a parent, a teacher, a prominent or popular figure, or any individual who inspires confidence and trust (cf. Gagné, 1973). The human model may present the "message" in person, or via a medium like television or the printed page; the model does not have to be "real," as is illustrated by the example of a fictional hero. The learner then perceives that the model is reinforced, or rewarded, for the action choice he has made, an event which is called "vicarious reinforcement."

The effectiveness of human modeling for attitude change contrasts markedly with the ineffectiveness of anonymously delivered messages conveying information, or verbal commands. Adjurations such as "Be a safe driver" are, according to the evidence, almost entirely ineffective for attitude learning. They remain similarly ineffective even when placed in larger contexts of emotional appeals and rational arguments. While information may need to be acquired by the learner as a *prerequisite* to attitude change, its learning does not in and of itself produce the desired change. Students may need to know what a *prothonotary* is before they acquire an attitude toward this class of persons. But such knowledge does not establish or change the students' attitude to an appreciable degree—it only makes such change possible. Similary, drug education, if it is designed to establish attitudes of rejection of harmful drugs, cannot be effective if it simply conveys to the students additional knowledge about drugs.

GENERAL REFERENCES

ATTITUDES AND ATTITUDE CHANGE

Bandura, A. *Principles of behavior modification.* New York: Holt, Rinehart and Winston, 1969.

Bem, D. J. *Beliefs, attitudes, and human affairs.* Monterey, California: Brooks/Cole, 1970.

Fishbein, M. (Ed.). *Attitude theory and measurement.* New York: Wiley, 1967.

Kiesler, C. A., Collins, B. E., and Miller, N. *Attitude change.* New York: Wiley, 1969.

Krathwohl, D. R., Bloom, B. S., and Masia, B. B. *Taxonomy of educational objectives. Handbook II: Affective domain.* New York: McKay, 1964.

Ringness, T. A. *The affective domain in education.* Boston: Little, Brown, 1975.

Rokeach, M. *Beliefs, attitudes and values.* San Francisco: Jossey-Bass, 1969.

Thornburg, H. D. *Development in adolescence.* Monterey, Calif.: Brooks/ Cole, 1975.

Triandis, H. C. *Attitude and attitude change.* New York: Wiley, 1971.

ATTITUDE MEASUREMENT
Shaw, M. E., and Wright, J. M. *Scales for the measurement of attitudes.* New York: McGraw-Hill, 1967.

11

ANALYZING THE REQUIREMENTS FOR LEARNING

Previous chapters have described the conditions of learning that are optimal for the five major varieties of learning outcomes: intellectual skills, cognitive strategies, verbal information, motor skills, and attitudes. The principles and generalizations we have been able to assemble from learning research theory are believed to be those which make possible the selection and design of appropriate conditions for effective human learning. Events which facilitate learning can accordingly be planned to activate and support the processes of learning envisaged in contemporary learning theory (Chapter 3). It is possible for such planning to take account of *internal* conditions (the contents of long-term memory accessible to the learner) and of *external* conditions (the relevant stimulation from the learner's environment).

Proper usage of the principles of learning to achieve effectiveness of outcome requires, first, that the *class of learning outcome* be identified for any specific learning task that the learner undertakes. Once this is done, steps can be taken to discover what internal conditions are applicable to the learning task, and further, to arrange the external conditions so that the expected outcome will be achieved.

Evidently, then, when an instructional plan for learning is to be made, an initial step is to conduct a *learning analysis* of the particular learning outcome to be expected. In this chapter, we shall consider how such a learning analysis, or *learning task analysis*, may best be done.

TASK DESCRIPTION

The tasks that human beings undertake are of many sorts. Most of them are learned. They range from the apparently simple actions of a young child in locomotion and object manipulation to the most complex intellectual ratiocinations that may enter into the invention of a scientific theory. The description of human tasks may also be done in various ways, to meet different needs. Describing a human task for purposes of classifying a job, for example, requires a different approach than does describing a task in order to reveal what is necessary for its learning. We need to consider here the kind of description which is most appropriate for revealing the requirements of planning for the internal and external conditions of learning.

Describing Job-Tasks

Human tasks can be described with differing degrees of specificity. One can describe a performance in general terms as "installing a shingle roof," its components in more specific terms as "nailing a shingle to a roofing board," or in even more detail as "striking a roofing nail with a hammer." The problem of choosing a degree of specificity for the description of human tasks has been a puzzling one. It appears to be best solved by considering the *communication purpose* of the description (cf. Gagné, 1965). That is to say, the degree of specificity of description should be determined by consideration of the question, *What* is being communicated *to whom?*

Clarifying principles of the analysis of human tasks for purposes of description have been greatly augmented by the work of R. B. Miller (1963). He made a careful distinction between "job-task description" and "learning task description" in terms of their different communication purposes. In general, the level of specificity needed for describing the tasks that make up a human job is not as detailed as the level needed for describing the learning task (that is, what has to be learned). In communicating an electronic equipment technician's job-task, for example, it may be sufficient to state, "adjusts the gain of amplifier X to a prescribed standard." In terms of the total job, this may be one fairly "small" specific performance out of many. However, if one asks what the electronic technician has to learn in order to adjust the gain of amplifier X, one gets an entirely different answer. It may be found, for example, that the adjustment task requires the technician to use a voltmeter, and that this is something he has to learn how to do. Thus, the job-task "adjusts an amplifier gain" does not by itself indicate the learning task "measures voltage with a voltmeter." The job-task must be further *analyzed* to reveal the requirements of the learning task.

The basic notion of "job-task" need not be confined to human tasks that are parts of identifiable occupations. Job-tasks occur much more generally. There is no reason why this basic conception should not be applied to all aspects of human life—to performances that make up one's human roles as citizen, as family member, as a social being, and as one who seeks enjoyment in living. Job-tasks in this general sense might reasonably be called *life tasks* and include descriptions of such human activities as the following:

Reads with comprehension accounts of events printed in daily newspaper

Records deposits and withdrawals to maintain an accurate balance in a personal checking account

Seeks enjoyment in watching a variety of sports events and dramatic shows

Feeds baby with bottled formula

Selects fresh vegetables for family meals in supermarket

Orally expresses opinions and communicates information in meetings as member of neighborhood council

Seeks opportunities to engage in scuba diving.

The significance of a general meaning for the concept of "life task" is that human activities described at this level of specificity often correspond to *educational goals*. When one attempts to achieve greater specificity in educational planning than exists in the "Seven Cardinal Principles" (Commission on the Reorganization of Secondary Education, 1918), the result is typically a list of human tasks that can reasonably be called "life tasks," if the broad meaning of that phrase is accepted. In this sense, *a life task is any task that a human being would reasonably be asked to do while in the course of fulfilling one or more purposes understood as contributing to his or her life goals.*

With this broadened definition of job-task, the degree of specificity intended becomes apparent. One would not ask an individual to perform a task so insignificant in purpose, and at the same time so general in its occurrence, that its particular relation to one or more life goals could not be perceived. "Lifting an arm," "sitting in a chair," and "holding a pencil" are not life tasks, whereas those given in the previous list do qualify. However, human tasks such as "reads a daily newspaper with comprehension" and others in the list of life tasks still do not have the level of specificity needed for the planning of learning conditions. In order to reveal learning requirements, these tasks must be analyzed further. Educational programs designed to insure optimal learning conditions cannot be planned by dealing only with tasks that express educational goals. Such statements must be subjected to additional analysis to make clear the components of what is to be learned.

Human Tasks as Procedures

The first analysis of human tasks is likely to reveal that a set of different actions must be performed in a sequential or steplike fashion. That is to say, the task goal is achieved by following a *procedure,* as described in Chapter 9. T. F. Gilbert's account (1962) of procedures ("chains") includes analyses of long division, reading color-coded electrical resistors, multiplying with the slide rule, and bal-

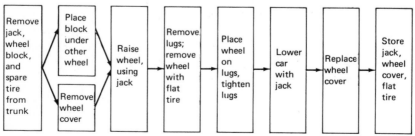

FIGURE 11.1   Analysis and description of the procedure of changing a tire.

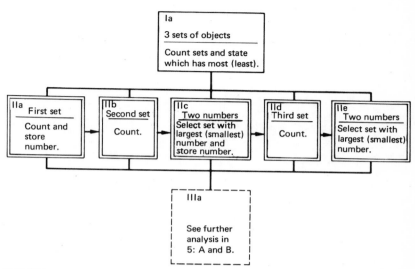

FIGURE 11.2   Procedure for a mathematics task to be accomplished by young children: Identifying which of three sets of objects has most (least). (Adapted from L. B. Resnick, M. C. Wang, and J. Kaplan, *Behavior analysis in curriculum design: A hierarchically sequenced introductory mathematics curriculum.* Pittsburgh, Pa.: University of Pittsburgh, Learning Research and Development Center, 1970, Figure 27.)

ancing teller's accounts. A simple procedure, changing a tire on an automobile, is illustrated in Figure 11.1.

Step-like procedures may also be involved in what appear to be very simple tasks, such as those learned by preschool children. Examples of procedures of this sort are described by Resnick, Wang, and Kaplan (1970), and one illustration is shown in Figure 11.2.

Procedures often require that decisions be made about alternative steps. That is, the outcome of one step gives a clue to the choice of the next step. Such procedures are sometimes called *conditional procedures*, and they are frequently described in more complicated flow charts, an example of which is shown in Figure 11.3. This distinguishes the *inputs* to the procedure (trapezoidal boxes), the *decision points* (diagonal boxes), and the *actions* (rectangular boxes). Some of the steps taken are conditional upon the decision which must be made, whereas others simply follow in a regular order.

The analysis of tasks to reveal their procedural characteristics has two major implications for learning. First, it is evident that each

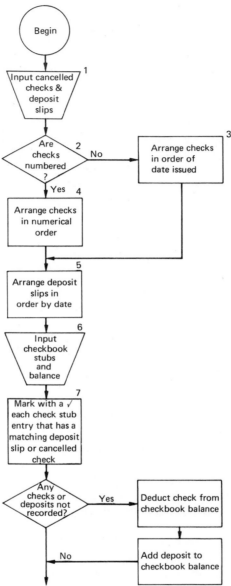

FIGURE 11.3   A vertically arranged flow chart showing initial steps in the procedure of reconciling a bank statement with checkbook records. In such a chart, diagonal boxes indicate decision points for choice of alternative steps. (From Merrill, P. F., *Task analysis: An information processing approach.* Technical Memo No. 27. Tallahassee: Florida State University, CAI Center, 1971, Figure 2. .)

step, or "link," in the procedure must be a capability of the learner. Sometimes the step is highly familiar (such as removing a jack from the trunk of a car); sometimes it is not familiar and must be newly learned (such as operating the jack to raise the car). In order to institute the entire procedure, the learner must have learned to perform each step, including the steps which require a decision about what action is appropriate next.

The second implication for learning is equally important: the learner must acquire the *executive routine* that governs the procedure as a whole. He must be able, in other words, to institute the steps of the procedure in the proper order, so that one follows another in a sequence that will accomplish the task goal. As we have seen in Chapter 9, learning the routine may constitute a separate event from learning the individual steps in the procedure. Even so, the entire task can sometimes be learned "as a whole." The latter circumstance most frequently occurs when the procedure is a short one, and its component steps are mostly familiar. The learning of executive routines for longer procedures is often aided by the mediation of verbal sequences, which provide cues to the ordering of the steps.

The results of analysis of human tasks (job-tasks) in terms of their procedures reveal (1) the executive routine which must be learned in order for the learner to carry out the task; and (2) the individual steps, or "links" of the procedure, each of which must be recalled from previous learning, or learned newly. The latter steps may be motor skills (as we have seen in Chapter 9); or they may be intellectual skills, that is, concepts or rules. For example, the steps in long division (using the algorithm most widely known) include the intellectual skills of (1) multiplying several-place numbers by single-place numbers, (2) subtracting one several-place number from another, and (3) estimating single-place quotients of several-place divisors. These individual skills, as well as the executive routine for the procedure, become *instructional objectives* for learning the task as a whole.

LEARNING ANALYSIS

It might be supposed that the analysis of human tasks into their procedural steps is all that is needed to discover the requirements for learning; but this is not the case. Consider what is revealed by the methods of analysis described up to this point. A broad educational goal, such as "maintaining health" is broken down into parts called job-tasks, an example of which is "brushing teeth to remove accumulated food particles." When analyzed as a procedure, this task is seen to consist of a sequence of several steps, some of which are familiar ("grasping the toothbrush"), while others may need to be learned by a child ("identifying crevices between inner surfaces of teeth"). When completed, this analysis results in a detailed *task description*.

Viewed broadly, a task description of a human activity has a number of applications. It may be used, for example, to construct a detailed guide to the actions required, in printed or pictorial form. When a task forms a part of a job or occupation, a task description may be of value for describing the job to applicants, for classifying the job within a career ladder, or for developing standards of performances to be used by a job incumbent (cf. R. B. Miller, 1963). From the standpoint of learning, a task description represents a description of "terminal" or "targeted" learning outcomes; that is, it describes the performances which a program of learning is designed to insure that the learner acquires as a result of completing the program.

A detailed task description of a useful human activity, however, does not tell us all that we need to know about how to arrange optimal conditions for learning. Two additional operations are needed. First, the task must be *categorized* as a learning outcome into one of the five categories described in this volume—intellectual skill, cognitive strategy, information, motor skill, or attitude. This classification is necessary in order to plan the internal and external conditions of learning differentially for each type of learning outcome, as discussed in previous chapters. Second, each procedural component of the task must be further analyzed to reveal its *prerequisites*. This procedure has the purpose of specifying the internal conditions of learning which pertain to the *recall of previously learned entities* from the long-term memory. These substantive components are recalled so that they can become a part of what is to be newly learned.

Categorizing Learning Outcomes

A human task described at the level of specificity of a job-task may be categorized in terms of the type of learning outcome it represents. Examples of such tasks, including some from the previous list of life tasks, is displayed in Table 11.1. It may be noted that the kind of *action* described by the task does not provide a certain clue to its nature as a learning outcome. The individual who performs the task may be standing or sitting; alone or in a social group;

TABLE 11.1   Examples of Useful Human Tasks and the Categories of Learning Outcomes They Represent

Task	Category of Learning Outcome
Reads with comprehension accounts of events printed in daily news-paper	*Intellectual skills*—applying rules for the decoding of words and the comprehension of language
Seeks enjoyment in watching a variety of sports events and dramatic shows	*Attitudes*—choosing courses of personal action toward particular kinds of entertainment
Communicates the precautions necessary in installing fiberglass ceiling insulation	*Information*—stating information so that its propositional meaning is preserved
Manually lowers the needle onto a phonograph record so as to engage the initial groove	*Motor skill*—executing a smoothly timed motor performance
Originates a game of "Ecology," to be played on family outings in an automobile	*Cognitive strategy*—solving a novel problem by invention

using hands, feet, or head. The learning outcome must be *inferred* from the kind of *mental processing* required. The mental processing which is to be learned as an internal state is what we have called a *capability.*

Describing Tasks as Learning Objectives

The necessity for making an inference about capabilities to be learned has led to the suggestion (Gagné and Briggs, 1974) that tasks be described by statements using *standard verbs*. Of course, capabilities do not have to be described in that fashion. The important point is simply that a correct inference be made about category of learning outcome. Nevertheless, standard verbs can provide an automatic clue to the type of capability to be inferred.

The description of tasks as learning objectives has been the subject of many books and articles (e.g., Bloom, Hastings, and Madaus, 1971; Mager, 1962; Popham and Baker, 1970). A fundamental necessity for good description proposed by Mager (1962) is the use of verbs that are unambiguous. Examples of ambiguous verbs are "knows," "appreciates," "understands," as opposed to verbs denoting definite action such as "selects," "calculates," or "writes." However, although action verbs are clearly useful in describing the tasks which are the objects of learning, they do not always provide the necessary clues for inferring the human capabilities which are to be learned. For example, one task may require "writing" the answer to an arithmetic problem (an intellectual skill), whereas another may require "writing" a sentence to express a fact (verbal information).

The suggestion made by Gagné and Briggs (1974) is that standard verbs be used in statements of human tasks to imply the type of capability (learning outcome) that they involve. Examples of such descriptive statements are reprinted from that source in Table 11.2. It will be evident that each of the learning outcomes de-

TABLE 11.2   Verbs To Describe Human Capabilities, with Examples of Phrases Incorporating Them

Capability	Verb	Example
Intellectual Skill		
Discrimination	DISCRIMINATES	Discriminates, by matching, the French sounds of "u" and "ou"
Concrete Concept	IDENTIFIES	Identifies, by naming, the root, leaf, and stem of representative plants
Defined Concept	CLASSIFIES	Classifies, by using a definition, the concept "family"
Rule	DEMONSTRATES	Demonstrates, by solving verbally stated examples, the addition of positive and negative numbers.
Higher-order Rule (Problem Solving)	GENERATES	Generates, by synthesizing applicable rules, a paragraph describing a person's actions in a situation of fear
Cognitive Strategy	ORIGINATES	Originates a solution to the reduction of air pollution, by applying model of gaseous diffusion
Information	STATES	States orally the major issues in the presidential campaign of 1932
Motor Skill	EXECUTES	Executes backing a car into driveway
Attitude	CHOOSES	Chooses playing golf as a leisure activity

Source: From Table 2, p. 85, Gagné, R. M., and Briggs, L. J., *Principles of Instructional Design.* Copyright © 1974 by Holt, Rinehart and Winston. Reproduced by permission of Holt, Rinehart and Winston.

scribed in this book, and their subvarieties, is represented in Table 11.2. The *major verb* in each task statement, listed in the middle column, immediately suggests the kind of human capability to be learned. Most of the statements, it may be noted, also employ *action verbs* in the form of gerunds, as in the phrases "by matching," or "by naming."

Analyzing Tasks for Prerequisites

When tasks representing learning outcomes have been adequately described and categorized, it then becomes possible to conduct a further step, which constitutes *learning analysis*. This step identifies the prerequisites for the learning of the capability represented by the task description.

Most investigators of the process of instruction acknowledge the importance for planning of finding out what the learner *brings to* the learning situation. Glaser (1967), for example, has often emphasized the importance of *entering behavior* as a critical element in instructional design. The point of view elaborated here is that certain previously learned capabilities need to be retrieved from the long-term memory and need to be readily accessible in the working memory, whenever a new capability is learned. These resultants of prior learning may *support* the new learning; an example is the retrieval of a cognitive strategy which permits the encoding of to-be-learned information. At least an equally important function of retrieval of previously learned entities, however, is their *incorporation* into new learning. When the intellectual skill of adding integers is learned, the previously acquired skill of subtracting whole numbers is incorporated as a part of the new capability. Similarly, when the intellectual skill of making the subject of a clause agree in number with its verb, the previously learned skills of identifying subject and verb are incorporated into the newly learned skill.

PRIOR LEARNING AS SUPPORT FOR NEW LEARNING.   A case can be made for the idea that certain previously learned capabilities provide necessary *support* for new learning, regardless of what is being learned. For example, cognitive strategies of one kind or another must be brought to bear upon the phases of the learning process—attending, perceiving, encoding, retrieving, problem solving. Whatever strategies are available to the learner, as a result of prior learning, must be retrieved and activated as executive control processes for the new learning. Although these strategies may be refined by the learning exercise, they do not themselves become a part of what is learned—which may be a new intellectual skill, a new motor skill, a new set of information, or an attitude.

In a similar sense, certain intellectual skills, often those learned years ago, may be seen to give *support* to the learning of any or all kinds of capabilities. The learner who is acquiring new information, or a new attitude, from reading, must be able to use the intellectual skills needed in the decoding of words and the comprehension of printed prose. Attitudes provide another source of support for learning, in that they engender choices of action toward particular subject matter to be learned, and preferences for achievement in the attainment of expected goals.

PREREQUISITES AS COMPONENTS OF WHAT IS LEARNED. While previously learned capabilities may facilitate learning in a number of different ways, the true meaning of *prerequisite* is a *capability of prior learning which is incorporated into new learning.* The previously learned entity actually enters into the newly learned capability, becomes and remains a part of the behavior which results from the events of learning.

The most obvious examples of prerequisites as components of new learning occur in the domain of intellectual skills, some examples of which have already been mentioned. When the new skill of pronouncing printed words having a final "e" and a medial "a" is learned, this skill *incorporates* the prerequisite skills of (1) identifying a final "e," (2) identifying a medial "a," and (3) naming the long "a" sound. When the new skill of subtracting multiple-place numbers is acquired, it incorporates the prerequisite skills of (1) subtracting single place numbers, (2) subtracting zero from a number, and (3) "borrowing" (or another operation having this purpose). As pointed out in Chapter 6, these prerequisites may be considered *subordinate* skills to the new and more complex skill that is being learned. A complex rule may actually be composed of simpler rules and concepts. The latter may be learned as prerequisites immediately prior to the new skill, or they may have been learned some time ago. When the new and more complex skill is being learned, they must be accessible in the working memory of the learner.

Incorporated prerequisites also become involved in the learning of other kinds of capabilities. In the case of motor skills, prerequisites are often the *part-skills* which compose the total skill; the skill of handwriting, for example, includes the part-skills of forming each of the letters. Attitudes, too, have prerequisites incorporated into their learning. Intellectual skills in the form of *concepts* of the categories of objects toward which the attitudes are directed are essential to the learning of attitudes. Thus, to acquire a positive attitude toward the maintenance of health, the learner must have prerequisite concepts which provide meaning to "good health" in terms of the functioning of various parts and organ systems of the body. Another kind of prerequisite for the learning of attitudes, as described in Chapter 10, is information about the situations in which the attitude will operate. An attitude towards "obeying the speed limit" in automobile driving incorporates prerequisite knowledge about the range of speed limits and the situations in which they are posted (highways, urban streets, school zones, etc.).

Does the learning of cognitive strategies, such as those of productive thinking, require prerequisites which are incorporated into the newly acquired (or newly refined) strategy? As indicated in Chapter 7, this is a matter of theoretical controversy and cannot be given a final answer at the moment. According to the views of Piaget (1970) and others, cognitive strategies require prerequisite intellectual growth, in the sense of the maturation of capabilities of logical thought. Learned intellectual skills *support* this intellectual growth, since they make possible the variety of specific performances required in the practice of the cognitive strategies. A contrasting view (Gagné, 1968b) is that intellectual skills (rules and concepts) are incorporated into cognitive strategies by cumulative generalization, and thus are true prerequisites in the learning of problem-solving strategies (see the discussion of learning hierarchies, Chapter 6).

What prerequisites are required for information learning? Let us suppose that the fact being learned is "Jack captured a squirrel." A first thought might be that the meaning of the individual words (that is, the concepts the words represent) must be known as prerequisites. However, we noted in Chapter 8 that information can be acquired when word meaning is not known, as in the sentence "Turlop glavered renstil." It would appear that the conceptual meanings of words, while supportive of learning, are not necessarily incorporated into the learning of new propositions, and are therefore not true prerequisites. What is essential is the basic skill of identifying the *syntactic relations* in strings of words. By this is meant the identification (not by name, of course) of *agent-action-object* and their transformation into *subject-predicate*. The sentence "Turlop glavered renstil" is learned as a proposition because "turlop" appears to be a subject, "glavered" appears to be a verb, and "renstil" appears to be the object of the verb. It is reasonable to conclude, then, that the specific intellectual skill of "taking in" a sentence as a set of words having subject-predicate relations with each other is an essential prerequisite for information learning. The identification of subject and predicate is *incorporated* into what is learned.

Enabling Objectives for Learning

We have seen that job-tasks may be analyzed as procedures into the individual steps that compose them. Each of these actions steps may be considered a prerequisite to the total performance, since each must be learned before the whole performance can be exhibited. Then again, each step may have its own prerequisites, not in the sense of comprising a sequence, but as entities of prior learning which are incorporated into the new learning.

Sometimes, the prerequisites of learning make sense as separate job-tasks, each of which a human learner might perform in and by itself. Sometimes, however, the prerequisite capabilities are not of this sort, but are useful *only* because they enter into the learning of a new capability. Learning outcomes that are prerequisite to other learning objectives are called *enabling objectives*. It is important to recognize, though, that although some enabling objectives may stand by themselves as useful human tasks (life tasks), others have *only* the enabling function.

For the task of subtracting multiple-place numbers, one of the enabling objectives is subtracting single-place numbers. But this is by itself a useful human task, which may be required in identifying innings in a baseball game, in making up shortages of goods, and in many other situations. In contrast, the enabling objective of "borrowing" (or whatever operation takes its place) is *only* enabling for the operation of subtracting multiple-place numbers, and is not useful for other purposes. Nevertheless, it is an *essential prerequisite,* and therefore deserves to be called an enabling objective. In the reading of words with final "e", the identification of a final "e" is an essential enabling objective, even though it fails to stand by itself as a useful human task.

The importance of this distinction among learning prerequisites is simply this: in order to discover the requirements for learning, *the capability to be learned must be analyzed into enabling objectives,* including those which serve *only* this purpose. Some enabling objectives which are themselves life tasks will be found, by analysis. Others will be found which are not life tasks, but which are equally essential as learning prerequisites. A teacher might report to a parent that a child has learned to subtract single-place numbers, but would probably not report that the child had learned "borrowing." Reporting the former makes sense because it is in itself a useful human task. Yet the latter, although not reported, is an equally essential enabling objective for learning to subtract multiple-place numbers.

The Results of Learning Analysis

Analyzing human tasks with the goal of learning in mind results in the identification of prerequisites for learning. Along the way, prior learning that *supports* the new learning, such as the possession of certain cognitive strategies and attitudes, may be noted. True prerequisites, however, are the previously learned entities that deserve to be called *enabling objectives*, because they are *incorporated* into the new learning. These may have been learned long ago, or only a few minutes ago. At the time the new learning is to occur, they must be retrieved from the learner's long-term memory to his working (short-term) memory, to be accessible for involvement in the new learning.

A summary of learning prerequisites that constitute necessary "entering behavior" of the learner is given in Table 11.3. From the example shown, the prerequisites of a newly learned intellectual skill are clearly other intellectual skills (rules, concepts). Notable, however, is the frequency with which intellectual skills appear as prerequisites for other kinds of learning outcomes, such as the learning of information and attitudes. As we have noted, in the case of motor skill, the executive routine which is an essential component is an intellectual skill in the form of a procedural rule. As for the cognitive strategy described in Table 11.3, we propose that this strategy is derived by the learner from a number of previously learned specific rules of categorizing.

LEARNING HIERARCHIES AS STATEMENTS OF PREREQUISITES.   As we recall the topic of learning hierarchies in Chapter 6, a special word needs to be said about their representation of prerequisites. As our discussion of rules and concepts (Chapter 6) has indicated, these intellectual skills can be readily analyzed to reveal subordinate skills, which are either simpler rules or concepts. Such subordinate skills are true prerequisites; that is, they are *incorporated* into a newly learned skill which is more complex. The subordinate "boxes" of a learning hierarchy are intended to represent only these kinds of essential prerequisites. The process of analysis may be continued on each of the prerequisite skills, so as to reveal rules or concepts

TABLE 11.3   **Prerequisites of Learning for Five Kinds of Learning Outcome, with Examples**

Type of Learning Outcome	Example	Prerequisites
Intellectual Skill	Finding the hypotenuse of a right triangle	Subordinate intellectual skills: rules for squares and square roots, concepts of right angle, adjacent sides, etc.
Cognitive Strategy	Originating a novel set of categories for non-fiction books	Rules for classifying and constructing superordinate categories
Information	Stating "Ontogeny recapitulates phylogeny"	Syntactic rules of Subject-Verb-Object relations, and rules for transforming these relations; previously organized information (knowledge)
Motor Skill	Punting a football	Part-skills of holding ball, dropping ball, aiming kick; executive routine for total action
Attitude	Choosing "careful" actions in automobile approach to stop-lights	Rules pertaining to customary stop-light operation; information about traffic situations in which stop-lights occur

which in turn are subordinate to these. In general, the analysis is conducted by asking the following question about each skill: "What [skill] should the learner already know how to do and be able to recall, when faced with the task of learning the new rule; the absence of which would make it impossible for him to learn the new rule?" (cf. Gagné, 1968c).

By means of such an analysis, successively carried out for each intellectual skill and for its subordinates, a learning hierarchy is defined. It is clear, however, that the prerequisites so derived are only *minimal essentials* for learning any new intellectual skill.

A learning hierarchy represents only the prerequisites which must be available to the learner because they are to be incorporated in the newly learned skill. The previously learned entities which simply *support* the new learning are not represented. There are, of course, a number of possible supports which may be available to the learner—previously learned information, for example, or previously learned cognitive strategies. A considerably more complex

diagram would be needed to represent successive learning prerequisites in this broader meaning of the term.

An additional example of a learning hierarchy, applicable to
a basic skill to be learned by preschool children, is shown in Figure
11.4 (Resnick, 1967). The "target" task to be learned by the children
is that of demonstrating the division of a set of objects into halves,
and also into thirds. Notice that the child must put together two
subordinate skills in order to achieve this complex rule. One is the
concrete concept of identifying a "half" (made by two equal subsets), or alternatively a "third" (made by three equal subsets). The
second subordinate skill is the *rule* which enables the child to demonstrate equality of the subsets (by showing a one-to-one correspondence of members of the subset). When these two prerequisite
skills are combined, they are incorporated into the newly learned
target skill of demonstrating the division of a total set into halves,
or thirds. When the prerequisites are themselves analyzed, they too

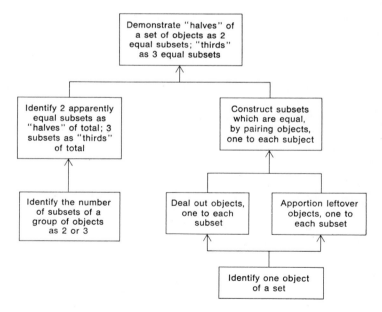

FIGURE 11.4   A learning hierarchy for a prekindergarten mathematical
skill. (Suggested by the work of Resnick, L. B. *Design of an
early learning curriculum.* Working Paper No. 16. Pittsburgh,
Pa.: University of Pittsburgh, Learning Research and Development Center, 1967.)

are found to be composed of other prerequisite concepts or rules.

This example serves to illustrate the specific meaning of prerequisite reflected in learning hierarchies. Obviously, these prerequisites are intended to represent only the essential previously learned skills that the child *must* be able to recall in undertaking the learning of a new intellectual skill. They do not include other kinds of previously learned entities (information, strategies) which may support the learning as *internal* conditions. Nor do they make any mention of the *external* conditions (those arranged by the teacher) which are also brought to bear in support of the new learning.

The validity of prerequisites revealed by this kind of analysis can, of course, be tested empirically, and has been tested for different kinds of target skills (see Gagné and Briggs, 1974; R. T. White, 1973; R. T. White and Gagné, 1974). When such prerequisites are identified, they become one of the important elements in the design of instruction, particularly with reference to *instructional sequence* (Gagné and Briggs, 1974) for the learning of intellectual skills. Learning hierarchies, however, do not appear to be an appropriate way of diagramming prerequisites for other kinds of learned capabilities, as Table 11.3 indicates. Modified versions of them, however, have been tried with this purpose in mind (Cook and Walbesser, 1973).

THE USES OF LEARNING ANALYSES.   When a learning analysis is completed, the information derived (as suggested by the final column of the table) may be used for the planning of conditions for learning; that is, for the *design of instruction*. Depending on other factors in the situation, two alternatives are available to the designer. One way of using prerequisites in planning is to select learners who have acquired the necessary capabilities through prior learning, and proceed with the design of learning conditions on that assumption. This method is sometimes used in vocational or industrial training programs. For public education, however, a second alternative is usually followed: the conditions of instruction are planned so that students who have not acquired the prerequisites may learn them before undertaking the "new" learning. Essential to optimal effectiveness for the latter method is careful identification of prerequisite learning for each student, or for groups of students having common capabilities. Various educational arrangements, including "homogeneous grouping" and programs called "compensatory" or "remedial," may be used to accomplish this purpose. In programs of *individualized instruction*, the progress of each individual student is assessed, and is made dependent upon the learning of necessary prerequisites (Gagné and Briggs, 1974).

DERIVING EXTERNAL CONDITIONS FOR LEARNING

Analysis of human tasks to reveal the prerequisites of learning yields a large portion of the information needed for design of optimal learning conditions. The other major part, the external conditions, is also implied by the classification of human tasks in terms of the categories of learning outcomes to which they belong. Previous chapters have been devoted to discussions of the ways in which external events can be used to *activate* and *support* internal processes of learning. Chapter 3 specifically relates the external events of a learning occasion to the internal processes of selective perception, coding, retrieval, and response organization.

Some of the external conditions for effective learning are common to all kinds of expected learning outcomes. External provisions made to stimulate the learner's *alertness*, or *attention*, for example, may be very similar regardless of the capability being learned. Likewise, whatever *performance* is associated with the learned capability—whether a motor act, a verbal statement, or the application of a rule—must be elicited as one essential event in learning. Some external conditions, however, are *specific* to the nature of what is being learned, and differ with the learning outcome expected. For example, the kind of event which supports the encoding process for a motor skill is quite different from that which facilitates the learning of verbal information. As we have seen in previous chapters, the encoding of a motor skill is critically affected by stimulation arising in the muscles, and resulting from performance of muscular movement. In contrast, encoding verbal information does not depend upon the act of "stating," but is affected by the contextual meaning to which it can be related.

Differential External Conditions for Learning

In summary fashion, it will now be possible to take a look at the external conditions of learning that differ from each other depending upon the outcome expected. We shall describe what appear to be critical conditions for each category of learned capability, in terms of the kind of instructional event which these conditions represent.

STIMULATING RECALL OF PREREQUISITES.   The condition of stimulating recall of prerequisites is common to all kinds of learning outcomes. As we have seen in Chapter 3, stimuli for recall have the purpose of activating retrieval of previously learned entities to the working (short-term) memory, so that they can be incorporated into the new learning. However, the nature of *what* must be retrieved obviously differs among learning outcomes. The basic requirements are described in Table 11.3.

It should be noted also that other kinds of previously learned material may support learning differentially, depending upon what the learner has in store. For example, the "larger meaningful context" for (new) information learning often comes mainly from the store of organized (old) information in the learner's memory. Different degrees of learning support can be expected from this organized knowledge, depending upon its amount, its degree of organization, and its relevance to the new learning. Likewise, the nature of previously stored information available to the learner may be expected to affect the ease of learning intellectual skills, and to facilitate the processes of problem solving and thinking.

PROVIDING LEARNING GUIDANCE (ENCODING).   External conditions exhibit critical differences for different learning outcomes when they pertain to the guidance provided to support the encoding process. A summary of these conditions is presented in Table 11.4. Despite a number of other features common to the learning situation (such as presentation of the stimulus, eliciting learner per-

TABLE 11.4   External Conditions Which Support Encoding Processes for Five Kinds of Learning Outcome

Learning Outcome	External Conditions
Intellectual Skill	Verbal or symbolic statement of rule or concept
	Demonstration of application of rule or concept
Cognitive Strategy (Problem Solving)	Periodic presentation of novel problem situations
Information	Presentation within a larger meaningful context
Motor Skill	Practice of total skill
Attitude	Experience of success
	Observation of human model

formance, providing reinforcement), it is evident that the conditions of learning which relate to the encoding process are indeed very different. These critical differences in encoding, in fact, most clearly distinguish the five kinds of learned capabilities and argue against the idea that "all learning is the same."

ENHANCING RETENTION AND TRANSFER.   The internal process supported by these external conditions is *retrieval*. This process is activated by external *cues*, and the more that can be provided, the better. Thus the condition that best supports retrieval of what is learned is a variety of external cues. In practice, this means that besides the essential stimuli for learning, the surrounding context of stimulation helps retrieval by providing additional cues. Since recall, and also transfer of learning, take place in situations different from that of original learning, *variety* of contextual cues raises the probability of effective performance in these new situations.

For intellectual skills, variety is provided by requiring the learner to apply a newly learned rule or definition to several kinds of examples. For cognitive strategies, problems varying in their content are used to enhance retention and transfer. Motor skills may be practiced in a variety of surrounding conditions, including noise and distractions, to aid their transfer to situations in which they will be used.

Variety in the cueing function can also be provided by requiring the learner to reinstate the learned capability at various times following initial learning. This is done in the technique of *spaced review*. Even a "next-day" recall and review of a learned rule or concept, for example, may greatly enhance its retention over longer periods. By reviewing after a period of time, the learner must utilize new cues not present at the time of original learning. Thus the variety of cues for retrieval is increased by such reviews. Deliberate introduction of varied contextual cues during review likewise serves to enhance the transferability of what is learned.

Learning Conditions and Instructional Design

In the manner indicated in the previous section, learning analysis leads to the identification of external conditions which are critically related to the attainment of different types of human capabilities. These conditions can be incorporated into the planning and *design* of instruction intended to bring about any of these learning outcomes. Techniques for accomplishing instructional design, based upon these principles, have been described by Gagné and Briggs (1974). A similar account, abbreviated in scope, is contained in the following chapter. There we shall show how instruction having various purposes can be designed for optimal effectiveness by using knowledge of learning conditions, internal and external.

EDUCATIONAL IMPLICATIONS

Programs of education are typically designed or selected with certain broad goals in mind. Sometimes these goals are specifically formulated, sometimes not. Their further analysis is always necessary if one wishes to answer the question, What is required of human learning in attaining these goals? The purpose of analysis is to make possible the detailed specification of what must be learned, in other words, the human tasks that the learner will be able to accomplish when he has completed a period of learning.

Several degrees of specificity are possible in the description of human tasks. This state of affairs is not inherently deplorable, for task descriptions serve many different purposes. For educational planning to be based on sound learning principles, description must begin with a fairly specific level of detail for human performance, sometimes called the *job-task*. A job-task is the kind one might reasonably ask another person to do as a single act, as a part of a larger human undertaking (such as a job). Examples of job-tasks are "typing a letter," "writing a descriptive report," "constructing an alphabetical file." Acts too specific to be so classified are "striking an e on the typewriter," "stating a sentence," "finding a folder labeled *M*."

The human task at this level of description is equally meaningful when *life task* is substituted for job-task. Such a substitution makes the concept applicable to human activities which are not solely vocationally oriented. Reading the newspaper, feeding the baby, watching a football game, are examples of life tasks which are described at a level of specificity comparable to the tasks that comprise a job. They are human tasks that one expects other human beings (depending on their ages) to do, and to be able to do. Specific goals of educational programs are often expressed at the level of specificity of life tasks (Gagné, 1975).

Beginning at this point, it is possible to proceed with analyses having the purpose of designing educational programs which take account of the conditions for learning. Job-tasks or life tasks usually involve *procedures*, in which one human action (or step) precedes another. Some procedures are quite short, others are quite long. Procedures may involve fixed sequences of steps, or more often, steps contingent upon the outcomes of previous steps. Analysis which identifies individual human actions, their dependencies, and their sequence, is a desirable, and often essential, first step in the specification of the required outcomes of learning. Whether the human task to be accomplished is long division or parallel parking an automobile, the delineation of its "steps" and their sequence provides the initial revelation of what must be learned. Usually, this turns out to be two things: (1) the procedure itself, or more specifically, the *executive routine* that enables the learner to perform the procedure; and (2) the component steps of the task (which are sometimes called *subtasks*).

In contrast to the analysis of human tasks into procedural steps, a *learning analysis* seeks to identify the *prerequisites* for the learning of the total task and any of its subtasks which are not already well established. This kind of analysis asks of each component of the total task, What must the learner have acquired by previous learning, and be able to recall, when the new learning is undertaken? Some prerequisites are merely *supportive* of the new learning. The learner may be able to use certain previously learned cognitive strategies to advantage, or may be able to recall a useful set of organized information. Other prerequisites, however, are *essential*, in that they actually become incorporated into the newly learned capability. Clearest examples of these are intellectual skills; the learning of a complex rule involves the combining of simpler rules or concepts. When successively applied to prerequisites of intellectual skills and their subordinate skills, learning analysis results in a description called a *learning hierarchy*.

Learning hierarchies indicate the essential prerequisites for the learning of new rules and concepts, and may for this reason be useful in the planning of sequences of instruction. Several precautions, however, should be noted. First, rational methods have not been devised to develop learning hierarchies for the four other kinds of learning outcomes (for example, information, motor skills); nor have valid hierarchies been demonstrated in these areas of human capability. Thus, methods of describing and diagramming *essential* prerequisites for these other capabilities, if feasible, have yet to be developed. Second, learning hierarchies for intellectual skills are intended to indicate *only* essential subskills; they do not depict supportive prerequisites such as information, attitudes, cognitive strategies. For this reason, they do not contain all the information needed for the planning of instructional sequence.

One of the important results of a learning analysis, then, is the identification of prerequisites not only for intellectual skills, but for all five kinds of learning outcomes. Prerequisites are kinds of learning outcomes that an "entering" learner is expected to possess as a result of prior learning. Once these are identified, the planning of instruction may proceed in one of two ways. An instructional program may be designed for learners who are *selected* to have the essential (and supportive) prerequisite capabilities. Alternatively, the program may be designed to teach the prerequisites in a sequential fashion before teaching of the "target" capabilities is attempted. In practice, all educational programs incorporate some combination of these two alternatives.

A second result of learning analysis is the identification of critical *external* conditions for the learning of different kinds of human capabilities. In particular, the classification of the type of capability to be learned makes it possible to specify the external events which are *differentially effective* for each kind of learning outcome. In this way, the conditions of learning described in previous chapters can be applied to the design of programs of instruction on any topic.

GENERAL REFERENCES

EDUCATIONAL GOALS

Commission on the Reorganization of Secondary Education. *Cardinal principles of secondary education.* Department of the Interior, Bureau of Education. Bulletin No. 35. Washington, D.C.: GPO, 1918.

Gagné, R. M. Taxonomic problems of educational systems. In W. T. Singleton and P. Spurgeon (Eds.), *Measurement of human resources.* London: Taylor and Francis, 1975.

Gardner, J. W. National goals in education. In *Goals for Americans: The Report of the President's Commission on National Goals.* Englewood Cliffs, N.J.: Prentice-Hall, 1960.

Popham, W. J., and Baker, E. L. *Establishing instructional goals.* Englewood Cliffs, N.J.: Prentice-Hall, 1970.

Tyler, R. W. *Basic principles of curriculum and instruction.* Chicago: University of Chicago Press, 1949.

TASK DESCRIPTION AND ANALYSIS

Miller, R. B. Task description and analysis. In R. M. Gagné (Ed.), *Psychological principles in system development.* New York: Holt, Rinehart and Winston, 1963.

LEARNING ANALYSIS

Briggs, L. J. *Handbook of procedures for the design of instruction.* Monograph No. 4. Pittsburgh, Pa.: American Institutes for Research, 1970.

Gagné, R. M., and Briggs, L. J. *Principles of instructional design.* New York: Holt, Rinehart and Winston, 1974.

Mechner, F. Behavioral analysis and instructional sequencing. In P. C. Lange (Ed.), *Programmed instruction.* Sixty-sixth Yearbook, Part II. Chicago: National Society for the Study of Education, 1967.

12

DESIGNING INSTRUCTION FOR LEARNING

Knowledge of the learning process combined with the analysis of tasks for learning finds a direct application to the *design of instruction*. In this chapter, we take the viewpoint of an instructional designer, who may be a teacher, a curriculum planner, or a writer of instructional texts or other materials. This is, of course, a different viewpoint from that of a person who is examining the process of learning in order to understand it. The reader will need to keep in mind this shift in orientation. We shall, of course, need to mention many of the conditions of learning that have been described in previous chapters, in order to put them into a framework of application.

The analysis of human tasks, as described in Chapter 11, makes possible their classification into types of capabilities to be learned. These classes, in turn, imply different conditions for effective learning which depend not only on the specific content of what is to be learned, but upon differential characteristics of the categories of learning outcomes. We have seen that optimal conditions differ particularly in relation to the *prerequisites* required for learning the different types, and also in relation to the provisions made for the activation and support of *encoding* processes. Other conditions may provide differential amounts of support for learning, depending on the nature of the stored memories of the learner.

The results of learning analyses provide essential information for the design of instruction relevant to any and all kinds of expected learning outcomes. In this chapter, we intend to examine how such results can be practically applied to instructional design. To do this systematically, we shall need to recall the events of learning derived from the information-processing model described in Chapter 3. We intend to describe how instruction can be planned for each of the *events of learning*, so as to make them of optimal effectiveness for the total act of learning. In doing this, we shall be dealing with the external conditions (such as attention, motivation, reinforcement) generally applicable to all learning outcomes, as well as with the conditions that must be different for each variety of outcome.

PLANNING FOR PHASES OF LEARNING

The model of learning and memory described in Chapter 3 involves different phases of learning, which roughly correspond to the input-output transformations of each of the model's structures. Thus a very brief phase of learning, occurring early in the entire process, is the *selective perception* that transforms the output of the sensory register to the input of the short-term memory. *Encoding* for storage in the long-term memory is a succeeding phase, and *storage* is still another. Relations between the phases of learning implied by the model, and the *events of instruction* implied by them, is shown in Figure 12.1. The right-hand column of the figure indicates the instructional events that must be designed in order to provide support for internal processes, during each phase of learning.

The kinds of instructional events listed in the right-hand column of Figure 12.1 can perhaps best be understood with the help of an example. Suppose that what is to be learned is an intellectual

LEARNING PHASE   INSTRUCTIONAL EVENTS

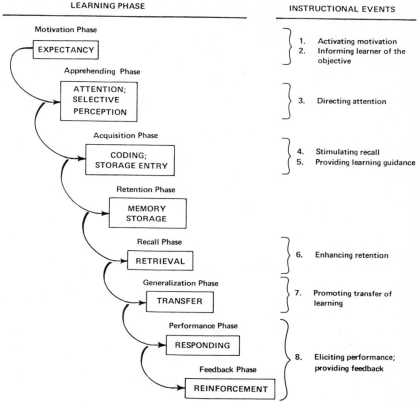

Motivation Phase
EXPECTANCY   1. Activating motivation
                                       2. Informing learner of the
                                           objective
Apprehending Phase
ATTENTION;
SELECTIVE   3. Directing attention
PERCEPTION

Acquisition Phase
CODING;   4. Stimulating recall
STORAGE ENTRY   5. Providing learning guidance

Retention Phase
MEMORY
STORAGE

Recall Phase
RETRIEVAL   6. Enhancing retention

Generalization Phase
TRANSFER   7. Promoting transfer of
                                          learning

Performance Phase
RESPONDING

Feedback Phase   8. Eliciting performance;
                                          providing feedback
REINFORCEMENT

FIGURE 12.1   Relations between phases of learning and events of instruction. The latter events represent the functions performed by
instruction which support internal learning processes.

skill described by the rule "In a written sentence, a singular indefinite pronoun ('any,' 'each,' 'someone,' etc.) as subject requires a singular verb." As the figure indicates, an *expectancy* first needs to be
established by activating the learners' motivation and informing them
of the objective (performance) to be achieved by the learning. This
may be done by telling the learners of the personal advantages of
correct, as opposed to incorrect, writing. Further, the teacher would
probably indicate what kind of sentence "sounds right" (such as
the sentence "Someone has to go") and what "sounds wrong" (such
as "Someone have to go"). Next, events need to be planned for
arousing *attention*, and directing it so as to accomplish *selective
perception*. In terms of the example, attention must be drawn to the

indefinite pronoun as a subject, and to the verb which follows it. Several sentences with these parts printed in bold type, and with other nondistracting parts, might be employed.

The process of *encoding* calls upon external events which stimulate the recall of prerequisites. In the example employed here, what this amounts to is reminding the learner of the previously learned concepts *subject, verb, pronoun,* and *singular.* The next step in encoding suggests one or more schemes to the learner; these schemes should preferably add distinctiveness to the concepts being learned. Each indefinite pronoun, for example, might be contrasted with a plural noun or pronoun, as "each" may be contrasted with "all," and "something" with "some things". *Retrieval* is facilitated by events which provide cues for the enhancement of recall; and *transfer of learning* by contextual variety in external stimulation. Typically, such events take the form of a variety of examples, using a number of different sentences for each of the indefinite pronouns to which the rule applies.

The remainder of instructional events appear straightforward. The learners must *respond* with the performance that reflects their newly learned capability. In practice, learners are given several sentences containing indefinite pronouns, and asked to supply the missing verb. Alternatively, they may be given sentences containing indefinite pronoun subjects, some correct and some incorrect, and asked to make them all correct in agreement of subject and verb. Following such an exercise, corrective feedback is given to provide *reinforcement* to the learners.

This example serves to make the point that properly designed instruction does not necessarily have to be unconventional. On the contrary, what is done in instruction is probably what any good teacher has learned to do. However, a teacher or instructional designer who is intent on "adequate coverage" of the subject may easily lose sight of one or more of the events that support learning processes. This is particularly true of the events which pertain to coding, storage, and retrieval (the external conditions of learning) as they have been described in preceding chapters. The reasons for careful design of these events of instruction can now be seen to be clearly related to the internal processes of learning and memory, as identified by information-processing theories of learning.

A Broad View of Instructional Events

By referring again to the structures and processes of learning described in Chapter 3, we will now present a broad view of the influences of external events on learning. We have described the conditions of learning that are distinctive for each general class of learning outcome. We now ask the question, What are *all* the circumstances that must be considered as composing what is called "instruction"? The answer is a more inclusive one than is suggested by the individual chapters.

The following sections of this chapter take the point of view of a designer who is engaged in planning instruction for an educational enterprise—a program of training for a vocation, a school program, or perhaps an adult education program. In a comprehensive sense, what must such a designer plan, and what general specifications can be given for the arrangement of instructional events? The plan for instruction, perhaps not surprisingly, begins with the problem of motivating the learner.

MOTIVATION

The motivation of human behavior is a large and complex subject, of which only a small portion can be treated here. Of course it is of great interest to try to know what varieties of motives exist, how they originate and develop within the individual, and how they determine the "force" and direction of human behavior. Psychologists continue to study these matters intensively. Many investigations of motivation have been and are being made, and there are many books on the topic (Cofer and Appley, 1964; Hall, 1961; McClelland, Atkinson, Clark, and Lowell, 1953).

Given the fact of multiple kinds and sources of motivation, the task of the instructional designer is one of *identifying* the motives of students, and of *channeling* them into activities that accomplish educational goals. Three ways of viewing the approach of harnessing existing motivation are described as incentive motivation, task motivation, and achievement motivation.

Incentive Motivation

Essentially, the use of incentives to change the directions of motivated behavior is a matter of employing *reinforcement contingencies* wisely (Skinner, 1968, pp. 160–168). In the elementary grades, for example, the young child may receive reinforcement for *social* activities: working with other children and relating appropriately to the teacher become essential for effective learning. The child comes to be motivated by a desire to gain the approval of others, to avoid their disapproval, and to establish a position of social esteem among peers (cf. Hewett, 1968). Beyond this, there is the acquisition of motivation for *mastery,* involving the learning of intellectual skills that enable the child to function independently. Reinforcement for such learning is provided by accuracy and completeness of accomplishment of tasks the child undertakes. Higher in a developmental sequence is motivation for *achievement.* This calls for the development of true self-motivation, in which the successful mastery of more and more difficult tasks becomes a source of self-satisfaction and generates a desire for greater improvement. When students attain this level of functioning, they possess the motivation required to become true "self-learners."

Practical motivational programs utilizing incentive motivation have been described by Bereiter and Engelmann (1966, pp. 81–91) and by Mager (1968), among others. Rather than waiting until exactly the correct response is made, emphasis is on the reinforcement of behavior that initially approximates the desired behavior. Providing students with information that enable them to judge their own success and failure is another suggestion commonly put forth. And finally, the idea of proceeding in steps, or "stages," from very concrete rewards to those that require a sense of satisfaction derived from self-imposed standards is frequently recommended. None of these techniques, of course, provides a magic key to the insurance of student interest in learning. However, if they are understood as contributing to the establishment of states of expectancy themselves acquired according to principles of reinforcement contingencies, these techniques can be of great value in establishing the necessary preconditions for school learning.

Task Motivation

Although motives of a social nature, sometimes called *affiliative needs,* are a part of the individual's makeup, some writers consider them of less importance to programs of instruction than the motivation of *task mastery and achievement.* Ausubel (1968, pp. 363–433) has reviewed the evidence concerning various forms of social motivation, and points out that these do not always constitute a dependable basis for learning readiness. In contrast, he believes the advantages of achievement motivation for learning lie, first, in the fact that such motives are intrinsic to the task, and hence the reward (the attainment of new knowledge or skill) is capable of wholly satisfying the underlying motive. Second, achievement is ego-enhancing, because the status achieved by individuals is in proportion to their achievement or competence level, affecting directly their self-esteem and feelings of adequacy.

This view of motivation also emphasizes the power of intrinsic and positive motives, including curiosity and exploration, as well as mastery. Such "cognitive" motives may be the most important kind of motivation in school learning. Consideration of their potential effects leads Ausubel (1968) to make the following statement:

> The causal relationship between motivation and learning is typically reciprocal rather than unidirectional. Both for this reason, and because motivation is not an indispensable condition of learning, it is unnecessary to postpone learning activities until appropriate interests and motivations have been developed. Frequently, the best way of teaching an unmotivated student is to ignore his motivational state for the time being, and to concentrate on teaching him as effectively as possible. Some degree of learning will ensue in any case, despite the lack of motivation; and from the initial satisfaction of learning he will, hopefully, develop the motivation to learn more. In some circumstances, therefore, the most appropriate way of arousing motivation to learn is to focus on the cognitive rather than on the motivational aspects of learning, and to rely on the motivation that is developed from successful educational achievement to energize further learning (pp. 365–366).

It is interesting to note that despite great differences from Ausubel in his theoretical point of view toward school learning, Skinner (1968, pp. 145–168) holds an essentially similar view about the importance of motivation intrinsic to the performance of the task. Skinner states that the problem of motivation for the schools is not a matter of imparting motivation, but of arranging conditions for study and learning so that they will be reinforcing. The teacher must often invent and use "contrived proximate reinforcers," to aid not only in the imparting of knowledge but also in getting the student to acquire diligent behavior of the learning-readiness variety ("precurrent management behaviors").

ACHIEVEMENT MOTIVATION. Motivation to achieve is carried far beyond the idea of "task mastery" by some theorists. These writers propose that individuals may acquire, to a greater or lesser degree, a persisting trait of striving to achieve that provides motivation for a great many of their activities, including those pertaining to school learning.

McClelland (1965) describes twelve propositions, derived from a variety of sources, that have been employed in studies designed to heighten the achievement motivation of groups of business people, and more recently, groups of disadvantaged students. It is McClelland's view that a combination of techniques—including those leading to clear definition of individual goals, perception of self-improvement, an increasing trend toward the assumption of responsibility for one's performance, and a supportive social environment—can lead to the acquisition of persisting motivation for achievement. It appears a distinct possibility that beneficial effects may be obtained by a program designed to increase this "general" form of achievement motivation in certain categories of students, for example, high school dropouts.

Another theory about achievement as a general motivational state is that of R. W. White (1959), who describes the concept of *competence*. In White's view, competence motivation has a broadly based biological origin, related to such sources as exploration, activity, and manipulation, as they have been studied in animal behavior. Many investigators of motivation have expressed the need to identify a similar source of positive motivation, variously termed *mastery, ego-development, a sense of industry*, and *dealing with the environment*. White maintains that many human activities must be explained not through the operation of need satisfactions (e.g., hunger, thirst, sex), but through the persistence of activities that constitute effective interaction with the environment, and that are accompanied by a "feeling of efficacy." In other words, human individuals have a need to master their environment, in some small or large way, throughout their lives.

Competence motivation can obviously be put to use in the educational process. According to this conception, when the situation is properly arranged for learning, mastering the problem of multiplying two-place numbers or of constructing passive forms of sentences or of producing a white precipitate from a mixture of chemical solutions will provide a rewarding experience to the learner. The problem is not primarily one of "acquiring" new motivation, according to this view. Rather, it is one of cleverly arranging situations for learning in such a way that competence will be displayed and the feeling of efficacy experienced.

It can be seen from this discussion that several possible ways have been proposed to account for the operation of motivation that is either intrinsic, or closely related, to performance resulting from learning. Despite differences in language, these approaches have practical implications that are very similar: the learners can be rewarded, and their subsequent learning can be enhanced, by the accomplishment of learning tasks within their capabilities. Achievement, successful interaction within the learning environment, and mastery of the objectives of an educational program can themselves lead to persisting satisfaction on the part of the learner, and can therefore become a most dependable source of continuing motivation. Even beyond this, evidence reported by Kifer (1975) strongly suggests that continued success in achievement over several years of schooling leads to the establishment of positive self-concepts and attitudes of self-esteem that become stable aspects of the individual's personality.

Informing the Learner of the Objective

If incentive motivation is to be used effectively for instructional design, the learner must be informed of the nature of the achievement expected as an outcome of learning. In terms of the learning model being followed here, the purpose of such a communication to the learner is to establish an expectancy of the performance to be achieved as a result of learning. If the learner is to acquire information about the process of reproduction, for example, such verbal directions as these may be used: "There are several different ways in which living organisms reproduce themselves. What you will be learning is how to describe each of these ways and to give some actual examples of them." Or, if someone is to learn the intellectual skill of adding decimals, instructions may say, "What you will learn is how to add numbers such as 124.27 and 16.743 to obtain the sum 141.013."

The primary effect of providing learners with an expectancy of the learning outcome is to enable them to match their own performances with a class of performance they expect to be "correct." Thus the reinforcement, in the form of informative feedback, confirms the learners' expectancy. For example, the performance expected in adding decimals, learners know, must be an expression that contains a decimal point and otherwise has the general form 141.013. It connot be of the form 141013, nor 141 1/77. Sometimes, the objective of learning is perfectly obvious to the learner, and does not have to be explicitly stated. For this reason, studies that contrast "telling" with "not telling" the objective may fail to indicate an advantage for the former procedure (cf. Duchastel and Merrill, 1973). When there are alternatives to be chosen, however, the effects of informing the learner about the objective can be clearly shown in resulting achievement (Rothkopf and Kaplan, 1972).

Under many circumstances, the clearest directions about expected performance following learning may be those that actually show the learners, before learning begins, what such a performance looks like. Is this "telling the learners the answer"? Obviously, the answer is not really being supplied, because learners are expected to learn a whole class of performances, not just the single one used to illustrate the class. However, if in fact learners can acquire all they are supposed to learn by simply being told about this class (not a rare occurrence), surely this is economical learning! Presumably, keeping learners in the dark in such instances serves no useful function.

DIRECTING ATTENTION

Among the first steps to be taken in designing instruction is making provision for directing attention. It is commonly recognized that there are two kinds of attention, two separate meanings for this term. The first is a general *alerting* function, by means of which the learner's posture and general muscular tone assume a state of readiness to receive stimulation. In addition, she may turn her head, and direct her sense organs so as to be in line with the source of stimulation. Alerting is accomplished by many different means—by sounds, by light changes, and in general by sudden changes in stimulation. Teachers use various techniques—including the introduction of novel stimuli, changes in voice pitch—to bring about alertness on the part of students. In television programs, the sudden changes in pictures produced by rapid "cutting" of successive scenes are used to maintain alertness on the part of student viewers.

The second meaning of attention is *selective perception*. The stimulation delivered to the learner is arranged to give emphasis to the distinctive features of the presentation, that is, to the features to be stored and processed in the *short-term memory*. Again, this function is accomplished in various ways. In a printed text, words and phrases may be underlined, italicized, or printed in bold type. Pictures and diagrams may use heavy outlining, arrows, circled portions, or different colors in order to highlight the features to be selectively perceived. When auditory communications are being employed, the use of meter and rhyme are often effective means of directing attention. Animated techniques in motion pictures and television provide many additional ways of insuring selective perception of the material to be learned.

The designer of instruction needs to be highly aware of the variety of ways that can be employed to give selective emphasis to stimulus presentations for learning. The "information" that is processed in learning is a *selected set* from the total stimulation presented to the learner. Using techniques of highlighting components and features of the communication to the learner—whether verbal, pictorial, auditory, or whatever—can be an important early step in laying the foundation for what is learned.

LEARNING GUIDANCE
FOR ENCODING

The next phase of learning for which instruction may be planned consists of the encoding process which transforms the information into the form in which it is stored in long-term memory. The guidance of learning may present actual schemes for encoding (such as tables, graphs, pictures), or it may simply suggest such schemes. Often, learning guidance consists of verbal communications to the learner, which may be given the general name *verbal directions*. Their function is not "instruction," in a strict sense (since this word is used to apply to the total set of events accompanying learning), but telling the learner what to do at any given time. Directions are not themselves a part of the content to be learned, but have a *mathemagenic* function (Gagné, 1974b; Rothkopf, 1970). Of course, learning guidance *can* be given without verbal directions, as happens when the learner is a young child who does not understand words. Verbal communication is, however, a frequently used mode for most instruction.

As indicated in Figure 12.1, two aspects of learning guidance affect the encoding process. One consists in the stimulation of recall of necessary prerequisites and other supportive material from the learner's long-term memory. The process involved is retrieval from the long-term memory to the working (short-term) memory. The second function for learning guidance is the presentation or suggestion of an encoding scheme, which affects the form in which the newly learned material will be stored in the long-term memory.

Stimulating Recall of Relevant
Prerequisites

If a new intellectual skill is being learned, subordinate skills must be retrieved so that they can be re-coded as parts of the new skill. If verbal information is being learned, previously learned organized knowledge may need to be retrieved, to become a part of the larger meaningful context for the newly acquired information. The various prerequisites that must be recalled for the five different types of learning outcome have been described in the previous chapter (see Table 11.3).

Two different kinds of verbal directions can be used to induce retrieval of previously learned entities, and each may be preferable in particular instances. When a relatively simple concept definition is being learned, it may be sufficient for directions to stimulate *recognition* of what has previously been learned. For example, in connection with the learning of a definition for "sodium," the directions might say, "You remember what sodium looks like; you also remember what a metal is." When more complex rules are being acquired, it may be desirable for directions to require *recall* (reinstatement) of the subordinate intellectual skills. Thus, if the learner is acquiring a rule about the hypotenuse of a right triangle, it may be desirable to require the *recall* of subordinate rules by saying, "Draw a right triangle," and asking "Which sides enclose the right angle?" The learning of the new rule can then proceed satisfactorily with the assurance that the necessary subordinate concepts are accessible in the working memory.

Guidance for Encoding

Guidance for the encoding of material to be stored in long-term memory may take a number of forms, depending to a large extent on the learning outcome expected. The essential functions to be performed by such learning guidance have been summarized in the previous chapter, and specifically in Table 11.4 (Gagné and Briggs, 1974).

SUGGESTING SCHEMES FOR ENCODING. The learning of procedures is often accompanied by a form of learning guidance called *prompting*. For example, if a child is learning to spell words having the common suffix "—ate," the suffix may be initially suggested by the stimulus "a_e," as in the word "infla_e." Subsequently, the cues may be reduced ("faded") as in the word "summa___," and finally eliminated for the word "dict___." This example illustrates a form of learning guidance that uses extra cues —cues which are eliminated in a step-by-step fashion.

Verbal directions are often employed in learning guidance to *suggest*, rather than to specify, the form of encoding to be used by the learner. When this is done, instruction is said to be using the technique of *guided discovery*. Many rules are learned by providing verbal cueing. For example, one can make the verbal statement, "Current flows in the direction of higher to lower electric potential." In contrast, when discovery of an encoding scheme is being suggested to the learner, a statement such as the following may be made: "Remember that a given point in a circuit may have a greater potential than another point. In which direction would you expect current to flow?" The first of these statements is designed to stimulate retrieval. The second is a question asking the student to *discover* the rule governing the flow of electric current. It is an example, then, of a verbal instruction of *guiding* discovery.

Directions that guide the learner's discovery of encoding schemes are very often in the form of questions. Of course, more than one question may be needed, in contrast to the rather simple example just given. In general, questions used for this purpose do not include all the language needed in the "answer," but are designed to suggest the answer required. Guidance provided by this kind of verbal communication is a method familiar to every teacher. It has been found to be effective in experimental studies of rule learning (Gagné and Brown, 1961; Gagné, Mayor, Garstens, and Paradise, 1962), although the question of how much or how little guidance is most effective has not yet received a satisfactory answer. Presumably, the effect of such verbal questioning is to channel the thinking of the learner away from the extreme incorrect hypotheses that would otherwise be tried. The effect of such guidance may be, therefore, to speed up the learning, since the learner does not waste time on discovered rules that are wildly wrong. Questions are also effective in suggesting encoding schemes for information learning, as the work of Rothkopf (1970) and Frase (1970) suggests.

CODING IN TERMS OF IMAGES.   The process of encoding may utilize images, as well as words and propositions. Diagrams and graphs, for example, may be presented to the learner to represent rules and definitions, procedures, or collections of information. Many learning theorists who operate within the information-processing model are inclined to favor a *dual-process* model of long-term memory, which acknowledges the possibilities of encoding in terms of both verbal propositions and images (J. R. Anderson and Bower, 1973; Paivio, 1971). Pictures and diagrams may be used in instruction to provide concrete visual images to serve an encoding function. Alternatively, the use of images as coding schemes can simply be suggested to learners, who then form their own.

The use of pictures in instruction serves the important function of support for the encoding process. Pictures are used in still or moving forms in various instructional media, which will be further discussed in a later portion of this chapter.

ENHANCING RETENTION AND
TRANSFER OF LEARNING

Instructional design provides for retention of what is learned, and for transfer of the learning to new situations. Various techniques may be employed to insure that *cues for retrieval* are available to the learner. The organization of material to be learned into categories or in the form of tables, graphs, and diagrams provides a source of cues that serve to enhance later retention. Such cues may be a part of what is initially learned, as when lists of words are categorized and later retrieved with the cues of their category names (Tulving and Osler, 1968). Cues may also have their origin in previously learned associations (Bahrick, 1970) or in the organized cognitive structures which Ausubel (1968) describes. The employment of pictures and diagrams in presentations for learning often constitutes an effective part of instructional design for the provision of cues to be used by the learner in recall.

Cues which favor transfer of learning to new tasks and new situations are taken into account in instructional design by providing a *variety* of features of the learning task, as well as a variety of contexts in which the learning occurs. The more broadly based a learned capability, the better chance it will have to transfer to new and different situations. Accordingly, the usefulness of any learned capability will be increased if it is practiced in as wide a variety of situations as possible. The learning of the intellectual skill of finding the cosine of an angle, for example, has a greater probability of being transferable if it is practiced in situations that are widely different from each other. The transferability of foreign words and phrases will be increased if they are practiced in a wide variety of contexts. The transferability of the scientific skill of "formulating operational definitions" will be increased if the skill is practiced in connection with a wide variety of natural phenomena. The implication for instructional design is quite clear: provision needs to be made for encouraging the learner to apply the learning in as great a variety of new situations as can be devised.

LEARNER PERFORMANCE
AND FEEDBACK

Instruction designed to achieve a learning objective begins with the establishment of a state of expectancy in the learner. Each single act of learning, having involved a number of intervening processes, is completed when the performance of the learner is followed by a *reinforcing event.* In theory, such an event provides learners with information concerning the correctness, and often with the *degree* of correctness, of their performances.

The Learner's Performance

The elicitation of the performance which reflects the newly learned capability seems a reasonably natural event. The learner who has acquired the motor skill of tracing a figure eight on ice skates exhibits this performance readily. If the student of algebra has learned to transform terms from one side of an equation to another, provision is made for him to demonstrate the skill by application to a new example. The principle of requiring a performance, in one or more instances, is equally applicable to other kinds of learning outcomes—cognitive strategies, attitudes, and information learning. The situations for eliciting performance may not be quite so clear-cut for these latter capabilities, but the importance of provisions for the relevant performing is not diminished. Performances to exhibit what has been learned provide evidence to an instructor, and to the learner, that learning has attained its objective.

Besides the exhibition of a performance in one or two instances following learning, performance of the learner may be appraised in a more formal way by means of a test. Usually, a test is designed to appraise the learning of several instructional objectives over an extended period. It therefore gives an indication of the retention of what has been learned, as well as the immediate outcome of instruction. Techniques of assessment by means of tests have been thoroughly described in such volumes as Bloom, Hastings, and Madaus (1971) and Popham (1975). It may be noted here that while tests have several important functions in programs of instruction, they are not substitutes for the elicitation of performance which occurs as an end-point in the learning act. The immediate performance of the learner can best be observed by an instructor, or by the learner himself, on an occasion which permits the natural and smooth completion of a sequence of learning processes.

Feedback

Closely associated with the elicitation of a performance that exhibits the new learning is the provision of feedback to the learner. In the most typical instance, the learner exhibits a performance that reflects the newly learned capability and then is "told" whether he is right or wrong. However, this does not mean that the words *right, wrong, correct, incorrect* have to be used. In the classroom, a correct performance may be indicated by the teacher's going on to the next point in the lesson. Many other subtle cues may be employed—a nod, a smile, a glance. There is no need to specify all the possibilities. Presumably, the learner must have previously learned that these events signify a correct performance. This can be assumed under most circumstances, since such knowledge is probably learned quite early in life. For some learning outcomes, such as motor skills and cognitive strategies, feedback must convey the *degree* to which the learner's performance approaches some standard.

The usefulness of frequent feedback during the acquisition of newly learned capabilities should not be overlooked. This is particularly the case when sequences or interrelated sets of components are being learned (for example, procedures, information in connected discourse). The designers of programmed instruction frequently emphasize the importance of confirming responses for each "frame" of the program (Skinner, 1968). Many instructional programs are composed of single sentences containing blanks to be filled by the learner and a printed answer that may then be checked against the filled-in response. When entire topics are being learned, feedback for the correct accomplishment of each subtopic can be of considerable value in increasing the efficiency of learning. The use of feedback in the form of "correction procedures" is a way of adapting instruction to the needs of the individual student. Several procedures having this purpose are discussed by R. C. Anderson and Faust (1974).

Feedback need not always come from the external situation, but may arise from concepts or rules previously acquired and recalled by the learner. There are many instances in which learners know they are right because of an internal check that they can apply to their own performances. For example, in completing the chemical equation the compounds on the right are (let it be as-

$$HCL + NaOH \rightarrow H_2O + NaCl$$

sumed) familiar ones, with previously learned chemical compositions. Furthermore, the number of atoms of each element in the equation is the same on the right as on the left. Thus a learner who discovered how to complete this equation would be pretty confident of its correctness without being told. Of course, she might like further verification at a later time. But she would be able to use recalled rules in supplying her own reinforcement immediately after completing the performance.

THE PROCEDURES OF INSTRUCTION

The instructional process as a whole may be thought of as a set of procedures designed to support learning in each of the phases just described. Once the learning task has been analyzed and classified (as described in Chapter 11), planning instruction becomes a matter of arranging the external situation for optimal support of each learning phase, beginning with the establishment of motivation and a specific expectancy, and ending with feedback for the learner's performance. The order in which these instructional events take place is not precisely fixed, although some must obviously come before others. Each of the functions is essential; however, it should be noted that a greater or lesser amount of self-instruction can be assumed, depending on the learner's sophistication (cf. Gagné, 1974a, pp. 131–138).

How do these procedures fit together in a typical instructional exercise? This can be illustrated by an analysis of an instructional sequences in elementary science, entitled "Inferring the Presence of Water Vapor in Air" (AAAS Commission on Science Education, 1963). This exercise has the objective of teaching the child to identify an inference, namely, that the liquid accumulating on a cold surface exposed to the air comes from the air. From the instruction provided, the child is expected to be able not only to state the inferred rule but also to demonstrate the operations that make possible the checking of the inference. The analysis of instruction for this exercise is given in Table 12.1.

Table 12.1 makes it clear that each step in the instructional procedure can be accounted for as an event designed to activate and support internal learning processes. First, it is apparent that a state of *motivation* is aroused and made specific as an *expectancy* of the outcome of learning. *Attention* and *selective perception* are directed by verbal communications from the instructor. A number of previously learned rules and concepts, prerequisite to the new learning, are *recalled*. Schemes for *encoding* the concepts and rules are suggested, although there is considerable dependence on discovery of these by the learner. *Performance* of the learner is called for, and followed by *reinforcement*. The *transferability* of the newly learned skills is tested, again with suitable feedback informing the learner of success in achieving a new capability.

TABLE 12.1   Instructional Procedure for an Exercise on "Inferring the Presence of Water Vapor in Air"

Instructional Event	Function
1. Teacher directs attention to clouding of windows on a cold day, the ring of water left by a glass of ice water, the cloud left by breathing on a mirror. Questions students about why these events happen.	1. Establishment of *achievement* motivation, based on curiosity and the desire to display knowledge to other children and to parents.
2. Children are given tin cans and ice cubes.	2. Providing *stimulus objects*.
3. Students are told to put the ice cubes in the cans, and to watch what happens to the outside of the cans.	3. Completion of stimulus situation. Directions to focus *attention, selective perception*.
4. Students are asked to describe what they see. "Fog"; "drops of water"; "large drops running down"; "ring of water at base of can."	4. Verbal directions to stimulate *recall* of previously learned concepts.
5. Students are asked what they can infer from their observations. "Liquid is water from the air."	5. Learning of a rule by discovery; for some students, this may be *recall*. Feedback provided.
6. Other alternatives are pointed out to students. Could it be some other liquid? Could it come from the metal of the can? *How can one test an inference?*	6. Verbal directions to inform the learners of the expected outcome of instruction (how to test this inference). Establishing an *expectancy*.
7. "How can we tell whether this liquid is water?" ("Taste it.")	7. Requiring *recall* of previously learned rule.
8. "If the water comes out of the metal, what should happen when it is wiped off?" ("Can should weigh less.")	8. Requiring *recall* of previously learned rule.
9. Students are asked, "if the water comes from the air, what should happen to the weight of the can after the water collects on it?" ("Can should increase in weight.") Direct observation is made of increase in weight of can by ice, by weighing on an equal-arm balance.	9. Requiring *recall* of previously learned rules.

TABLE 12.1   Instructional Procedure for an Exercise on "Inferring the Presence of Water Vapor in Air" (Continued)

Instructional Event	Function
10. Students are asked to recall that steam consists of water droplets and water vapor (an invisible gas). Air can contain water vapor.	10. Requiring *recall* of previously learned rules.
11. Students are asked to state (a) what they observed; (b) what they inferred; and (c) how they checked their inference.	11. Verbal guidance to suggest *encoding* for concepts of observation and inference; and of rules for checking inferences. *Feedback* provided.
12. Students are asked to make and test inferences in two or three other new situations, and to describe the operations and reasoning involved. These might be (a) water evaporation; (b) the extinguishing of a candle in a closed cylinder; (c) the displacement of water by gas in an inverted cylinder.	12. Additional *examples* of the concepts and rules learned, for the purpose of insuring *retention* and *learning transfer*.
13. Another new situation is presented to the students and they are asked to describe it in terms of (a) what they observed; (b) what they inferred; (c) how they checked their inference.	13. *Appraisal* providing *feedback*.

Source: Based on an exercise of the same name occurring in AAAS Commission on Science Education. *Science: A Process Approach, Part 4.* Washington, D.C.: American Association for the Advancement of Science, 1963.

Instructional procedures for adult learners take account of the same learning phases. However, those who are used to learning will undoubtedly have developed strategies of self-instruction. Mature learners are likely to approach the learning situation with motivation already well established. They may be able to realize immediately what the expected outcome of learning should be (although information about objectives is often helpful in confirming their expectancy). They have learned to perceive the stimulus selectively. They have a variety of encoding schemes and cues for retrieval at their command. They make provision for their own performances, and are able to provide their own feedback. External events of instruction are frequently helpful, but evidently not essential, for the learning of these "truly sophisticated" learners. As a result, such learners are able to acquire many new capabilities simply from reading a book (like this one). The important point for the instructional designer, however, is that not all learners can do all these things, whether they are children or adults. Hence there is a need for insuring that external means are available to actively support the internal transformations required in each learning phase.

CHOOSING INSTRUCTIONAL MEDIA

One of the most important practical decisions involved in the design of instruction is *choice of media*. Many events of instruction are designed as oral communications to the learner, usually to be delivered by a teacher. Alternatively or in addition, instruction may be given by a printed text. Although the entire content of instruction is sometimes communicated in one of these ways, supplementary means of delivery are commonly used. The other media of instruction range from actual objects to pictures and moving pictures (cf. Briggs, 1970; Briggs, Campeau, Gagné, and May, 1967; Dale, 1969).

The basic form of instruction must be considered to be *language*, whether in oral or printed form. Language in its propositional form can be employed to *direct* the learners' behavior, and thus to bring about any or all of the conditions needed to activate and support internal processes. Language communications can channel the learners' motivation, inform them of the learning objective, stimulate (by questions) the retrieval of prerequisites, provide guidance for encoding and cues for retrieval, ask for the relevant performance, and provide feedback. Oral or printed language, however presented, is therefore the most universal and versatile form for the delivery of instruction.

Of course, instructional events *can* be designed without the use of language, and they may be so designed for young children or for the mentally retarded who are unable to respond to language. When instruction must be designed in this way—using demonstrations, dolls and puppets, actual objects, and the like—it is a most challenging task for the designer. The limitations of what can be accomplished without language become starkly apparent. One of the most important sets of skills for the young child to learn is "following directions" conveyed by language. This set of competencies, usually acquired in nursery school or kindergarten, enables the child's subsequent learning to be carried out in instructional situations that are most efficient.

In the delivery of instruction, language in oral or printed form is often combined with, and supplemented by, *objects* and *representations of objects*. In this supplementary function, actual objects may sometimes be the best media. Examples are manipulable objects like blocks and beads, when number concepts are being taught to children; and objects like automobile fenders, when the vocational skills of body repair are to be learned. The range of nonlanguage stimuli for instruction is enormously extended, however, by object representations in the form of *pictures* and *diagrams*. In these forms, concrete objects and events—which would otherwise be expensive, difficult, or even impossible to introduce in their actual form—can be presented (or "represented") to the learner. Mount Everest can be shown to students who cannot travel to see it; the internal parts of cells can be shown to those who cannot use a microscope; the flow of blood to the capillaries can be shown to students who have no opportunity to observe the actual event.

In choosing media, then, the instructional designer has first to choose the kind of *language medium* which will be able to perform all of the functions required in establishing the instructional events described in previous sections of this chapter. (As has been mentioned, the assumption is made that learners are able to respond to the directions conveyed by language). The basic choices pertain to the delivery of oral language, printed language, or some combination of these. This decision, having been made, a further choice may be made regarding the additional requirements for the presentation of *objects* or their representation in *pictures* or *diagrams*. Such choices depend largely upon the specific objectives of the learning to be accomplished.

Language Media

Language communications designed to bring about appropriate events for instruction may be presented orally or in printed form. Each is sometimes employed in this "pure" fashion, as in a lecture or textbook, but each is commonly combined with object representations such as pictures or diagrams. We shall consider here the instructional functions which can be provided by each of these language media.

ORAL COMMUNICATION.　　All of the required instructional functions can be performed by oral communication, provided that objects or pictures are included when required by the learning task.
Typically, oral communication is given by a teacher, and in that
form achieves greatest versatility and flexibility in its adaptation to
particular requirements of students and situations. Instruction may
also be delivered orally by means of tape recorders, which have
many valuable uses in classroom instruction. Oral language may
also be delivered by radio, and this means of delivery has been
shown to have great effectiveness when the intended students are
widely dispersed, as in sparsely settled areas.

Oral communications can be used to good effect in channeling motivation toward instructional aims. A teacher or another
person in the role of a human model can perform this instructional
function effectively. In *informing the learner of the expected learning outcome*, oral communication sometimes needs to be supplemented by printing or pictures. For example, if the objective is
"computing the normality of chemical solutions," the printed example ".5 N" is evidently a good model for the kind of performance required. Oral communication may suffice, however, when the
learned performance is an oral one, as in constructing sentences in
a foreign language, or in making a speech.

The *guidance of learning* including the suggestion of encoding schemes, can often be accomplished by means of oral language.
Procedural steps involved in children's printing or writing of letters
may be prompted by a teachers' oral directions; for example,
"First a long line down," "Next, a line across the top," and so on.
Guidance in the form of questions may be used in the discovery of
new rules, as in the following example. Asked to demonstrate the
truth of the statement

$$8 \times 3 + 16 = 5 \times 8,$$

the students' thinking may be guided by such questions as, "Can
you think of another name for 16?"—and others as needed—to
enable them to arrive at the expression

$$8 \times 5 = 8 \times 5.$$

For the more mature learner, adequate learning guidance
can often be given in oral form. The earth's orbit around the sun
can be described rather than being directly observed. The passage
of a bill through Congress can be verbally described. But oral communications are often more effective when supplemented by pictures or by actual objects. The science teacher would feel grossly

handicapped if the concept of wave motion could not be pictured. The description of a town meeting may not be as satisfactory for encoding purposes as the direct observation of a town meeting, or a filmed record of one.

Questions that are designed to enhance *retention* and *transfer* can be presented orally. If students have learned information and concepts pertaining to the distribution of powers among the legislative, executive, and judiciary branches of government, a question such as the following can be asked: "What possible means could there be of legislative restraint on judicial powers? When actual objects and events are used in instruction (as in simulation games), they set the stage for transfer of learning, a process which is continued by oral discussion.

Teachers often employ oral questions to *elicit the performance* of the learner, and oral statements to *provide feedback*. For young children, a good deal of the teacher's conversation may consist in statements of "Yes," "Good!," "That's right," as the pupils attain successive goals of instruction. At later ages, the necessity for such "oral reinforcement" is greatly reduced, since students are able to match their performances with external standards, or with those they themselves supply.

All of these functions, then, *can* be performed by oral communication. Perhaps this is the reason why the model of the teacher and student talking to each other from two ends of a log seems so appropriate for the instructional situation. But many of these functions can be more readily and more efficiently accomplished when pictures or actual objects are added to the stimulus situation for learning. And, of course, the same instructional events can be carried out by the use of printed media.

PRINTED LANGUAGE. Books, pamphlets, and leaflets are also a traditional part of the instructional situation. For the later years of formal education, dependence on books as media of instruction is very high relative to dependence on other media. It is noteworthy, however, that oral discussion still has an instructional function at the level of postgraduate education. The instruction of an experienced university scholar may be derived mostly from the printed media of books and learned journals; yet the scholar finds it necessary to discuss with colleagues the ideas so obtained. At the other extreme of the educational scale, printed communication can accomplish very little; the presentation of actual objects accompanied by oral communication is the typical mode of instruction for children in the elementary grades. Accordingly, learning the skill of reading is the crucial event that determines the increasing dependence on printed media from the early grades of school onward.

Assuming that the student possesses the necessary prerequisite skills, instruction by means of a book is usually a remarkably rapid and efficient process. Although no figures are available, the time required for oral communication must surely be three or four times as much as that needed for instruction by means of a book. For the vast range of subject matters taught following the primary school years, printed communication can certainly be the major medium of instruction, and often is. When pictures and diagrams are combined with printed text (as, for example, in a good high school physics text), the dangers of excessive verbalism can largely be overcome, and the book can impart a great deal of instruction in a relatively short time when used by a suitably prepared student. At this level of schooling, in fact, whatever ineffectiveness books possess as instructional media may often be attributed to difficulties not inherent in the medium: the student has not acquired the necessary background knowledge or has not learned how to read or both.

The printed medium, however, does have other limitations. These have to do with the ways in which the sentences on the printed page function in the instructional situation. Textbooks, after all, are not always well written in terms of properly supporting the processes involved in each learning phase. For example, does the printed text introducing a topic direct attention to the proper stimuli? Does it inform the learner of the nature of the performance expected from learning? Does it supply, or suggest, useful schemes for encoding? Does it require the learner to exhibit what has been learned, and provide corrective feedback for this performance? Many printed texts would score quite low in their accomplishment of these necessary instructional functions. What happens, usually, is that learners carry out these functions themselves by the time they have as much experience as a college student. But, it is perhaps too much to expect that fifth-graders will have acquired this much sophistication about self-instruction through reading.

The potentialities of printed texts for instruction are very great, and it is doubtful that they are always well exploited. Designing a printed text that will efficiently instruct ten-year-olds is not simply a matter of matching their vocabulary. Primarily, it is a matter of *organizing* the statements in such a way that they will perform the instructional functions described in this chapter. Unless one is simply "telling a story" (that is, seeking to have learners acquire information organized in a meaningful context), it is doubt-

FIGURE 12.2 Vessels of different shapes, each containing a liquid.

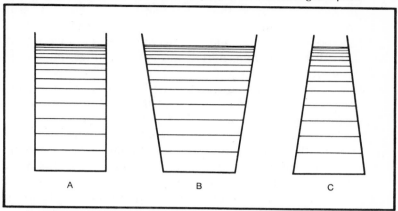

ful that the proper sequence of printed statements is much like a story. Each sentence or question may have a distinct purpose in suporting a particular internal learning process. The reader will perhaps be able to identify the instructional functions of the propositions in the following sequence, applicable to Figure 12.2.

1. Look at the pictures.
2. How is the pressure at the bottom of a vessel full of liquid related to the shape of the vessel?
3. Remember that pressure is the ratio of a force to (what?).
4. In a vessel whose walls flare outward (B), where is the force of the central cylindrical portion of water exerted?
5. The areas of the bottoms of the vessels are equal.
6. What can you say about the pressure at the bottom of the two vessels A and B?
7. State the relationship in general terms. (Answer: The pressure at the bottom of the vessel of liquid is not affected by the shape of the vessel.)
8. Now look at the other vessel, with walls flaring inward (C).
9. Etc.

Nonverbal Media

As we have seen, oral or printed language is seldom employed by itself to accomplish all instructional functions. Typically, verbal communications are accompanied by actual *objects*, or by representations of objects in the form of *pictures* or *diagrams*. One primary reason for the use of objects in instruction is that they are *involved directly* in the performance expected as a result of learning. For example, if the outcome is skill in using a microscope, evidently an actual microscope must be employed in the instruction; if the outcome pertains to map reading, actual maps must be used in the instruction.

A second and much broader reason for the use of objects or pictures in instruction is that they are the means by which the learner can acquire the *visual images* that are a very important type of memorial encoding and storage. Thus, objects and pictures are frequently used to perform the function of providing *encoding schemes*, even when the capability being learned is not itself to be displayed in a performance involving these objects (or pictures).

It will be useful here to explore more fully the second important function of objects and pictures of objects—the *image-making* function. In order to simplify the complex interactions of verbal communications and their nonverbal accompaniments, we shall confine our attention here to a common combination: oral communication accompanied by pictures. Such a combination occurs in (1) sound motion pictures used for instruction, in (2) slide-tape presentations, and particularly in (3) instructional television programs. Assuming that many of the functions of instruction in such presentation are provided by *oral language*,we need to address the question of what the picture contributes. What is added to the oral instruction by the inclusion of a picture?

WHAT DOES A PICTURE CONTRIBUTE? What a picture basically contributes is an *image*. As an encoding scheme, this image has certain important properties. First, it is an image of a *specific* object, person, or event. If the picture shows a tree, for example, the image generated in the learner is not that of a "generalized" tree, but of the tree depicted. Of course, the process of perceiving this particular tree may be selective; and consequently the image may not exactly match the picture in all its features. Some features may be omitted from the image, while others may be added from previously stored memories. Nevertheless, the image derived from the picture is of a specific tree. Similarly, if a diagram is pictured, the image generated is of the specific diagram.

The image that is formed and stored as a result of viewing a picture can be, and is, *retrieved* in its specific form. It does not have to be "constructed," as is the case when one says "Imagine a tree." In contrast to the generalized and variable image of a tree which would typically arise from such instructions, the image of the tree derived from viewing a picture is retrieved with the features and form it took when originally perceived. This is not to deny that certain minor changes, or losses of detail, may occur in the process of retrieval; nevertheless, what is retrieved is the same specific object or scene shown in the picture. In sum, then, the addition of a picture to oral verbal instruction makes it possible for the learner to encode the objects or events depicted as *specific, retrievable images*. For convenience, these images may be referred to in abbreviated form as SRI's.

Table 12.2 summarizes the contributions that can be made in support of the encoding process by SRI's generated within the learner as a result of the inclusion of pictures as accompaniments to orally presented instruction. Since the form of encoding also affects later retrieval, the effects of the SRI on this process are assumed to be included.

As Table 12.2 indicates, when an intellectual skill is being learned, an SRI may first of all aid the retrieval of prerequisite skills. For example, if the skill being learned is the placement of a dependent clause within a sentence, a diagram of the sentence may be used to stimulate recall of the prerequisite concepts of subject, predicate, object, and so on. The diagram which includes the dependent clause (and shows its placement) may then generate an SRI which aids in retrieval of the rule for placement of the dependent clause.

TABLE 12.2   Effects of Specific Retrievable Images (SRI's) on Encoding and Retrieval Processes When Derived from Pictures Included in Oral Instruction

Learning Capability	Contribution of SRI
Intellectual Skill	(1) SRI's of application examples enhance recall of prerequisite skills (2) SRI's add cues for retrieval of a newly learned skill, including its correct sequence
Cognitive Strategy	Variety of SRI's adds cues for transfer of strategy to new situations
Information	SRI's broaden and add detail to the meaningful context in which new information is embedded
Motor Skill	SRI of sequence or movement encodes the "executive subroutine"
Attitude	(1) SRI's of situations to which attitude is relevant add cues for retrieval (2) SRI of human model's choice behavior, plus vicarious reinforcement, encodes the attitude

Suppose that a cognitive strategy of problem solving is being learned, such as "waiting until all the evidence is in." Various problem situations to which this strategy is applicable may be presented in pictorial form (as in television scenes). These pictures generate an equal variety of images which, when retrieved by the learner, provide cues for the transfer of the strategy to new situations in which it may be employed.

When information is being learned, a great deal of added meaningful material may be contributed in a short time as a context for the encoding of the newly learned propositions. For example, if new facts are being learned about a state's agricultural products, a considerable variety of scenes depicting the growing of these products can be shown. The specific images formed from such pictures are capable of adding a great many additional cues for the retrieval of the new information.

In the case of a motor skill, pictures often depict the sequence of actions and the movements involved in them. Essentially, this amounts to a display of the executive subroutine (the "motor plan"). The image formed from such a picture can probably not be derived in any better way.

Pictures are particularly supportive of attitude learning and attitude change. They can establish SRI's which aid the learner's retrieval of the variety of situations in which the attitude may be displayed. And they produce images of the human model's behavior in choosing a course of action within these situations, as well as the reinforcement that follows such choice. Suppose an attitude toward "disposing of personal trash" is the aim of instruction. Pictures (shown in television scenes, in movies, or on slides or filmstrips) can display situations in which personal trash must be disposed of—including walking on a sidewalk, and traveling in an automobile. Pictures can show a respected human model behaving in desirable ways in disposing of trash—saving aluminum cans, depositing gum wrappers in trash receptacles, and so on. The reinforcing events for the model, also shown in pictures, could be views of clean streets and of unspoiled forest trails. The SRI's thus established contribute features to the encoding and retrieval of the attitude.

PROPERTIES OF THE VERBAL INSTRUCTION–PICTURE COMBINATION. Many of the features of media which combine pictures with oral instruction are duplicated when pictures are added to printed text. It should be noted also that the functions we have described for the oral instruction–picture combination, as listed in

Table 12.2, pertain only to the support of encoding and retrieval processes involved in various learning outcomes. The same combination, as embodied in television programs, for example, has many other valuable characteristics for the support of learning. In this combination, rapid changes of scenes and unusual visual stimulation are highly effective in controlling attention. Many techniques of pictorial emphasis are available to direct selective perception. Motion and sequences of action can be portrayed in ways that make possible specific retrievable images of these events. The implications of these characteristics of the oral instruction–picture combination have been explored by a number of writers (e.g., Gropper, 1963; Levie and Dickie, 1973; Lumsdaine, 1963).

The conception of pictures (or actual objects, when appropriate) in combination with oral instruction as generators of encoding schemes by way of specific retrievable images implies that pictures typically play a critical role in learning. Oral instruction without pictures ordinarily has limited effectiveness for encoding. Its effects are greatly enhanced when pictures enable the learner to use concrete images as an encoding device and as a source of cues for the retrieval of what has been learned.

EDUCATIONAL IMPLICATIONS

This chapter has attempted to draw together practical implications of our description of *varieties of learned capabilities*, and of the *phases of processing during learning*. The applications of these ideas has been to the *design of instruction*.

The sources of knowledge about learning and its conditions described in previous chapters may be put to use in the process of instructional design. To be carried out effectively, such a process must include attention to the details, as well as to the general characteristics, of human learning. Instructional design requires that two major questions be answered as bases for design procedures. The first is, What kinds of capabilities are to be learned? And the second is, What kinds of stimulation external to the learner will best support the internal processing necessary for learning?

Having identified the intended learning outcome, the instructional designer undertakes to specify the external conditions of learning, and to embody them in a series of events given the general name of *instruction*. The events of instruction are planned as stimulation to the learner during the phases of learning, as indicated in Figure 12.1. The purpose of these external events is to activate, support, and maintain the internal processes of learning (cf. Gagné, 1974a; Gagné and Briggs, 1974).

Instructional design draws the specifications for events which support the processes of (1) motivation channeling and the establishment of expectancies, (2) attention and selective perception, (3) encoding, (4) retrieval and recall, (5) learning transfer, and (6) performance reflecting the learned capability. Finally, the event of (7) reinforcement serves to complete the learning act by confirming the learner's expectancy. Each of these events requires a specific design. Some (such as the direction of attention) have common features which are applicable in the learning of any or all types of capabilities. Others (such as encoding and provisions for retrieval) require different arrangements of events for each kind of learning outcome. Naturally, these events take many forms, as determined by the learning task and also by the characteristics of the learner. The *functions* of these events in support of learning processes are the critical features that determine their planning and selection.

External stimulation constituting events of instruction often takes the form of *verbal communication*. In fact, this is the typical form of these events, with exceptional planning being necessary when verbal instruction cannot be understood by learners (as in the case of very young children, the mentally retarded, etc.). The *choice of media* for the instructional designer thus involves an initial decision of the use of *oral* or *printed communication* or a balance between them. Typically, oral communication is delivered by a teacher, printed communication by a textbook or other printed source; other combinations are, of course, possible.

As the word "media" is generally understood, most vehicles for the delivery of instruction include both verbal communication and the representation of objects by means of pictures and diagrams. When they are appropriate and available, actual objects may be used in preference to pictures. Pictures add many valuable features to instructional events, when employed in combination with either printed or oral communications. Their function in supporting *encoding* and *retrieval* functions is considered critical. Their operation is conceived as one of generating *specific retrievable images* in the learner, which in turn constitute a means of encoding and memory storage, and a source of cues for retrieval of what has been learned. The planning of these functions in media such as television requires the instructional designer to take account of the particular category of learning outcome intended, in order to achieve optimal effectiveness of the pictures' role in learning support.

GENERAL REFERENCES

FOUNDATIONS OF INSTRUCTIONAL DESIGN

Anderson, R. C., and Faust, G. W. *Educational psychology: The science of instruction and learning.* New York: Dodd, Mead, 1974.

Gagné, R. M. *Essentials of learning for instruction.* New York: Holt, Rinehart and Winston, 1974.

Merrill, M. D. *Instructional design: Readings.* Englewood Cliffs, N.J.: Prentice-Hall, 1971.

DESIGNING INSTRUCTION

Briggs, L. J. *Handbook of procedures for the design of instruction.* Monograph No. 4. Pittsburgh, Pa.: American Institutes for Research, 1970.

Gagné, R. M., and Briggs, L. J. *Principles of instructional design.* New York: Holt, Rinehart and Winston, 1974.

MEDIA IN INSTRUCTION

Dale, E. *Audiovisual methods in teaching,* 3rd ed. New York: Holt, Rinehart and Winston, 1969.

Gropper, G. L. Why is a picture worth a thousand words? *AV Communication Review,* 1963, *11,* 75–95.

Levie, W. H., and Dickie, K. E. The analysis and application of media. In R. M. W. Travers (Ed.), *Handbook of research on teaching,* 2nd ed. Skokie, Ill.: Rand-McNally, 1973.

Lumsdaine, A. A. Instruments and media of instruction. In N. L. Gage (Ed.), *Handbook of research on teaching.* Skokie, Ill.: Rand-McNally, 1963.

May, M. A., and Lumsdaine, A. A. *Learning from films.* New Haven, Conn.: Yale University Press, 1958.

REFERENCES

AAAS Commission on Science Education. *Science: A Process approach, Part 4*. Washington, D.C.: American Association for the Advancement of Science, 1963.

Adams, J. A. *Human memory*. New York: McGraw-Hill, 1967.

Allport, G. W. Attitudes. In C. Murchison (Ed.), *Handbook of social psychology*. Worcester, Mass.: Clark University Press, 1935.

Anderson, J. R., and Bower, G. H. Recognition and retrieval processes in free recall. *Psychological Review*, 1972, *79*, 97–123.

Anderson, J. R., and Bower, G. H. *Human associative memory*. Washington, D.C.: V. H. Winston, 1973.

Anderson, N. H. Information integration theory applied to attitudes about U.S. Presidents. *Journal of Educational Psychology*, 1973, *64*, 1–8.

Anderson, R. C., and Faust, G. W. *Educational psychology: The science of instruction and learning.* New York: Dodd, Mead, 1974.

Anderson, R. C., and Myrow, D. L. Retroactive inhibition of meaningful discourse. *Journal of Educational Psychology Monograph,* 1971, *62,* 81–94.

Atkinson, R. C., and Shiffrin, R. M. Human memory: A proposed system and its control processes. In K. W. Spence and J. T. Spence (Eds.), *The psychology of learning and motivation,* Vol. 2. New York: Academic Press, 1968.

Ausubel, D. P. The use of advance organizers in the learning and retention of meaningful verbal material. *Journal of Educational Psychology,* 1960, *51,* 267–272.

Ausubel, D. P. *Educational psychology: A cognitive view.* New York: Holt, Rinehart and Winston, 1968.

Ausubel, D. P., and Blake, E. Proactive inhibition in the forgetting of meaningful school materials. *Journal of Educational Research,* 1958, *52,* 145–149.

Ausubel, D. P., and Fitzgerald, D. Organizer, general background, and antecedent learning variables in sequential verbal learning. *Journal of Educational Psychology,* 1962, *53,* 243–249.

Ausubel, D. P., Robbins, L. C., and Blake, E. Retroactive inhibition and facilitation in the learning of school materials. *Journal of Educational Psychology,* 1957, *48,* 334–343.

Ausubel, D. P., and Youssef, M. The effects of spaced repetition on meaningful retention. *Journal of General Psychology,* 1965, *73,* 147–150.

Baer, D. M., Peterson, R. F., and Sherman, J. A. The development of imitation by reinforcing behavioral similarity to a model. *Journal of the Experimental Analysis of Behavior,* 1967, *10,* 405–416.

Bahrick, H. P. Two-phase model for prompted recall. *Psychological Review,* 1970, *77,* 215–222.

Bandura, A. Influence of model's reinforcement contingencies on the acquisition of imitative responses. *Journal of Personality and Social Psychology,* 1965, *1,* 589–595.

Bandura, A. *Principles of behavior modification.* New York: Holt, Rinehart and Winston, 1969.

Bandura, A. Vicarious and self-reinforcement processes. In R. Glaser (Ed.), *The nature of reinforcement.* New York: Academic Press, 1971.

Bandura, A., and McDonald, F. J. The influence of social reinforcement and the behavior of models in shaping children's moral judgments. *Journal of Abnormal and Social Psychology,* 1963, *67,* 274–281.

Bandura, A., and Mischel, W. The influence of models in modifying delay of gratification patterns. *Journal of Personality and Social Psychology,* 1965, *2,* 698–705.

Bartlett, F. C. *Remembering.* New York: Cambridge University Press, 1932.

Battig, W. F. Paired-associate learning. In T. R. Dixon and D. L. Horton (Eds.), *Verbal behavior and general behavior theory.* Englewood Cliffs, N.J.: Prentice-Hall, 1968.

Belmont, J. M., and Butterfield, E. C. What the development of short-term memory is. *Human Development,* 1971, *14,* 236–248.

Bem, D. J. *Beliefs, attitudes and human affairs.* Monterey, Calif.: Brooks/ Cole, 1970.

Bereiter, C., and Engelmann, S. *Teaching disadvantaged children in the preschool.* Englewood Cliffs, N.J.: Prentice-Hall, 1966.

Berlyne, D. E. *Structure and direction in thinking.* New York: Wiley, 1965.

Bilodeau, I. M. Information feedback. In E. A. Bilodeau (Ed.), *Acquisition of skill.* New York: Academic Press, 1966.

Bloom, B. S., Hastings, J. T., and Madaus, G. F. *Handbook on formative and summative evaluation of student learning.* New York: McGraw-Hill, 1971.

Bogardus, E. S. Measuring social distance. *Journal of Applied Sociology,* 1925, *9,* 299–308.

Bostrom, R., Vlandis, J., and Rosenbaum, M. Grades as reinforcing contingencies and attitude change. *Journal of Educational Psychology,* 1961, *52,* 112–115.

Bourne, L. E., Jr. *Human conceptual behavior.* Boston: Allyn and Bacon, 1966.

Bourne, L. E., Jr., Ekstrand, B. R., and Dominowski, R. L. *The psychology of thinking.* Englewood Cliffs, N.J.: Prentice-Hall, 1971.

Bousfield, W. A. The occurrence of clustering in the recall of randomly arranged associates. *Journal of General Psychology,* 1953, *49,* 229–249.

Bower, G. H. Mental imagery and associative learning. In L. Gregg (Ed.), *Cognition in learning and memory.* New York: Wiley, 1969.

Bower, G. H. Imagery as a relational organizer in associative learning. *Journal of Verbal Learning and Verbal Behavior,* 1970, 9, 529–533.

Bower, G. H. A selective review of organizational factors in memory. In E. T. Tulving and W. Donaldson (Eds.), *Organization of memory.* New York: Academic Press, 1972.

Bower, G. H. Cognitive psychology: An introduction. In W. K. Estes (Ed.), *Handbook of learning and cognitive processes,* Vol. I. Hillsdale, N.J.: Erlbaum Associates, 1975.

Bower, G. H., and Winzenz, D. Comparison of associative learning strategies. *Psychonomic Science,* 1970, *20,* 119–120.

Briggs, L. J. *Handbook of procedures for the design of instruction.* Monograph No. 4. Pittsburgh, Pa.: American Institutes for Research, 1970.

Briggs, L. J., Campeau, P. L., Gagné, R. M., and May, M. A. *Instructional media.* Monograph No. 2. Pittsburgh, Pa.: American Institutes for Research, 1967.

Briggs, L. J., and Reed, H. B. The curve of retention for substance material. *Journal of Experimental Psychology,* 1943, *32,* 513–517.

Bruner, J. S. The act of discovery. *Harvard Educational Review,* 1961, *31,* 21–32.

Bruner, J. S. *Toward a theory of instruction.* Cambridge, Mass.: Harvard University Press, 1966.

Bruner, J. S. *The relevance of education.* New York: Norton, 1971.

Bruner, J. S., Goodnow, J. J., and Austin, G. A. *A study of thinking.* New York: Wiley, 1956.

Campbell, D. T. Social attitudes and other acquired behavioral dispositions. In S. Koch (Ed.), *Psychology: A Study of a science,* Vol. 6. New York: McGraw-Hill, 1963.

Chittenden, G. E. An experimental study in modifying assertive behavior in young children. *Monographs of the Society for Research in Child Development,* 1942, 7 (Serial No. 31).

Clark, L. V. Effect of mental practice on the development of a certain motor skill. *Research Quarterly.* 1960, *31,* 560–569.

Cofer, C. N. A comparison of logical and verbatim learning of prose passages of different lengths. *American Journal of Psychology,* 1941, *54,* 1–20.

Cofer, C. N. (Ed.) Verbal learning and verbal behavior. New York: McGraw-Hill, 1961.

Cofer, C. N., and Appley, M. H. *Motivation: Theory and research.* New York: Wiley, 1964.

Cofer, C. N., and Musgrave, B. S. (Eds.) *Verbal behavior and learning: Problems and processes.* New York: McGraw-Hill, 1963.

Collins, A. M., and Quillian, M. R. How to make a language user. In E. Tulving and W. Donaldson (Eds.), *Organization of memory.* New York: Academic Press, 1972.

Commission on the Reorganization of Secondary Education. *Cardinal principles of secondary education.* Department of the Interior, Bureau of Education Bulletin No. 35. Washington, D.C.: GPO, 1918.

Cook, J. W., and Walbesser, H. H. *How to meet accountability with behavioral objectives and learning hierarchies.* College Park, Md.: University of Maryland, Bureau of Educational Research and Field Services, 1973.

Covington, M. V., Crutchfield, R. S., Davies, L. B., and Olton, R. M. *The productive thinking program.* Columbus, Ohio: Merrill, 1973.

Craik, F. I. M., and Lockhart, R. S. Levels of processing: A framework for memory research. *Journal of Verbal Learning and Verbal Behavior,* 1972, *11,* 671–684.

Crossman, E. R. F. W. A theory of the acquisition of speed-skill. *Ergonomics,* 1959, *2,* 153–166.

Crothers, E. J. Memory structure and the recall of discourse. In J. B. Carroll and R. O. Freedle (Eds.), *Language Comprehension and the acquisition of knowledge.* Washington, D.C.: V. H. Winston, 1972.

Crouse, J. H. Retroactive interference in reading prose materials. *Journal of Educational Psychology,* 1971, *62,* 39–44.

Crovitz, H. F. *Galton's walk.* New York: Harper & Row, 1970.

Crowder, R. G., and Morton, J. Precategorical acoustic storage (PAS). *Perception and Psychophysics,* 1969, *5,* 365–373.

Crutchfield, R. S., and Covington, M. V. Facilitation of creative problem solving. *Programmed Instruction,* 1965, *4,* 3–10.

Dale, E. *Audiovisual methods in teaching,* 3rd ed. New York: Holt, Rinehart and Winston, 1969.

Deese, J., and Hulse, S. H. *The psychology of learning,* 3rd ed. New York: McGraw-Hill, 1967.

Dewey, J. *How we think.* Boston: Heath, 1910.

Dixon, T. R., and Horton, D. L. (Eds.) *Verbal behavior and general behavior theory.* Englewood Cliffs, N.J.: Prentice-Hall, 1968.

Dong, T., and Kintsch, W. Subjective retrieval cues in free recall. *Journal of Verbal Learning and Verbal Behavior,* 1968, *7,* 813–816.

Duchastel, P. C., and Merrill, P. F. The effects of behavioral objectives on learning: A review of empirical studies. *Review of Educational Research,* 1973, *43,* 53–70.

Ebbinghaus, H. *Memory: A contribution to experimental psychology.* (Transl. by H. A. Ruger.) New York: Teachers College, 1913.

Ellis, H. C. *The transfer of learning.* New York: Macmillan, 1965.

English, H. B., Welborn, E. L., and Killian, C. D. Studies in substance memorization. *Journal of General Psychology,* 1934, *11,* 233–260.

Estes, W. K. The statistical approach to learning theory. In S. Koch (Ed.), *Psychology: A study of a science;* Vol. 2. *General systematic formulations, learning, and special processes.* New York: McGraw-Hill, 1959.

Estes, W. K. Reinforcement in human behavior. *American Scientist,* 1972, *60,* 723–729.

Festinger, L. *A theory of cognitive dissonance.* Stanford, Calif.: Stanford University Press, 1957.

Festinger, L. *Conflict, decision, and dissonance.* Stanford, Calif.: Stanford University Press, 1964.

Fishbein, M. (Ed.) *Attitude theory and measurement.* New York: Wiley, 1967.

Fitts, P. M. Perceptual-motor skill learning. In A. W. Melton (Ed.), *Categories of human learning.* New York: Academic Press, 1964.

Fitts, P. M., and Posner, M. I. *Human performance.* Monterey, Calif.: Brooks/Cole, 1967.

Fitts, P. M., and Seeger, C. M. S-R compatibility: Spatial characteristics of stimulus and response codes. *Journal of Experimental Psychology,* 1953, *46,* 199–210.

Flavell, J. H. *The developmental psychology of Jean Piaget.* New York: Van Nostrand, 1963.

Fleishman, E. A. *A factorial study of psychomotor abilities.* Research Bulletin TR-54-15. Lackland Air Force Base, Tex.: Air Force Personnel and Training Research Center, 1954.

Frase, L. T. Paragraph organization of written materials: The influence of conceptual clustering upon the level and organization of recall. *Journal of Educational Psychology,* 1969, *60,* 394–401.

Frase, L. T. Boundary conditions for mathemagenic behavior. *Review of Educational Research,* 1970, *40,* 337–347.

Gagné, R. M. Learning and proficiency in mathematics. *Mathematics Teacher,* 1963, *56,* 620–626.

Gagné, R. M. Problem solving. In A. W. Melton (Ed.), *Categories of human learning.* New York: Academic Press, 1964.

Gagné, R. M. The analysis of instructional objectives for the design of instruction. In R. Glaser (Ed.), *Teaching machines and programmed learning. II: Data and directions.* Washington, D.C.: National Education Association, 1965.

Gagné, R. M. Context, isolation and interference effects on the rentention of fact. *Journal of Educational Psychology,* 1968, *60,* 408–414. (a)

Gagné, R. M. Contributions of learning to human development. *Psychological Review,* 1968, *75,* 177–191. (b)

Gagné, R. M. Learning hierarchies. *Educational Psychologist,* 1968, *6,* 1–9. (c)

Gagné, R. M. Domains of learning. *Interchange,* 1972, *3,* 1–8.

Gagné, R. M. *Expectations for school learning.* Phi Delta Kappa Monograph. Bloomington, Ind.: Phi Delta Kappa, 1973.

Gagné, R. M. *Essentials of learning for instruction.* New York: Holt, Rinehart and Winston, 1974. (a)

Gagné, R. M. Task analysis—its relation to content analysis. *Educational Psychologist,* 1974, *11,* 19–28. (b)

Gagné, R. M. Taxonomic problems of educational systems. In W. T. Singleton and P. Spurgeon (Eds.), *Measurement of human resources.* London: Taylor and Francis, 1975.

Gagné, R. M., and Bassler, O. C. Study of retention of some topics of elementary non-metric geometry. *Journal of Educational Psychology,* 1963, *54,* 123–131.

Gagné, R. M., and Briggs, L. J. *Principles of instructional design.* New York: Holt, Rinehart and Winston, 1974.

Gagné, R. M., and Brown, L. T. Some factors in the programming of conceptual learning. *Journal of Experimental Psychology,* 1961, *62,* 313–321.

Gagné, R. M., and Fleishman, E. A. *Psychology and human performance.* New York: Holt, Rinehart and Winston, 1959.

Gagné, R. M., and Foster, H. Transfer to a motor skill from practice on a pictured representation. *Journal of Experimental Psychology,* 1949, *39,* 342–355.

Gagné, R. M., Mayor, J. R., Garstens, H. L., and Paradise, N. E. Factors in acquiring knowledge of a mathematics task. *Psychological Monographs,* 1962, *76,* No. 7 (Whole No. 526).

Gardner, J. W. National goals in education. In *Goals for Americans: The Report of the President's Commission on National Goals.* Englewood Cliffs, N.J.: Prentice-Hall, 1960.

Gates, A. I. Recitation as a factor in memorizing. *Archives of Psychology,* 1917, *26* (Whole No. 40).

Getzels, J. W., and Jackson, P. W. *Creativity and intelligence.* New York: Wiley, 1962.

Gibson, E. J. A systematic application of the concepts of generalization and differentiation to verbal learning. *Psychological Review*, 1940, *47*, 196–229.

Gibson, E. J. Retroactive inhibition as a function of degree of generalization between tasks. *Journal of Experimental Psychology*, 1941, *28*, 93–115.

Gibson, E. J. Intra-list generalization as a factor in verbal learning. *Journal of Experimental Psychology*, 1942, *30*, 185–200.

Gibson, E. J. *Principles of perceptual learning and development*. New York: Appleton, 1969.

Gibson, J. J. *The perception of the visual world*. Boston: Houghton Mifflin, 1950.

Gilbert, T. F. Mathetics: The technology of education. *Journal of Mathetics*, 1962, *1*, 7–73.

Gilbert, T. H. Overlearning and the retention of meaningful prose. *Journal of General Psychology*, 1957, *56*, 281–289.

Glaser, R. Some implications of previous work on learning and individual differences. In R. M. Gagné (Ed.), *Learning and individual differences*. Columbus, Ohio: Merrill, 1967.

Glaser, R. Concept learning and concept teaching. In R. M. Gagné and W. J. Gephart (Eds.), *Learning research and school subjects*. Itasca, Ill.: Peacock, 1968.

Glaser, R. Educational psychology and education. *American Psychologist*, 1973, *28*, 557–566.

Goss, A. E. Comments on Professor Noble's paper. In C. N. Cofer and B. S. Musgrave (Eds.), *Verbal behavior and learning: Problems and processes*. New York: McGraw-Hill, 1963.

Goss, A. E., and Nodine, C. F. *Paired-associates learning*. New York: Academic Press, 1965.

Greeno, J. G., and Bjork, R. A. Mathematical learning theory and the new "mental forestry." *Annual Review of Psychology*, 1973, *24*, 81–116.

Gropper, G. L. Why is a picture worth a thousand words? *AV Communication Review*, 1963, *11*, 75–95.

Guilford, J. P. *The nature of human intelligence*. New York: McGraw-Hill, 1967.

Guthrie, E. R. *The psychology of learning*. New York: Harper & Row, 1935.

Guthrie, J. T. Instruction versus a discovery method. *Journal of Educational Psychology*, 1967, *58*, 45–49.

Guttman, N., and Kalish, H. I. Discriminability and stimulus generalization. *Journal of Experimental Psychology*, 1956, *51*, 79–88.

Hall, J. F. Retroactive inhibition in meaningful material. *Journal of Educational Psychology*, 1955, *46*, 47–52.

Hall, J. F. *Psychology of motivation*. Philadelphia: Lippincott, 1961.

Harlow, H. F. The development of learning sets. *Psychological Review*, 1949, *56*, 51–65.

Harlow, H. F., and Harlow, M. K. Learning to think. *Scientific American*, 1949, *181*, 36–39

Hartshorne, H. and May, M. A. *Studies in deceit*. New York: Macmillan, 1928.

Hebb, D. O. *A textbook of psychology*, 2nd ed. Philadelphia: Saunders, 1966.

Heider, F. *The psychology of interpersonal relations*. New York: Wiley, 1958.

Hempel, W. E., Jr., and Fleishman, E. A. A factor analysis of physical proficiency and manipulative skill. *Journal of Applied Psychology*, 1955, *39*, 12–16.

Henderson, E. N. A study of memory for connected trains of thought. *Psychological Monographs*, 1903–1904, *5*, No. 6.

Hewett, F. M. *The emotionally disturbed child in the classroom*. Boston: Allyn and Bacon, 1968.

Hilgard, E. R., and Bower, G. H. *Theories of learning*, 4th ed. Englewood Cliffs, N.J.: Prentice-Hall, 1975.

Hovland, C. I. "Inhibition of reinforcement" and phenomena of experimental extinction. *Proceedings of the National Academy of Sciences*, 1936, *22*, 430–433.

Hovland, C. I. The generalization of conditioned responses. I. The sensory generalization of conditioned responses with varying frequencies of tone. *Journal of General Psychology*, 1937, *17*, 125–148.

Hovland, C. I., Janis, I. L., and Kelley, H. H. *Communication and persuasion*. New Haven, Conn.: Yale University Press, 1953.

Hovland, C. I., Lumsdaine, A. A., and Sheffield, F. D. *Experiments in mass communication*. Princeton, N.J.: Princeton University Press, 1949.

Hull, C. L. *Principles of behavior*. New York: Appleton, 1943.

Inhelder, B., and Piaget, J. *The growth of logical thinking from childhood to adolescence*. New York: Basic Books, 1958.

Insko, C. A. Verbal reinforcement of attitudes. *Journal of Personality and Social Psychology*, 1965, *2*, 621–623.

James, W. *Principles of psychology*. New York: Holt, Rinehart and Winston, 1890.

Jenkins, J. J. Mediated associations: Paradigms and situations. In C. N. Cofer and B. S. Musgrave (Eds.), *Verbal behavior and learning*. New York: McGraw-Hill, 1963.

Jensen, A. R. An empirical theory of the serial-position effect. *Journal of Psychology*, 1962, *53*, 127–142.

Johnson, D. M. *A systematic introduction to the psychology of thinking*. New York: Harper & Row, 1972.

Jones, H. E., and English, H. B. Notional vs. rote memory. *American Journal of Psychology*, 1926, *37*, 602–603.

Katona, G. *Organizing and memorizing*. New York: Columbia University Press, 1940.

Keele, S. W. Movement control in skilled motor performance. *Psychological Bulletin*, 1968, *70*, 387–403.

Keller, F. S., and Schoenfeld, W. N. *Principles of psychology*. New York: Appleton, 1950.

Kelly, G. A. *The psychology of personal constructs,* Vol. I. New York: Norton, 1955.

Kelman, H. C. Attitude change as a function of response restriction. *Human Relations,* 1953, *6,* 185–214.

Kelman, H. C. Compliance, identification, and internalization: Three processes of attitude change. *Journal of Conflict Resolution,* 1958, *2,* 51–60.

Kendler, H. H., and Kendler, T. S. Effect of verbalization on reversal shifts in children. *Science,* 1961, *141,* 1619–1620.

Keppel, G. Retroactive and proactive inhibition. In T. R. Dixon and D. L. Horton (Eds.), *Verbal behavior and general behavior theory.* Englewood Cliffs, N.J.: Prentice-Hall, 1968.

Kestin, J. Creativity in teaching and learning. *American Scientist,* 1970, *58,* 250–257.

Kiesler, C. A., Collins, B. E., and Miller, N. *Attitude change.* New York: Wiley, 1969.

Kifer, E. Relationships between academic achievement and personality characteristics: A quasi-longitudinal study. *American Educational Research Journal,* 1975, *12,* 191–120.

Kimble, G. A. *Hilgard and Marquis' "Conditioning and learning."* New York: Appleton, 1961.

Kimble, G. A. *Foundations of conditioning and learning.* New York: Appleton, 1967.

Kintsch, W. Notes on the structure of semantic memory. In E. Tulving and W. Donaldson (Eds.), *Organization of memory.* New York: Academic Press, 1972.

Klatzky, R. L. *Human memory: Structures and processes.* San Francisco: Freeman, 1975.

Klausmeier, H. J. Cognitive operations in concept learning. *Educational Psychologist,* 1971, *9,* 1, 3–8.

Klausmeier, H. J. *Learning and human abilities. Educational psychology,* 4th ed. New York: Harper & Row, 1975.

Klausmeier, H. J., Ghatala, E. S., and Frayer, D. A. *Conceptual learning and development: A cognitive view.* New York: Academic Press, 1974.

Klausmeier, H. J., and Harris, C. W. *Analyses of concept learning.* New York: Academic Press, 1966.

Koestler, A. *The act of creation.* London: Hutchinson, 1964.

Koffka, K. *The growth of the mind,* 2nd ed. New York: Harcourt, 1929.

Kohlberg, L. The contribution of developmental psychology to education: Examples from moral education. *Educational Psychologist,* 1973, *10,* 2–14.

Köhler, W. *The mentality of apes.* New York: Harcourt, 1927.

Köhler, W. *Gestalt psychology.* New York: Liveright, 1929.

Krathwohl, D. R., Bloom, B. S., and Masia, B. B. *Taxonomy of educational objectives. Handbook II: Affective domain.* New York: McKay, 1964.

La Piere, R. I. Attitudes vs. actions. *Social Forces,* 1934, *13,* 230–237.

Levie, W. H., and Dickie, K. E. The analysis and application of media. In

R. M. W. Travers (Ed.), *Handbook of research on teaching,* 2nd ed. Skokie, Ill.: Rand-McNally, 1973.

Lewis, D. Shephard, A. H., and Adams, J. A. Evidences of associative interference in psychomotor performance. *Science,* 1949, *110,* 271–273.

Lindahl, L. G. Movement analysis as an industrial training method. *Journal of Applied Psychology,* 1945, *29,* 420–436.

Lindsay, P. H., and Norman, D. A. *Human information processing: An introduction to psychology.* New York: Academic Press, 1972.

Lindsley, D. B. The reticular system and perceptual discrimination. In H. H. Jasper (Ed.), *Reticular formation of the brain.* Boston: Little, Brown, 1958.

Lovell, K. *The growth of basic mathematical and scientific concepts in children.* New York: Philosophical Library, 1961.

Lumsdaine, A. A. Instruments and media of instruction. In N. L. Gage (Ed.), *Handbook of research on teaching.* Skokie, Ill.: Rand-McNally, 1963.

Mager, R. F. *Preparing objectives for instruction.* Belmont, Calif.: Fearon, 1962.

Mager, R. F. *Developing attitude toward learning.* Belmont, Calif.: Fearon, 1968.

Maier, N. R. F. Reasoning in humans. I. On direction. *Journal of Comparative Psychology,* 1930, *10,* 115–143.

Masur, E. F., McIntyre, C. W., and Flavell, J. H. Developmental changes in apportionment of study time among items in a multitrial free recall task. *Journal of Experimental Child Psychology,* 1973, *15,* 237–246.

Mathews, D. K., and McDaniel, J. Effectiveness of using Golf-Lite in learning the golf swing. *Research Quarterly,* 1962, *33,* 488–491.

May, M. A., and Lumsdaine, A. A. *Learning from films.* New Haven, Conn.: Yale University Press, 1958.

McClelland, D. C. Toward a theory of motive acquisition. *American Psychologist,* 1965, *20,* 321–333.

McClelland, D. C., Atkinson, J. W., Clark, R. A., and Lowell, E. L. *The achievement motive.* New York: Appleton, 1953.

McGeoch, J. A. *The psychology of human learning.* New York: McKay, 1942.

McGeoch, J. A., and Irion, A. L. *The psychology of human learning,* 2nd ed. New York: McKay, 1952.

Mechner, F. Behavioral analysis and instructional sequencing. In P. C. Lange (Ed.), *Programmed instruction.* Chicago: National Society for the Study of Education, 1967.

Melton, A. W. Learning. In W. S. Monroe (Ed.), *Encyclopedia of educational research.* New York: Macmillan, 1940.

Melton, A. W. (Ed.) *Apparatus tests.* Army Air Forces Aviation Psychology Program Research Report No. 4. Washington, D.C.: GPO, 1947.

Melton, A. W. The taxonomy of human learning: Overview. In A. W. Melton (Ed.), *Categories of human learning.* New York: Academic Press, 1964.

Melton, A. W., and Martin, E. (Eds.) *Coding processes in human memory.* Washington, D.C.: V. H. Winston, 1972.

Merrill, M. D. *Instructional design: Readings.* Englewood Cliffs, N.J.: Prentice-Hall, 1971.

Merrill, P. F. *Task analysis: An information processing approach.* Technical Memo No. 27. Tallahassee: Florida State University, CAI Center, 1971.

Meunier, C. F., Ritz, D., and Meunier, J. A. Rehearsal of individual items in short-term memory. *Journal of Experimental Psychology,* 1972, *95,* 465–467.

Meyer, B. J. F., and McConkie, G. W. What is recalled after hearing a passage? *Journal of Educational Psychology,* 1973, *65,* 109–117.

Mill, J. *Analysis of the phenomena of the human mind.* (Ed. by A. Bain, A. Findlater, and G. Grote; ed. with additional notes by J. S. Mill.) London: Longmans, 1869.

Miller, G. A. *Language and communication.* New York: McGraw-Hill, 1951.

Miller, G. A. The magical number seven, plus or minus two: Some limits on our capacity for processing information. *Psychological Review,* 1956, *63,* 81–97.

Miller, N. E. Liberalization of S-R concepts. Extensions to conflict behavior, motivation, and social learning. In S. Koch (Ed.), *Psychology: A study of a science,* Vol. 2. New York: McGraw-Hill, 1959.

Miller, N. E. Laws of learning relevant to its biological basis. *Proceedings of the American Philosophical Society,* 1967, *111,* 315–325.

Miller, R. B. Task description and analysis. In R. M. Gagné (Ed.), *Psychological principles in system development.* New York: Holt, Rinehart and Winston, 1963.

Mowrer, O. H. *Learning theory and behavior.* New York: Wiley, 1960. (a)

Mowrer, O. H. *Learning theory and the symbolic processes.* New York: Wiley, 1960. (b)

Newcomb, T. M. *The acquaintance process.* New York: Holt, Rinehart and Winston, 1961.

Newell, A., and Simon, H. A. *Human problem solving.* Englewood Cliffs, N.J.: Prentice-Hall, 1972.

Newman, E. B. Forgetting of meaningful material during sleep and waking. *American Journal of Psychology,* 1939, *52,* 65–71.

Newman, S. E. A mediation model for paired-association learning. In J. P. DeCecco (Ed.), *Educational technology.* New York: Holt, Rinehart and Winston, 1964.

Noble, C. E. Meaningfulness and familiarity. In C. N. Cofer and B. S. Musgrave (Eds.), *Verbal behavior and learning.* New York: McGraw-Hill, 1963.

Olton, R. M., and Crutchfield, R. S. Developing the skills of productive thinking. In P. Mussen, J. Langer, and M. Covington (Eds.), *Trends and issues in developmental psychology.* New York: Holt, Rinehart and Winston, 1969.

Olton, R. M., Wardrop, J. L., Covington, M. V., Goodwin, W. L., Crutchfield, R. S., Klausmeier, H. J., and Ronda, T. *The development of productive thinking skills in fifth-grade children.* Technical Report No. 34. Madison, Wis.: University of Wisconsin, Center for Cognitive Learning, 1967.

Orlando, R., and Bijou, S. W. Single and multiple schedules of reinforcement in developmentally retarded children. *Journal of the Experimental Analysis of Behavior,* 1960, *3,* 339–348.

Paivio, A. *Imagery and verbal processes.* New York: Holt, Rinehart and Winston, 1971.

Paivio, A., and Yuille, J. C. Changes in associative strategies and paired-associate learning over trials as a function of word imagery and type of learning set. *Journal of Experimental Psychology,* 1969, *79,* 458–463.

Pavlov, I. P. *Conditioned reflexes.* (Transl. by G. V. Anrep.) New York: Oxford, 1927.

Penfield, W. Memory mechanisms. *Transactions of the American Neurological Association,* 1951, *76,* 15–31.

Piaget, J. *The construction of reality in the child.* New York: Basic Books, 1954.

Piaget, J. Piaget's theory. In P. H. Mussen (Ed.), *Carmichael's manual of child psychology.* New York: Wiley, 1970.

Piaget, J., and Inhelder, B. *The early growth of logic in the child.* New York: Harper & Row, 1964.

Popham, W. J. *Educational evaluation.* Englewood Cliffs, N.J.: Prentice-Hall, 1975.

Popham, W. J., and Baker, E. L. *Establishing instructional goals.* Englewood Cliffs, N.J.: Prentice-Hall, 1970.

Porier, G. W., and Lott, A. J. Galvanic skin responses and prejudice. *Journal of Personality and Social Psychology,* 1967, *5,* 253–259.

Postman, L. The present status of interference theory. In C. N. Cofer (Ed.), *Verbal learning and verbal behavior.* New York: McGraw-Hill, 1961.

Poulton, E. C. On prediction in skilled movements. *Psychological Bulletin,* 1957, *54,* 467–478.

Quillian, M. R. Semantic memory. In M. Minsky (Ed.), *Semantic information processing.* Cambridge, Mass.: MIT Press, 1968.

Rankin, R. E., and Campbell, D. T. Galvanic skin response to negro and white experimenters. *Journal of Abnormal and Social Psychology,* 1955, *51,* 30–33.

Razran, G. Conditioned response changes in rating and appraising sociopolitical slogans. *Psychological Bulletin,* 1940, *37,* 481.

Resnick, L. B. *Design of an early learning curriculum.* Working Paper No. 16. Pittsburgh, Pa.: University of Pittsburgh, Learning Research and Development Center, 1967.

Resnick, L. B., Wang, M. C., and Kaplan, J. *Behavior analysis in curriculum design: A hierarchically sequenced introductory mathematics curriculum.* Pittsburgh, Pa.: University of Pittsburgh, Learning Research and Development Center, 1970.

Reynolds, J. H., and Glaser, R. Effects of repetition and spaced review upon retention of a complex learning task. *Journal of Educational Psychology*, 1964, *55*, 297–308.

Richardson, A. Mental Practice: A review and discussion, Parts I and II. *Research Quarterly*, 1967, *38*, 95–107; 263.

Riley, D. A. *Discrimination learning*. Englewood Cliffs, N.J.: Prentice-Hall, 1968.

Ringness, T. A. *The affective domain in education*. Boston: Little, Brown, 1975.

Robinson, E. S. *Association theory today*. New York: Appleton, 1932.

Rohwer, W. D., Jr. Constraint, syntax and meaning in paired associate learning. *Journal of Verbal Learning and Verbal Behavior*, 1966, *5*, 541–547.

Rohwer, W. D., Jr. Images and pictures in children's learning. *Psychological Bulletin*, 1970, *73*, 393–403. (a)

Rohwer, W. D., Jr. Mental elaboration and proficient learning. In J. P. Hill (Ed.), *Minnesota symposia on child psychology*, Vol. 4. Minneapolis: University of Minnesota Press, 1970. (b)

Rohwer, W. D., Jr. Elaboration and learning in childhood and adolescence. In H. W. Reese (Ed.), *Advances in child development and behavior*. New York: Academic Press, 1975.

Rohwer, W. D., Jr., and Lynch, S. Semantic constraint in paired-associate learning. *Journal of Educational Psychology*, 1966, *57*, 271–278.

Rokeach, M. *Beliefs, attitudes and values. San Francisco:* Jossey-Bass, 1969.

Rosenberg, M. J., and Hovland, C. I. Cognitive, affective and behavioral components of attitudes. In C. I. Hovland and M. J. Rosenberg, *Attitude organization and change*. New Haven: Yale University Press, 1960.

Roshal, S. M. *Effects of learner representation in film-mediated perceptual-motor learning*. State College, Pa.: Pennsylvania State College Instructional Film Research Program, 1949.

Rothkopf, E. Z. The concept of mathemagenic activities. *Review of Educational Research*, 1970, *40*, 325–336.

Rothkopf, E. Z. Experiments on mathemagenic behavior and the technology of written instruction. In E. Z. Rothkopf and P. E. Johnson (Eds.), *Verbal learning research and the technology of written instruction*. New York: Teachers College, 1971.

Rothkopf, E. Z., and Bisbicos, E. E. Selective facilitative effects of interspersed questions on learning from written material. *Journal of Educational Psychology*, 1967, *58*, 56–61.

Rothkopf, E. Z., and Johnson, P. E. *Verbal learning research and the technology of written instruction*. New York: Teachers College, 1971.

Rothkopf, E. Z., and Kaplan, R. Exploration of the effect of density and specificity of instructional objectives in learning from text. *Journal of Educational Psychology*, 1972, *68*, 295–302.

Rumelhart, D. E., Lindsay, P. H., and Norman, D. A. A process model for long-term memory. In E. Tulving and W. Donaldson (Eds.), *Organization of memory*. New York: Academic Press, 1972.

Salatas, H., and Flavell, J. H. Behavioral and metamnemonic indicators of strategic behaviors under remember instructions in first grade. *Child Development*, 1976, *47*, 81–89.

Saltz, E. Compound stimuli in verbal learning: Cognitive and sensory differentiation versus stimulus selection. *Journal of Experimental Psychology*, 1963, *66*, 1–5.

Scott, W. A. Attitude change through reward of verbal behavior. *Journal of Abnormal and Social Psychology*, 1957, *55*, 72–75.

Sharp, S. E. Individual psychology. *American Journal of Psychology*, 1899, *10*, 329–391.

Shaw, G. B. *Adventures of the black girl in her search for God*. New York: Putnam, 1959.

Shaw, M. E., and Wright, J. M. *Scales for the measurement of attitudes*. New York: McGraw-Hill, 1967.

Shulman, L. S., and Keislar, E. R. *Learning by discovery: A critical appraisal*. Skokie, Ill.: Rand-McNally, 1966.

Sigel, I. E., and Hooper, F. H. *Logical thinking in children*. New York: Holt, Rinehart and Winston, 1968.

Simon, H. A., and Feigenbaum, E. A. An information processing theory of some effects of similarity, familiarity and meaningfulness in verbal learning. *Journal of Verbal Learning and Verbal Behavior*, 1964, *3*, 385–396.

Singer, R. N. (Ed.) *Readings in motor learning*. Philadelphia: Lea & Febiger, 1972.

Singer, R. N. *Motor learning and human performance*, 2nd ed. New York: Macmillan, 1975.

Skinner, B. F. *The behavior of organisms*. New York: Appleton, 1938.

Skinner, B. F. *The technology of teaching*. New York: Appleton, 1968.

Skinner, B. F. *Contingencies of reinforcement: A theoretical analysis*. New York: Appleton, 1969.

Slamecka, N. J. Studies of retroaction of connected discourse. *American Journal of Psychology*, 1959, *72*, 409–416.

Slamecka, N. J. Retroactive inhibition of connected discourse as a function of similarity of topic. *Journal of Experimental Psychology*, 1960, *60*, 245–249.

Smode, A. Learning and performance in a tracking task under two levels of achievement information feedback. *Journal of Experimental Psychology*, 1958, *56*, 297–304.

Spence, K. W. *Behavior theory and conditioning*. New Haven: Conn.: Yale University Press, 1956.

Sperling, G. The information available in brief visual presentations. *Psychological Monographs*, 1960, *74*, No. 6. (Whole No. 498).

Staats, A. W. An outline of an integrated theory of attitudes. In M. Fishbein (Ed.), *Readings in attitude theory and measurement.* New York: Wiley, 1967.

Staats, A. W., and Staats, C. K. Attitudes established by classical conditioning. *Journal of Abnormal and Social Psychology,* 1958, *57*, 37–40.

Staats, A. W., Staats, C. K., and Crawford, H. L. First-order conditioning of meaning and the parallel conditioning of a GSR. *Journal of General Psychology,* 1962, *67*, 159–167.

Stevens, J. C., and Savin, H. B. On the form of learning curves. *Journal of the Experimental Analysis of Behavior,* 1962, *5*, 15–18.

Taylor, C. W. *The second University of Utah research conference on the identification of creative scientific talent.* Salt Lake City: University of Utah Press, 1958.

Taylor, J. A. The relationship of anxiety to the conditioned eyelid response. *Journal of Experimental Psychology,* 1951, *41*, 81–92.

Thomson, D. M., and Tulving, E. Associative encoding and retrieval. *Journal of Experimental Psychology,* 1970, *86*, 255–262.

Thornburg, H. D. *Development in adolescence.* Monterey, Calif.: Brooks/Cole, 1975.

Thorndike, E. L. Animal intelligence: An experimental study of the associative processes in animals. *Psychological Review Monograph Supplements,* 1898, *2*, No. 4 (Whole No. 8).

Tolman, E. C. *Purposive behavior in animals and men.* New York: Appleton, 1932.

Trabasso, T., and Bower, G. H. *Attention in learning.* New York: Wiley, 1968.

Travers, R. M. W. *Essentials of learning,* 3rd ed. New York: Macmillan, 1972.

Triandis, H. C. Exploratory factor analyses of the behavioral component of social attitudes. *Journal of Abnormal and Social Psychology,* 1964, *68*, 420–430.

Triandis, H. C. Towards an analysis of the components of interpersonal attitudes. In C. W. and M. Sherif (Eds.), *Attitudes, ego-involvement, and change.* New York: Wiley, 1967.

Triandis, H. C. *Attitude and attitude change.* New York: Wiley, 1971.

Triandis, H. C., and Triandis, L. M. Race, social class, religion and nationality as determinants of social distance. *Journal of Abnormal and Social Psychology,* 1960, *61*, 110–118.

Tulving, E. Subjective organization and effects of repetition in multitrial free-recall learning. *Journal of Verbal Learning and Verbal Behavior,* 1966, *5*, 193–197.

Tulving, E. Episodic and semantic memory. In E. Tulving and W. Donaldson (Eds.), *Organization of memory.* New York: Academic Press, 1972.

Tulving, E., and Donaldson, W. (Eds.) *Organization of memory.* New York: Academic Press, 1972.

Tulving, E., and Osler, S. Effectiveness of retrieval cues in memory for words. *Journal of Experimental Psychology,* 1968, *77*, 593–601.

Tulving, E., and Pearlstone, Z. Availability versus accessibility information in memory for words. *Journal of Verbal Learning and Verbal Behavior,* 1966, *5,* 381–391.

Tyler, R. W. *Basic principles of curriculum and instruction.* Chicago: University of Chicago Press, 1949.

Underwood, B. J. Laboratory studies of verbal learning. In E. R. Hilgard (Ed.), *Theories of learning and instruction.* Sixty-third Yearbook, Part I. Chicago: National Society for the Study of Education, 1964. (a)

Underwood, B. J. The representativeness of rote verbal learning. In A. W. Melton (Ed.), *Categories of human learning.* New York: Academic Press, 1964. (b)

Underwood, B. J., and Schulz, R. W. *Meaningfulness and verbal learning.* Philadelphia: Lippincott, 1960.

Vanderplas, J. M. Perception and learning. In M. H. Marx (Ed.), *Learning: Interactions.* New York: Macmillan, 1970.

Watson, J. B. *Psychology from the standpoint of a behaviorist.* Philadelphia: Lippincott, 1919.

Watson, J. B., and Rayner, R. Conditioned emotional reactions. *Journal of Experimental Psychology,* 1920, *3,* 1–14.

Watts, G. H., and Anderson, R. C. Retroactive inhibition in free recall as a function of first- and second-list organization. *Journal of Experimental Psychology,* 1969, *81,* 595–597.

Welborn, E. L., and English, H. Logical learning and retention: A general review of experiments with meaningful verbal materials. *Psychological Bulletin,* 1937, *31,* 1–20.

Welford, A. T. *Fundamentals of skill.* London: Methuen, 1968.

Wellman, H. M., Ritter, K., and Flavell, J. H. Deliberate memory behavior in the delayed reactions of very young children. *Developmental Psychology,* 1975, *11,* 780–787.

Wertheimer, M. *Productive thinking.* New York: Harper & Row, 1945.

Westie, F. R., and de Fleur, M. L. Autonomic responses and their relationship to race attitudes. *Journal of Abnormal and Social Psychology,* 1959, *58,* 340–347.

White, R. T. Research into learning hierarchies. *Review of Educational Research,* 1973, *43,* 361–375.

White, R. T., and Gagné, R. M. Past and future research on learning hierarchies. *Educational Psychologist,* 1974, *11,* 19–28.

White, R. W. Motivation reconsidered: The concept of competence. *Psychological Review,* 1959, *66,* 297–333.

Whitely, J. D. Effects of practice distribution on learning a fine motor task. *Research Quarterly,* 1970, *48,* 576–583.

Wickelgren, W. A. *How to solve problems.* San Francisco: Freeman, 1974.

Wittrock, M. C. Replacement and nonreplacement strategies in children's problem solving. *Journal of Educational Psychology,* 1967, *58,* 69–74.

Wittrock, M. C. Learning as a generative process. *Educational Psychologist,* 1974, *11,* 87–95.

Worthen, B. R. Discovery and expository task presentation in elementary mathematics. *Journal of Educational Psychology Monograph Supplement,* 1968, *59,* No. 1, Part 2.

Yates, F. A. *The art of memory.* London: Routledge and Kegan Paul, 1966.

Zajonc, R. B. The concepts of balance, congruity, and dissonance. *Public Opinion Quarterly,* 1960, *24,* 280–286.

AUTHOR INDEX

SUBJECT INDEX

Advance organizer, in verbal information learning, 195
Affective domain (see Attitudes)
Association, role in learning, 75–76
Associationism, in learning psychology, 7–8
Attention, cognitive strategies in, 166
external events, 63
in information-processing model, 53
step in instruction, 286–287
Attitudes, affective component, 231
affective domain, 235–236
behavioral component, 231–235
beliefs, emotions, behavior, 236–237
change, 237–244
characteristics, 229–235
and classical conditioning, 238
cognitive component, 230
conceptual prerequisites, 244–245
conditions of learning, 45–47; 244–248
definition, 226–227
educational implications, 248–250
examples, 228–229
human modeling, 240–242; 246–248
information as prerequisite, 245–246
as learning outcomes, 44–47
message content, 242–244
message source, 243–244
occurrence, 227–229
operational definition, 237
personal action, 234–235
and reinforcement, 239–240
reinforcement of action choice, 248
scales, 232–234
and values, 235–236
vicarious reinforcement, 241

Basic forms of learning, chaining, 91–94
in everyday life, 87–89
S-R Theory, 74
varieties, 76
verbal association, 94–99
Behavior modification, 91

Capabilities (see Learning outcomes), 26–28
Chaining, as basic form of learning, 91–94

Chaining (cont.)
conditions, 92–93
uses, 93–94
Cognitive strategies, in attending, 166
in children's learning, 173–174
educational implications, 175–177
encoding, 167–168
executive control, 165
experimental questions, 174–175
internal and external conditions, 37–38
as learning outcomes, 35–38
in problem solving, 153–154; 170–171
retrieval, 36; 368–370
in thinking, 171–172
transfer of learning, 172–174
Concept learning, and verbal instructions, 115–118
Concepts, concrete, 111–122
defined (type), 126–133
(See also Concrete concepts, Defined concepts)
Concrete concepts, adult and child learning, 117–118
age differences in learning, 117–118
conditions of learning, 118–120
educational implications, 122–124
examples, 111–113
generalizing, 120–121
letters, phonemes, 121–122
relation to discriminations, 113–115
trial and error procedure, 113
verbal instructions, 115–118
Conditioned response, learning conditions, 79–80
in learning psychology, 10–11
rate of conditioning, 78
(See also Signal learning)
Conditioning, in attitude change, 238
classical, signal learning, 77–79
Connected discourse, as verbal information, 191–192
Context, in verbal information learning, 194–196
Control processes, in information-processing model, 59–60
Creativity, in problem solving, 163–165
Cumulative learning, 144–149